'This is a brave and beautiful book. Writing with a generous ecumenism, Chine McDonald offers a rich revisioning of Mary's motherhood, interweaving the theological tradition with a deeply personal and honest account of her own experiences of maternal life in all its complexity, struggle, vulnerability and joy. As a feminist theologian, mother and grandmother, I felt inspired and liberated by reading this.'

Tina Beattie
theologian, writer and broadcaster

'I was utterly riveted by *Unmaking Mary*. Beautifully written, richly layered and meticulously researched, this is a game-changing, much-needed corrective to the restrictive ideal of motherhood presented in the white, patriarchal myth of Mary. Chine McDonald deconstructs the perfect, passive motherhood Mary has long been saddled with, and clears the way for a maternal figure of profound humanity, power and beauty, as well as unspeakable pain. Astute, smart, witty and brave. A radical, deeply thoughtful and essential intervention.'

Lucy Jones
author of *Matrescence*

'With an honesty as painful as it is rare, *Unmaking Mary* is a book that will remain with you long after its close. A rigorous examination of motherhood and the ways our icons form us; and a site of truth-telling for those who have, for too long, mirrored postures never meant for us. My only fear is that the foolish among us will mistake it as a book only of interest to women. It is vital reading for all who were once born.'

Cole Arthur Riley
author of *This Here Flesh*

'There are many names for Mary in the Christianities of the world: Mother of the Word Incarnate, Mother of Sorrows, Mother of God. In her signature searing, incisive analysis, Chine McDonald explores other names: Mother of Rage, Mother of Childloss, Mother of Exhaustion, Mother of Grief, Mother of Joy, Mother of Solidarity, Mother of Racial Justice. This is a book for people of all genders to explore how ideas of religion and maternity influence our understanding of power, validity, truth and belief. At times a journalistic analysis, at times theological, at times narrative, at times historical, Chine McDonald's *Unmaking Mary* is – all the time – a powerful demonstration of theology speaking to contemporary society. Did I say it was part journalism, theology, narrative and history? Yes. It is also all fire; burning with conviction, clarity, scholarship and declaration.'

Pádraig Ó Tuama
poet, theologian and conflict mediator

'"Sometimes you don't have to make the cake." If actual flesh and blood mothers need liberating from impossible projections of perfection, so does the most famous mother of all. Dealing honestly and movingly with the complex emotions of motherhood, Chine McDonald offers us not only a deeply valuable reflection on the topic, but also a great deal of wisdom on how to use (and how not to use) myth and metaphor in understanding our humanity. A challenging, hope-filled book.'

Rowan Williams
theologian, poet and 104th Archbishop of Canterbury

'As a cultural historian and a mother, I found this book to be rich, provocative and powerful. It was also deeply comforting and freeing at a personal level. I wish I had read it a long time ago. McDonald's combination of intellectual argumentation and personal observation is superb and disarming. By the end of the book, the roadblocks of unrealistic maternal ideals long associated with Mary are cleared away to make way for a deep and rich encounter with the actual Mary of the Bible.'

Sarah C. Williams
historian and author of *When Courage Calls*

'This is a wonderful book. Sharp, funny and theologically rich on both Mary and motherhood – constructive theology at its best.'

Janet Soskice
Research Professor of Catholic Theology, Duke Divinity School and Professor Emeritus of Philosophical Theology, University of Cambridge

'I feel profoundly seen by Chine's words. Mothering is the most difficult work I've ever done, and she not only affirms me in this messy and mostly unseen holy task, but assures me that God is right there in the mess with me. Using historical, theological and contemporary examples to unmake the Mary we think we know, and through the vulnerable sharing of her own experiences, Mary is beautifully remade in the image of us all. This book not only made me feel better about being a mother, it made me feel more fully human. I encourage every imperfect mother to read her words and be comforted and inspired.'

Jayne Manfredi
Anglican deacon, writer and BBC Radio Four contributor

'In *Unmaking Mary*, Chine McDonald draws on an impressive range of sources – from theology to social media posts, and from literature to her own personal experiences – to deeply challenge oppressive archetypes and to recover more liberatory models of motherhood. Sweeping in its intellectual range, light in its touch, and discerning in its distinctions, this is a wise and illuminating book.'

Jennifer Banks
Senior Executive Editor at Yale University Press
and author of *Natality: Towards a Philosophy of Birth*

'I have the immense privilege of teaching, researching, writing, and contemplating the life of Mary, so it was not the truths of her life that initially grabbed me in this book. What captured me was McDonald's honesty. I read as one who had entered a new stage of motherhood, past the fog of the early years and the relative steadiness of the primary school era, to the complicated terrain of adolescence. In that new season, I had not resisted the voice in my head that charged, "failure!" frequently enough. I had begun to believe that damning voice was speaking truth. *Unmaking Mary* reacquainted me with a familiar friend. It is not that Mary, the Nazareth girl who became the mother of God, had changed, but I had, and needed to meet her anew, not only as the successful gospel proclaimer but also as a mother who on long days and sleepless nights probably also fought the demons of self-doubt. I learned a great deal from this book, but it touched me at many more levels than the intellect. I *connected* with this book and know that countless readers will do the same.'

Amy Peeler
author of *Women and the Gender of God* **and Professor of New Testament and the Kenneth T. Wessner Chair of Biblical Studies at Wheaton College**

'With *Unmaking Mary* Chine McDonald approaches a sometimes-contentious subject with endless grace. This book is affirming and enlightening; written with enough depth that will keep theological students engaged but with the strength of heart that will reach any mother caught in the tangle of shame, obligation and exhaustion. My soul was stirred with each turn of the page.'

Jendella Benson
writer, editor and creative

'This book is a marvel! In *Unmaking Mary*, Chine McDonald masterfully serves as both death doula and midwife. On the one hand, McDonald generously and incisively guides us to kill and release all of the ways we have been held hostage by toxic perfectionistic motherhood. On the other hand, McDonald graciously and wisely guides us to birth something new: a form of mothering that truly liberates, heals, and nurtures both ourselves and those we love. Remarkably, by being both death doula and midwife, McDonald shows us that we can truly reclaim and transform everything we think we know about Mary and mothering. Indeed, a part of my mother-related trauma was healed simply by reading this book. And I know that *Unmaking Mary* is going to save a lot of kids from unnecessary trauma. Read it, savour it, embody it – and be free!'

Christena Cleveland
author of *God Is a Black Woman*

Unmaking Mary

Shattering the Myth of Perfect Motherhood

CHINE McDONALD

HODDER &
STOUGHTON

First published in Great Britain in 2025 by Hodder & Stoughton
An Hachette UK Company

1

A CIP catalogue record for this title is available from the British Library

Hardback ISBN 978 1 399 81463 8
ebook ISBN 978 1 399 81465 2

Typeset in Bembo MT by Hewer Text UK Ltd, Edinburgh
Printed and bound in Great Britain by Clays Ltd, Elcograf S.p.A.

Hodder & Stoughton policy is to use papers that are natural, renewable
and recyclable products and made from wood grown in sustainable forests.
The logging and manufacturing processes are expected to conform
to the environmental regulations of the country of origin.

Hodder & Stoughton Ltd
Carmelite House
50 Victoria Embankment
London EC4Y 0DZ

www.hodderfaith.com

John Murray Press, part of Hodder & Stoughton Limited
An Hachette UK company

The authorised representative in the EEA is Hachette Ireland, 8 Castlecourt
Centre, Dublin 15, D15 XTP3, Ireland (email: info@hbgi.ie)

To my sons: Keir and Noah. My making and unmaking.

Author's Note

Before her book *Motherhood and God* was published in the year I was born, theologian and journalist Margaret Hebblethwaite's manuscript had been turned down by six publishers. Those that refused the book critiqued the fact that she was writing about both motherhood and theology. She had to pick one or the other, they said. It had to be either or. Definitely not both. For Hebblethwaite, however, this 'both' was precisely the point. Writing forty years later, this is my point, too. For most of history, women's experiences have been hidden. It is only really over the past century that women have had the means to write about their own stories, bringing to light the realities of what it is to be human and a woman. The experience of motherhood – together with its realities – has in very recent decades become less shrouded in silence, as writers and thinkers have seen it as their mission to tell the truth. This book is my contribution to these voices, but, like Hebblethwaite, I write in the tradition that brings together motherhood and theology, in the hope that we might gain new and profound insight into both ourselves and God.

Acknowledgements

Writing a book is a little like having a baby, and I have noticed how the two have shared imagery. We talk of conception, of book babies, and of bringing a book into the world. *Unmaking Mary* has been a *labour* of love. It is one of the hardest things I have ever done. The roller coaster of juggling motherhood and work and life continued while I breathed through the pain of early mornings and late evenings writing. But now that the book has been brought to birth, it's funny how I don't remember much of the challenge of delivering it. I remember that it was hard, and I remember that I had the support that made it possible. First, the midwives. I remember meeting Katherine Venn – the then editorial director at Hodder Faith – for lunch with my younger son when he was only a few months old and I was on maternity leave. It was a goodbye lunch, as she was leaving her long-time post. We spoke about what my next book might be on, and it was in that conversation, where my mind was dominated by feeds and changes and development milestones, that I realised there was only one thing I wanted to write about next: motherhood. Joanna Davey was passed the baton from Katherine at Hodder Faith and, like a midwife shift handover, she worked with me to take the spark of an idea to what became the book in your hands. I am so grateful to these women who have championed me and the book. For Joanna's gentle challenge, sharpening of the narrative, encouragement and kindness, and to all at Hodder, including Abigail Chatterjee and Rhoda Hardie. For Lydia Blagden, who designed the stunning book cover. I love it.

There have been many eyes and minds that have helped me write this book. I'm hugely grateful to my early readers Madeleine Pennington, Margaret Hebblethwaite, Paula Gooder, Madeleine

Davies and Donna Ford – for their honesty and encouragement, and for the time they put into it on top of everything else they were juggling. I was absolutely delighted and honoured that Professor Beth Allison Barr agreed to write the foreword for the book. When I read it the first time, I knew that she had understood the message I had laboured for months to try and communicate in the pages of this book.

I'm thankful to the NCT friends and the school mum friends, and the women friends who – whether they realised it or not – helped to shape my thoughts and ideas about what it is to be a woman, and the questions that I have attempted to ask and answer in this book. I'm thankful for those friends who let me tell their story – especially Alexandra and Chi.

A special thanks also to The Society of Authors and the Authors' Foundation for awarding me a grant in support of this work.

None of this would have been possible without the love and support of friends and family who have cheered me on, offered words of advice and checked in on me. Thanks to my parents, whose pride and belief in me have driven me on to do things I never thought possible. To my husband, Mark, who has been there every step of the way on my motherhood journey, and been my partner and rock throughout. And to my boys, Keir and Noah. Thank you for attempting to keep me in the present moment, with all its wonder. I love you.

Someone keeps stealing Mary. First from
the porcelain set bought on a
holiday, then in roadside nativity scenes.
She has been removed, disappeared
from the mall's store window, the church's
glass, Aunt Miriam's table
set. Have you noticed, I say to anyone who
will listen, that all the Marys are
gone? No one answers or tries to listen
(let's not talk politics). My nephew's
Plastic set sits above the fireplace. Where
is the mother? I ask, turning over
every figurine. But the wisemen keep their
silence, begging us to ask if, in fact,
she ran.

—*What Kind of Woman*, Kate Baer[1]

'We pray for the mothers who have protected us, who are weary,
who have stayed, who have left, who are grieving, who are proud
– understanding that the story of what it means to be a mother is
not singular.'

—*Black Liturgies*, Cole Arthur Riley[2]

Contents

Contents

Foreword

It was 29 July 2017. I was with my daughter in the unicorn tapestry room of the *Musée de Cluny* – a medieval monastic residence in Paris repurposed as a museum – when I heard my husband call out.

'Have you seen this?' he asked, beckoning to me. I found him standing in front of a fifteenth-century carving, about two feet tall, in a glass case. At first, I didn't understand his surprised tone. As I walked towards him from across the room, my perspective of the carving was different. It seemed a typical image of the Madonna. Serenity marked her perfect face as she stared straight ahead, her golden robes matching those of her child, who stood out a little way from her body. I couldn't see the red apple, loosely held in Mary's hand, as it was on the other side from my approach. But, when I did see, it only reinforced the ordinariness of the image. Mary redeems Eve. Or, more theologically accurate, the child of Mary redeems the sin of Eve.

Then I walked to the front of the case, joining my husband, and I understood his surprise. From her chest down, a line sliced the Virgin in half, breaking her body open to reveal the Trinity Enthroned: God the Father, God the Son – the crucified Christ, and God the Holy Spirit that (originally) emanated from the golden folds of God the Father's robes and directly behind God the Son. I later learnt that the image was called a Shrine Madonna or Opening Virgin – a devotional statue that became popular throughout late medieval Europe.

What startled my husband about the statue also startled me: the image of the Godhead literally contained within the broken body of a woman. Individually, all aspects of the image were familiar – the serene face of the Virgin Mary, the symbol of the apple contrasted with the Christ Child, the Trinity enthroned. But taken together – indeed, taken together inside the body of Mary, a body cut open for all to see – they became less familiar. I understood, perhaps for the first time, the gravitas of her title *Mother of God*.

In prose as vivid and beautiful and startling as the Shrine Madonna, Chine McDonald asks us to take another look at the Mother of God. Instead of as a paragon, McDonald invites us to see her as an ordinary woman whose broken brown body, covered in stretch marks, bleeding and leaking and tired, is anything but perfect. To help us see Mary from this different perspective, McDonald traces the rich, complexity of Marian history, from medieval through to modern, bringing the Mother of God down from an unreachable pedestal. No longer does Mary startle us with her unattainability, burdening mothers with shame about who we think we should be – the mum who snaps back into her pre-pregnancy jeans a week after birth, who loves breastfeeding, and revels in staying at home with a house full of children instead of secretly longing to return to the job she left behind. Through McDonald's words, Mary stops pressuring us into unrealistic conformity, but rather stands before us as a broken woman experiencing all the pain and anguish of motherhood, including the death of her child, yet still finding hope in the justice of God.

In perhaps my favourite line, McDonald explains that 'natality is a radical act, when all around is death, brutality, destruction and hopelessness'. The body of Mary, like the body of all women, breaks and bleeds; but it is also her body that offers hope of a better world.

As I stood before the Shrine Madonna that day so long ago, I remembered how medieval sermons repeated over and over to their audiences that God chose the body of a woman to bring salvation to all people.

In the same way, Chine McDonald reminds us of the beauty and holiness of our female bodies – our broken black, brown and white bodies – because 'it is here too where God lives'.

Beth Allison Barr
James Vardaman Professor of History, Baylor University
Author of *The Making of Biblical Womanhood: How the Subjugation of Women Became Gospel Truth* and *Becoming the Pastor's Wife: How Marriage Replaced Ordination as a Woman's Path to Ministry*.

Prologue

As I drive barefoot with my baby in the back seat, I wonder how I will explain my bleary-eyed ride up and down the A road near my house to the police, should they stop me for my erratic behaviour. It is not yet dawn. The roads are empty. Braless and shoeless, with my fourteen-month-old dressed in his sleepsuit and strapped in his car seat, blinking at his pyjama-clad chauffeur, I feel mad. This is an act of desperation. I have been up for hours, rocking and cuddling and burping and soothing and stroking his head. The baby just would not go to sleep. I knew I needed to take action after I held him up to my face, looked him straight in the eye and shouted, 'Go to sleep!' Not in the cheerful, sing-song way that I believed a mother should, but with the desperate rage of a sleep-deprived monster. I immediately felt shame. But I did need to do something – and something that would not wake my husband or my elder son. So I bundled the baby in my arms, crept down the stairs, opened the front door and got us into the car.

These sleepless nights will be familiar to those who have raised children. Babies have to be taught to understand the difference between night and day; and even when they have learnt, they might go through several rounds of dreaded sleep regressions before we can expect that we ourselves might be able to have a full night's sleep. On those nights it is difficult to keep a sense of perspective. At 3 a.m., the world can feel oppressive and dark and lonely. My baby – so delightful in the daytime (most of the time) – was now my night-time nemesis. Dark eyes blinking. Awake. Awake. Awake. I feel helpless; out of control. I just need to sleep.

Within a few minutes, the motion of the car successfully sends my little passenger into a slumber and I drive back and park in front of our house, hoping to get some rest before having to start my working day. I intend to sleep there while he sleeps, but all I can picture is the scene I have created. My mind retraces my steps, reruns the past few hours. I imagine looking down on myself and my behaviour in my son's bedroom. The agitation, a woman dishevelled, at her wits' end; a crazed mother shouting at her beautiful, chubby-thighed, bouncing baby boy. A far-from-perfect mother.

A bad mother.

I shut my eyes at the wheel of our car, as up and down our street, neighbours begin to wake up. My phone buzzes with a text from my worried husband: 'Where are you?'

PART ONE
Annunciation

Introduction

'What if we could enter motherhood
unattached to expectations?'

—*To Have and to Hold: Motherhood, Marriage and
the Modern Dilemma*, Molly Millwood[1]

Motherhood turned out to be a world away from what I had expected. Before I became a mum, I had assumed I would be a good one. Maybe not perfect, but not as far from perfection as I often feel that I am. I thought that intelligence, the care I had shown to my dolls as a child, love, grit, determination and prayer would get me through. No one warns you about the constant feelings of inadequacy; the failing at every turn.

I was raised in a faith tradition that warned me to stay away from men, lest I face the ultimate sin – becoming pregnant out of wedlock. So when it came to trying to get pregnant after I got married, I thought it must be easy. It turns out not to have been as easy as I had been led to believe, and that the assumption of flawless fertility was a myth. When I did get pregnant, I expected nine months of floaty dresses, bonding with the baby inside me, and eating whatever I wanted. But for me the pregnant glow was a myth. Instead, I battled months of debilitating pregnancy sickness, a diet of the blandest instant noodles I could find, the prodding and poking of medical professionals, a hyper-awareness of my body and the existential weirdness of growing a human animal inside me.

I was told that having a bad pregnancy would mean I would surely be due a good birth experience. I realised this had been an urban myth when I passed out while attempting to push my overdue baby out after three days of the most terrible pain I could imagine. In the days and weeks after my first son was born, I felt that the assumptions I had made about what all of it was going to be like were shattered daily. The breastfeeding, the sleep deprivation, the sheer relentlessness. This is not to say that it was for me a wholly negative realisation. I was shocked too at the force of love I had for my child. It took my breath away and I felt that the world could never and should never be the same again – the world that was all of a sudden full of danger, hazards everywhere I turned, things that could hurt my child. My baby was a china doll – too small and fragile for this world of catastrophe – and I was a mother bear.

I felt ill-equipped for motherhood; as if I had packed for the wrong trip. As if the forecast had been perfect sunshine, and when I arrived, I was standing in the cold rain with thunderclouds overhead, shivering in shorts and a T-shirt. That there were indeed the occasional pockets of sunshine did not completely eradicate the feeling that I had been misinformed. It felt not only as if I were ill-equipped, but that I was failing to live up to a standard – some notion in my head of what a perfect mother was like. It was only in the safest places that I felt able to confess this sense of inadequacy. To the world, I have selectively put forward those images of myself that conform to the trope of perfect motherhood. But it is among other mums, who are also bewildered, that the façade slips and I feel able to exhale and tell the truth. There, in that safety, I find that many of us are wrestling with this sense of maternal inadequacy.

But what is this standard against which we all feel we are failing? Where does it come from, and why does it feel so pervasive?

Before we enter into the world of mumhood ourselves, what we experience is a vacuum of real, earthy and gritty sharing about what it's really like. Our notions of motherhood come from cultural imagery that perpetuates myths about womanhood. When I think of a perfect mother, I might think of Carol in *The Brady Bunch*, or Caroline Ingalls in *Little House on the Prairie*. Mothers who are patient and kind and give all for their children. When I was not a mother, I judged those mums who shouted at their children in supermarkets, or who let them watch shows on their phones to keep them quiet, or who fed them chocolate. I would surely be different if I were ever to become a mum, I thought. I would be perfect. How hard could it be? Now, when I see pregnant mothers with 'Baby on Board' badges stroking their bumps on the train, or walking down the street, I wonder if this is their first time. I wonder if they know what is to come. If they are first-timers, I hope they enjoy this all-too-brief moment – this state of blissful unawareness; pregnant with possibility.

Great expectations

It's a truth universally acknowledged that if you are a middle-class British couple and have discovered you are pregnant, then you simply must sign up to the National Childbirth Trust (NCT). Even there, despite my husband, Mark, and I learning about the practicalities of becoming parents, we were left with expectations about what it would be like that left us floundering when it came to the existential, psychological, spiritual and emotional whirlwind of the real thing. The NCT has been running courses for soon-to-be parents since 1961. Originally designed to get them through the first thousand days of a baby's life, they guide you through the birthing process – providing hints, tips and tricks, what to expect when you're expecting, what the stages of labour are, and how to change a baby's nappy. When we first arrived at our group in Greenwich, south-east London, I was taken aback by how beautiful the other seven couples were. These immaculate, stylish men and women were the cream of the crop of mid-thirties would-be parents, all well educated, with good jobs: lawyers, diplomats, events planners. Over coffee, we shared photos of our oh-so-unique wedding days. We were all in strong relationships and lived in one of the most sought-after areas of London. And now we were having babies. I could feel my own smugness levels rising as we approached the end of our first session. We were women who were about to have it all.

NCT cohorts are organised with the intention that you all give birth within a few weeks of each other. Of the eight couples, our due date was the last, and even then, he ended up arriving nearly two weeks later than that. This meant I watched as, one by one, the other women became mothers. We celebrated each arrival on our WhatsApp group. It felt miraculous to see these little squished-up faces – once bumps, now living, breathing tiny human beings. The births were varied: there were waters breaking at restaurants, emergency C-sections; one or two of the babies seemed to fly out, while the others took their time in long and agonising labours. As each woman joined the sacred group of those with a birth story, those of us still sporting our bumps asked many, many questions. Did it hurt? What did it feel like? How long did it take? What should we pack in our labour bags?

One afternoon after everyone else's babies had been born, but mine still would not budge, I apprehensively joined the other mums and their newborns for lunch at a local pub. There was something different about the mothers, though. Something – quite a large thing – had changed since those first NCT classes in which we were excited and optimistic about our impending motherhood.

Now, even just a few days into their matrescence – a term which describes the metamorphosis that takes place when one becomes a mother – my new friends had changed. Behind the exhausted eyes, it was as if they knew something now that they did not know – could not have known –before. They had experienced the reality of motherhood that no NCT instructor could have prepared us for. It felt too that each of them was shielding me from the darkness – whether or not they had consciously or unconsciously intended to. They knew that my initiation into the identity-bending reality of motherhood would soon come.

I had no idea what was coming: a change so monumental and irrevocable that it shook the very foundations of who I was and what I believed. Becoming a mother turned my world – and my living room, and my office and bedroom and bathroom, come to think of it – upside down; it caused me to see the world in a completely different light, to think and feel and believe differently. What made it so unsettling was the lack of preparedness for it, the dissonance between the expectation and the reality. I'm convinced it is this that made my journey into motherhood all the more challenging, and that many other women feel the same about motherhood. Wonderful, yes, but challenging all the same. It's the surprise of it; the tremor of bewilderment. The constant feeling: *why did no one tell me about this?* Rachel Cusk, in *A Life's Work*, says that no one would have children if they knew what it was like. She describes the shock of motherhood perfectly when she writes: 'I have observed several times an expression of polite, horrified surprise on the faces of new mothers, as if they had just opened an inappropriate Christmas present: clearly they were unprepared.'[2]

For me, part of what made the initial foray into motherhood so world-altering was that it felt so very alien. It was eliciting in me feelings that I had never felt before, nor could describe. I once asked mothers on social media to tell me the main feeling that came to mind for them in those first few minutes, hours and days of becoming parents. So aware was I of the fear of judgement that can feel debilitating for mothers – the fear of sounding too happy (*smug mother*), the fear of sounding too negative (*well, you brought it on yourself*) – that I made it clear that there would be no judgement – that they could share whatever it was they had been feeling, whether negative or positive. Every single one of the feelings shared with me that day I too had felt and recognised in that early phase. *Relieved. Overwhelmed. Alone. Grief. Daunted. Exhausted. Confused. Grateful. Discombobulated.*

My word? Shock. Not merely the shock that you feel when something surprising happens, but a shock more like that of an earthquake: *a violent shaking movement caused by an impact, explosion or tremor.*[3] A feeling of unsteadiness caused by a fundamental fracture; a shift in perception. The world was all of a sudden and forever not as I thought it was. The shock for me also came from an overwhelming feeling of not having been adequately prepared for any of it; and it seems I am not alone. For many people, parenting is far harder than they thought it would be. A 2023 Pew Research study on parenting in the USA found that most parents (62%) found it at least somewhat harder than they expected, with around a quarter (26%) saying it was a *lot* harder. Mothers were more likely than fathers to think parenting was harder than they had expected.[4]

In her book *Matrescence: On the Metamorphosis of Pregnancy, Childbirth and Motherhood*, Lucy Jones describes her own entry into the world of motherhood and her prior expectations versus the reality: 'I thought that I must be going mad. I searched desperately for ways of understanding what was happening to me. I started to realize that my mind had been colonized by inadequate ideas about womanhood, about motherhood, about value, even love: there was canker in the roots of my habitat.'[5]

What is it about the reality of motherhood that feels so at odds with what we had expected? Where do the expectations come from? I am convinced that the 'institution of motherhood', as feminist author Adrienne Rich described it, the ideal of motherhood that shapes our expectations of what motherhood is *supposed* to be, is most vividly displayed in the ways in which Mary, the mother of Jesus, has been constructed throughout art, history, culture and theology over the centuries. In Mary we can see the dominant ideals of motherhood that have been projected onto her, and which shape our ideas about the maternal – in good ways, and in bad.

The ways in which Mary has been portrayed represent therefore a depiction of what we *expect* motherhood to be like. Often, the reality is so far removed from this divine ideal that it causes a fracture in our sense of self, as too often we judge ourselves for the failure to live up to the impossible standard. Writer Molly Millwood explains it well when she writes:

> Expectations can be helpful if they are realistic – they allow us to prepare in both psychological and practical ways for what is to come, and to avoid the emotional discomfort of being caught unaware. But when they are not realistic or, worse, are simply false, they set us up for disappointment, frustration and anger. They restrict the quality and flow of our internal experiences, because if any of those experiences was unexpected, we may be viewed as bad or wrong or unfair or shameful . . . The human tendency to expect generates a whole host of distorted perceptions and self-critical judgments.[6]

I think the myth of perfect motherhood, which I see reflected in the character and construction of Mary, set me up for disappointment, and for a regular feeling of not being good enough.

There's something about Mary

We are in Advent and images of Mary, the perfect mother, are everywhere. We find her on saccharine Christmas cards complete with scenes of mangers in stables, in nativity scenes in candlelit churches. A friend texts her pride at her daughter having been chosen to play Mary in the school nativity, and I try to suppress my irrational jealousy. I do not have a daughter, but two very boisterous little boys; and my elder is not Joseph, the leading male role in the school performance; instead, he is a sheep. Ridiculously, the text evokes in me feelings of never having been able to measure up to an impossible standard. The same feelings of inadequacy I find myself having in lonely moments in cars with finally-sleeping babies on A roads in the middle of the night.

In my school days, it seemed it was always the prettiest girl – at least pretty by some arbitrary standard of western beauty – who was chosen to play Mary. Even as a child, I had some level of awareness that – ironically –- a brown immigrant child did not fit into the nativity scene. Because the mother of God was surely white. Because whiteness is divine; whiteness is perfection.

In my most frazzled and broken moments of mothering, those times when I am full of regret and shame, I feel far from perfect. Those moments in which I am surrounded by soiled nappies and pieces of Lego feel far away from those paintings of Mary: a serene, quiet, doting, caring mother. A woman with not a hair out of place, skin porcelain-white, eyes fixed on her precious child. A mother so gentle, so loving. A woman who would never shout at her baby because he refused to sleep. A tender-hearted young woman who, when she held him in her arms, knew she held the world. Mary's image has become the standard for mothers in the Anglo-American world. What she represents has been used to beat mothers – and all women – over the head; an impossible standard we must all meet. We have all fallen short of her glory.

Mary represents the archetype of Perfect Motherhood. In her, I see a sister – a mother like me; yet at the same time I feel judged by the unrealistic picture she represents. Catholic theologian Mary C. Gray writes: 'Mary has been used in Christian spirituality as icon, ideal and role-model for *all* women: the ideal has been that of virgin-mother, which is an impossible one for ordinary women to follow.'[7]

Though Christianity's historical influence over society is waning, Anglo-American societies in the twenty-first century continue to be shaped by the Christian imagination, whether we realise it or not. As historian Tom Holland puts it: 'All of us in the West are a goldfish, and the water that we swim in is Christianity.'[8] A culture that clings – however lightly – to the nativity scenes found on Christmas cards and in art galleries and on TV screens sears our collective consciousness.

The ideas about what it is to be a woman, and a mother, that infuse our societies have been shaped by what art historian Catherine McCormack describes as 'an avalanche of Christian devotional images of the Virgin Mary that define mothering as something sacrosanct, monumental, self-sacrificing, subservient, and de-sexualised'.[9] *Matrescence* author Lucy Jones describes the way in which Mary represents a passive receptacle of motherhood ideals: 'She is there as a container, a prop, a dummy.'[10] Writes theologian Nicola Slee: 'It is hardly possible to exist as an inhabitant of the western world, with even half an eye open to the visual and cultural heritage of Christendom, and not to have been in some way affected by this woman, *the* woman of the Christian tradition.'[11]

But who do we see in these portrayals of Mary? A woman who is at once so familiar, yet so unreachable. Her ubiquitous image derived from just a few verses in the Bible, yet hard to grasp beyond the two-dimensional. As Slee notes, despite her lifelong familiarity with Mary, 'somehow her presence remained tacit, shadowy, unexplored'.[12] Mary – or at least Mary in the versions we have come to understand – presents us with something paradoxical. She is at the same time replete with divine qualities and an empty vessel; she is both the prophetic voice railing against injustice in the Magnificat and a passive receptacle without agency. She is whatever the world wants her to be, or indeed whatever the world wants all women to be. Slee puts it like this:

I've come to think [. . .] that Mary functions iconographically, symbolically and theologically in western culture (and perhaps in other cultures too) in much the same way that Christ does in the psyche of Christendom, as a kind of reflective screen upon which has been projected a culture's shifting ideals and aspirations around humanity, sanctity and deity. Specifically, Mary has functioned as a mirror for society's notions of the female, of the holy and of the divine feminine at any one time.[13]

Despite her elusiveness, there's something about Mary – and, in particular, these archetypal notions of the female and of motherhood that she has come to represent – that has a chokehold on women, and not just in the Church. Mary's ubiquity as a maternal archetype in culture helps to explain the number of secular thinkers who, when relaying their experience of motherhood, at some point touch on the perfect ideal she represents. Lucy Jones, again in *Matrescence*, describes the image of a mother that she had before having children: 'Effectively, she was Mary, the mother of Jesus, her expression matching the gold icons we had on the walls and mantelpieces of my childhood home. The baby Jesus, on her lap, was never having a tantrum. His swaddling clothes were immaculate. Motherhood looked chilled.'[14]

In *Of Woman Born*, her iconic feminist rail against the institution of motherhood, Adrienne Rich recalled being pregnant for the first time and feeling that the expectations and views about motherhood were embodied 'in the booklet in my obstetrician's waiting room, the novels I had read, my mother-in-law's approval, my memories of my own mother, the Sistine Madonna or she of the Michaelangelo *Pietà*, the floating notion that a woman pregnant is a woman calm in her fulfilment or, simply, a woman waiting'.[15]

Coming to terms with Mary

The portrayal of Mary has in some ways seeped into secular consciousness more than it has into certain parts of the Church. I was raised in a conservative Christian tradition that did not pay much attention to her. But nevertheless, through, rather than despite, this lack of emphasis, I still absorbed some fundamental assumptions as to what it meant to be a woman and a mother from her portrayal. In my experience of these churches, Mary was – at best – incidental in the muscular story of salvation. She was merely a vessel in which the incarnation took place. The Messiah made his home in her body, squatting there until he was ready to make his divine entrance, in a manger, among the cattle and oxen in a stable in Bethlehem. In these nativity scenes, Mary – with a serenity that would feel completely alien to any twenty-first-century woman who has gone through the wide-eyed craze of the later stages of labour – sits side-saddle on a donkey, hand resting on bump, head covered. Totally fine with the far from sufficient birthing environment. No birthing playlist or midwife; no fairy lights or birth plan. In the tradition in which my faith was forged, Mary was she who carried God, but there was nothing particularly remarkable – and certainly nothing divine – about her. We did not pay attention to her story because it got in the way of the main events. We did not hear her cry for justice, nor did we see her righteousness and strength. The Magnificat – Mary's manifesto for justice and a vision of a world turned upside down, which is found in Luke's Gospel (1:46–55) – was described merely as 'Mary's song' – the warbles of a chaste and obedient woman rather than a rallying cry to dethrone the mighty and turn the world order on its head.

When our gaze *was* turned towards Mary, what was highlighted was her obedience. When the angel visits her to tell her of God's miraculous mission, what was emphasised were these words in Luke 1:38: 'I am the Lord's servant.' It was Mary's 'yes' that set her apart from all others.

But this subservient Mary just would not do for any Christian women who thought of themselves as independent and intelligent, or who did not want to conform to the Church and society's stereo-types of what a woman should be. In her 1982 essay *Coming to Terms with Mary*, author Mary Gordon writes that such women rejected the Virgin Mary in the same way that early feminists might have felt they had to 'radically reject those things that were associated exclu-sively with the female: dresses, make-up, domestic work, relations with men, children'.[16] These questioning women might, however, be more drawn to Mary's initial question in the Annunciation: 'How will this be, since I am a virgin?' (Luke 1:34). Glossed over more often than not, these words express the doubt of a woman who won't simply accept her place; one who dares to question God. This questioning contradicts the narrative of perfect motherhood, which implies that a good mother doesn't question her place. A good mother is steadfast in her role in this, 'the mother of all jobs'; a bad mother isn't so sure. A good mother is unwavering; a bad mother has ups and downs.

For centuries, patriarchal societies have built up a picture of the Bad Mother, and the Good Mother. What constitutes good or bad mothering has seen significant variations over the years, depending on what has been required by national or societal propaganda at the time. But for around two thousand years, the Virgin Mary and the myth of perfect motherhood that surrounds her have both been influenced by the societal norms of the day, and Mary has represented a paragon of womanhood that continues to have an influence on how we are seen, even today.

These are not just saccharine ideals; rather, they give us glimpses into the grittiness of the maternal experience. We can recall Mary gazing into the warmly lit crib, surrounded by shepherds and wise men and angels and animals. But we might also be able to call to mind her sorrow as she cradles her dying son, in the imagery of the pietà, or her openness to wonder and the miraculous in the imagery of the Annunciation, or the solidarity of sisterhood in her visit to her cousin Elizabeth depicted in the many paintings of the Visitation. If we refocus our gaze on who Mary really is – a woman whose motherhood points the way to a God of love, care and justice – we see in Mary, the mother of Jesus, what God is like, and the way in which motherhood itself provides a glimpse into the nature of God. As Amy Peeler writes in *Women and the Gender of God*, '[Mary] flourishes in the roles of mother, as well as proclaimer, presenting the robust possibility of God's yes to other women who are called to do the same. This God who honours women and does not favour men is revealed with dazzling clarity in the pregnancy that is the epicentre of the Christian faith.'[17]

In many ways Mary of Nazareth was extraordinary; but what has drawn me – a Black, twenty-first-century, evangelically raised

Protestant mother – to her is that this Mary reflects back the extraordinary nature of so many of the everyday mothers I see around me. There is the Mary myth that acts as an archetype of perfect motherhood and has oppressed women for centuries. It is she who must be unmade. But there is also the myth, in the sense of a falsehood, which fools us into thinking that this was all that Mary was. Women through history have sensed this falsehood. They have seen in Mary an icon for their own liberation, and a paragon of womanhood that points towards a God whose arms are open to all. These contradictions are why Mary has been both critiqued and hailed by feminist movements at different points in history.[18]

A word about myths

This is a book that attempts to unmake, to deconstruct, the unhelpful narratives about women, and – in particular – mothers, that arise from myths about Mary, and to elevate the helpful truths that arise from what she symbolises. I hope that, in so doing, I can go some way towards shattering the myth of perfect motherhood that is acutely seen through two millennia of portrayals of the mother of God – a myth that hovers over many homes and makes women feel they are constantly failing. This is not a book about whether or not Mary existed, nor whether the Immaculate Conception happened; nor will it explore the arguments for or against the validity of the claim of Mary's perpetual virginity. This is a book about the myth of Mary's perfect motherhood, and the impact of this maternal ideal on women, in both positive and negative ways. It recognises the part the Church has historically played in the subjugation of women through the construction of Mary, but also sees the ways in which the Christian faith and Mary's story – if we can see past the trappings of patriarchy – can free women from the boxes into which we have all been placed.

In today's common parlance, to describe something as myth is often to describe it as fiction, or untrue. But in exploring the myth of Mary's perfect motherhood, I am concerned with the original sense and meaning of the term 'myth' – which goes beyond whether or not something is empirically true.

Mary is one of the greatest myths in human history. So profound is her influence that people have worshipped her, created great artworks depicting her, and erected monuments and churches in her honour. Remembering his Catholic upbringing, US academic and novelist Theodore Roszak writes: 'The early and medieval Church remained pliable enough to accommodate to some degree the widespread need for myth. The major manifestation of this was the cult of the virgin, which elevated the inconsequential figure of Mary to a stupendous symbolic stature.'[19]

The myths of Mary's perfect motherhood are good if they help us rather than hinder us. Comparative religion commentator Karen Armstrong explains:

> If [a myth] does not give us new insight into the deeper meaning of life, it has failed. If it *works*, that is, if it forces us to change our minds and hearts, gives us new hope, and compels us to live more fully, it is a valid myth [. . .] A myth is essentially a guide; it tells us what we must do in order to live more richly.[20]

I believe there is much in Mary's story and in the transcendent beauty of motherhood that can lead us to this deeper richness. As a Protestant reflecting on my own relationship with Mary, there is so much that I had missed; so much of her story that can help women – and in fact, all of us – to gain new insight into the nature of God, and who we are in the light of that nature. We need to unmake the patriarchal trappings of perfect motherhood that have surrounded her to get to these liberating truths for women.

In his 1977 book *The Mary Myth*, Catholic priest Andrew Greeley writes of the usefulness of the myth – by 'myth' he means a symbolic archetype that tells a deeper truth – of Mary, not in pointing us to Mary, but in demonstrating something of the nature of God – that God is not just masculine, but feminine too. 'The theologians may have missed the point or have been afraid to touch it,' he writes, 'but the poets and the painters have not – nor have the Christian faithful.'[21]

It was this deeper truth represented in the person of Mary that drove novelist Toni Morrison away from the African Methodist

Episcopal (AME) Church in which she was raised, and towards Catholicism. Writing about Morrison's conversion, Jennifer Banks suggests: 'Catholicism's emphasis on mothers, bodies, miracles and a lineage of saints that stretches far back into history like holy ancestors must have appealed to her [Morrison].'[22] Mary is a hero of the Christian faith from whom many of us have been told to avert our eyes. But she is worth a second glance.

While by many Mary has been seen as an oppressive – and regressive – standard women are expected to imitate, some see the fact of Mary's motherhood of God as liberating for women. In her study of cross-cultural approaches to Mary, Finnish theologian Elina Vuola suggests that beliefs about Mary are not confined to the doctrines of the Catholic Church, which 'presents Mary to women as a perfect model to follow'.[23] But neither is Mary confined to the subservient, passive, wallflower image that arouses the ire of feminists. Vuola writes that 'believing Christian women in very different contexts tell the same story of a Mary who is both like them and unlike them – and is therefore both a point of deep identification and a source of help and empowerment'.[24] Much of the myth of Mary is helpful. But the idea that leads from a perfect Mary to the belief that there can be such a thing as 'perfect' motherhood for the rest of us – that is the myth. It is the invisible myth that drives much of the challenge of motherhood today. It is the myth that exposes our maternal imperfections, making us feel inadequate, or ashamed. Before becoming mothers, women are shaped by the myth of Mary's divine motherhood, and they are surprised, on attaining motherhood themselves, to find theirs is nothing like they had imagined.

What follows includes my personal reflections on what feminist writer Adrienne Rich describes as 'the institution of motherhood', through meditating on Mary – both her reality and the constructed myth of Mary that pervades our collective consciousness. I attempt to free motherhood from the chokehold of perfection. Throughout the book, I draw on theological ideas, as well as on art, culture, literature and music. I do not pretend to be an expert on motherhood. I am certainly not; and in many ways I am conscious that I am another mother writing another book about motherhood. I have felt the self-consciousness in my answers to people asking what this book is about. *'It's a book about motherhood, but not just motherhood.'* My caution reflects an awareness of a world in which motherhood is mundane, the most ordinary of occurrences; not worthy of further exploration that could tell us anything profound about existential truths. What I hope to offer here is something different: in holding up Mary as a case study, I want to suggest a curiosity about the invisible forces at work (through theology and the Church, art, popular culture, and even the ways in which our societies are structured) that play a part in putting undue pressure on women to meet an impossible standard. Books about motherhood and Christian faith have too often presented a light and insincere picture of what it is to be a good mother. Recent years have seen more women giving voice to the realities of maternity, laying bare the challenges and rejecting the silence that was required of our foremothers. I lend my voice to the growing chorus of women speaking up so that others who come after us – those who face pregnancy and birth and baby loss and infertility and the mental load in the future – might feel less fractured, more forewarned and better held. So that the myth of Mary, and the idea of perfect motherhood, might be helpful rather than oppressive.

Motherhood has given me the highest of highs and the lowest of lows. My hope is that in sharing the realities of the shadow side of motherhood, this book might enable women everywhere to exhale, but also realise that in these shadows we can gain new and profound understanding. I recognise that, for some, what I write in these pages will expose deep personal pain and highlight a profound grief about what has not been, despite being much longed for. I am very aware of my privilege in having children. Giving voice to these experiences might, I hope, let us all give ourselves permission to share beyond binaries, recognising life in all its texture: pain and euphoria, sorrow and beauty, rage and hope.

This book is my breaking cover, with the aim of helping women to break free from the collusion. The Christian faith attempts to confront us with the truth of ourselves, with all our faults and wonder, our brokenness and beauty, and invites us to stand in the light of a God whose love envelops us with a womb-like holding. By breaking cover, I'm attempting to break free from the false and restrictive motherhood ideals that choke and shame and oppress and torment. It's time to tell the truth; to unmake this cloak of perfection that surrounds Mary and shames the rest of us. It is the constructed Mary that I want to 'unmake' – the one onto whom every idea about the maternal ideal has been projected. By unmaking this Mary and the myths of perfect motherhood that surround her, we can find space to see the beauty of the true Mary, and in reflecting on who she is, gain a deeper understanding of the realities – rather than the unhelpful myths – of being a mother, and acquire new insight. Many women through many centuries have found this new insight and liberation in the person of Mary: she who sings of casting down the mighty in the Magnificat. The question for us is the same as the one posed by American academic Kimberly VanEsveld Adams: 'Has the Virgin Mary served only as a distorted and repressive female ideal because of her close links to the practices and politics of a patriarchal church and male-dominated societies, or is she a symbol that can empower women?'[25]

PART TWO

Conception

Chapter 1

The Making of Mary

A Short History of Our Lady

'Vergine madre, figlia del tuo figlio'
('Virgin mother, daughter of your son')

—*Paradiso 33*, Dante[1]

'It's as though, over time, Mary's feet have
gotten farther and farther off the ground.'

—*A Year of Biblical Womanhood*, Rachel Held Evans[2]

Right in the heart of one of the most contested and conflicted places on earth, I held Mary in my hands and felt a sense of peace. I had picked up this serene figure carved out of olivewood at a little shop run by a Palestinian Christian woman, which sat right on the separation wall in the West Bank. It was 2013 and I was on a press trip to Israel and the Occupied Palestinian Territory. Over those ten days, I had stood and prayed at the Western Wall in Jerusalem, experienced the claustrophobia-tinged anxiety of going through a crowded checkpoint guarded by soldiers alongside Palestinians heading in to work in Israel, joined a mobile clinic of Israeli physicians providing medical assistance to those living in poverty, and experienced the crazed religious fervour of tourists visiting the Church of the Nativity. It was there that we glimpsed the place where Jesus is alleged to have been born, his birthplace marked with a fourteen-point star, representing the fourteen generations in the genealogy of Jesus. *Hic De Virgine Maria Jesus Christus Natus Est* – the Latin inscription translating as 'Here Jesus Christ was born to the Virgin Mary'.

It was in this land, amid the violence and political unrest of occupation, that Mary gave birth to her baby – a baby that was to be the Saviour of all humankind. Among the many figures of the Holy Family on sale in that little gift shop on the separation wall, the serenity with which the olivewood Mary figure enveloped her baby spoke to me – a moment of quiet, reassuring love, despite the surreal reality of the huge wall erected as a symbol of humanity's division.

We all know that the Holy Land has been a site of conflict for the three Abrahamic faiths for centuries. In a similar way, Mary too is contested, as is what she tells us about humanity and motherhood and women and God. Though her significance crosses Judaism, Islam and Christianity, she herself was of course Jewish. She was devoted to Yahweh and lived her life according to the Torah and the cultural traditions handed down to her over generations. In that sense, as the Reverend Lucy Winkett describes it, she is 'a literal umbilical link between Judaism and Christianity'.[3] She is also revered in Islam. Maryam bint Imran, as she is known, is mentioned around seventy times in the Qur'an – many more times than she appears in the Bible. The 19th chapter in the Qur'an, Surah Maryam, is named after her, and it is within the Qur'an that she is identified as the greatest woman ever to have lived.

Christian thinkers from across denominations and traditions have wrestled with Mary – her identity and her significance – ever since Jesus' nativity. There is the historical figure, Mary of Nazareth, the mother of Jesus, and then there is Mary the shapeshifting myth, whose identity is formed and promoted to reflect what a culture believes – or wants people to believe – about women, and about God. Marina Warner writes: 'A myth of such dimension is not simply a story, or a collection of stories, but a magic mirror like the Lady of Shalott's, reflecting a people and the beliefs they produce, recount, and hold.'[4] In a way, Mary functions like an 'everywoman' – she is a character who can represent what we want her to. Because of the lack of material that exists in the canon about who Mary really was, there has been a lot of room to create different versions of her. A 'towering female presence in theology, art and worship', as Clarissa Atkinson describes it, has been built 'using scraps of evidence' both from the Gospel accounts and from apocryphal material from outside the Bible.[5]

As we do with most of the people mentioned in the Bible, we get to know Mary through the actions she takes and the words she says, analysing her responses for hidden meanings, based on what we know about human nature. So what does the Bible's description of Mary tell us about who she truly is, and what can we learn from how she has been constructed and characterised in popular culture, right up to the present day? How did we go from the few verses about Mary in the Bible to her being described as the Queen of Heaven, the God-bearer, the Mother of Mercy, the Star of the Sea, Our Lady? This chapter does not attempt to be an exhaustive commentary on two millennia of Marian devotion, but highlights some key moments in the making of Mary and, in particular, the potential impact of them on the idea of perfect motherhood.

Here, I should make it clear that I do not believe that Mary is a mythical character. There is much historical evidence to prove that she was a living, breathing person. She is not like the tooth fairy, or a fairy godmother, or Father Christmas. Instead, when I describe the myth of Mary, I see this as more akin to the myth that surrounds the person of Winston Churchill. There is the man, and there is the myth. There is Churchill the man who was born in November 1874 and died in January 1965, and whose political career spanned fifty-five years, including two stints as prime minister of the United Kingdom. And then there is the Churchill who has come to symbol-ise good leadership, manhood, bravery and Britishness; the one who said, 'If you're going through hell, keep going' – although he did not. The one who has been hailed as a god-like hero, although he was very human. This is also not to say that a myth is necessarily bad. Myths help us find meaning, they unite nations and people, they help us tell stories about what it is to be human. The problem for me is when a myth becomes damaging rather than helpful; when it is draining rather than life-giving. On this question, when it comes to the myth of Mary and this myth's impact on mothers, I am undecided.

I want to shatter the myth that Mary only presents us, as women and mothers, with a patriarchal and restrictive view of who and what we should be; to shatter this idea of Mary as the archetypal mother whose perfection – a perfection mistakenly reduced to coyness, aesthetic beauty, self-sacrifice and domestic mastery – makes all of us feel like failures.

There are elements of Mary's story, however, that can provide strength and inspiration for mothers, and all women, today. The powerful Mary who gave birth to God, the thinking Mary who questioned the angel's proclamation about her impending mother-hood, the revolutionary Mary who declared that God has 'brought down rulers from their thrones, but has lifted up the humble' (Luke 1:52). The Mary of the pietà who provides comfort to heartbroken mothers, the brown-skinned, migrant Mary who is in solidarity with those who are oppressed and marginalised.

Shattering the myth of perfect motherhood that surrounds Mary will help us better see this more interesting, compelling and helpful Mary; and this just might change our lives.

To shatter the myth, however, we first have to see how it has been constructed.

Disciple, prophet, mother

One of the myths of Mary's motherhood as it has been presented to us over the centuries is the false idea that she was passive and submis-sive, and that her role was confined to that of being a mother. Rather, if we take off the lenses of western thought that have shaped how we view Mary and in turn how we predominantly view all women and mothers, and attempt to see her through the lens of the earliest followers of Jesus, we see a very different Mary emerging. This Mary was a mother, yes, but she was a mother who had power and author-ity; a mother who helped shape and lead the movement that would change the world.

Mary is not mentioned by name in the Old Testament, save for a reference to a virgin who will bear a son (Isaiah 7:14). 'Mary' being one of the most popular Jewish names at the time, the New Testament refers to at least five other women called Mary, besides Jesus' mother: Mary Magdalene, Mary of Bethany, Mary, the mother of Mark, Mary, the wife of Clopas, and the Mary who goes to a church in Rome. Mary, Jesus' mother, is given direct speech just seven times in the Bible. While this is more than many other characters, it is remarkable that so much devotion and oppression and inspiration and liberation have come from so few words. Nevertheless, the biblical narratives are rife with much symbolism, telling us a lot about who Mary is and what she signifies. But sometimes you have to look to find it. The master storytelling of Luke's Gospel account paints pictures that give us insight into his theological understanding of the life and times of Jesus. While in Matthew, Mary's role is limited to that of mother, albeit the mother of the Messiah, Luke paints a fuller picture of Mary, portraying her, as Beverly Roberts Gaventa describes it, in 'three distinct roles, those of disciple, prophet, and mother'.[6] Within the wider narrative of Luke, we see the writer place a special emphasis on the role of women in the kingdom of God, including in his presentation of Mary as the first follower of Jesus. She has faith in Christ before he is even born, her faithfulness made evident in her words at the Annunciation: 'I am the Lord's servant. May your word to me be fulfilled' (Luke 1:38). For early Jewish readers of Luke's Gospel, Mary echoed the heroes of the Old Testament, including the mothers who were also visited by angels before becoming pregnant and giving birth to great biblical figures. In John's Gospel, Mary comes to life even more, her prophetic instruction to Jesus to help out when the wedding at Cana runs out of wine instigating his first miracle (John 2:1–12). As his mother, she wielded the power to tell him what to do.

The dominant myth of Mary – a myth which has promoted a view of women as submissive, with motherhood a woman's main redemption – would not have been possible without centuries of biblical translation having happened within patriarchal contexts. Most of those who have translated the Bible since the first century have been men whose context was one in which women were subordinate. It would have taken a great deal of effort – or perhaps divine revelation through the Holy Spirit – for them to have taken off the patriarchally tinted glasses and translated or read Scripture in the context of an imagined world where women were equal; and yet despite the scarce likelihood of that happening, we can still find surprising glimpses of Mary's discipleship and prophetic role within Jesus' ministry, alongside the important stories about her motherhood.

When Christian feminists in recent history have sought to liberate the faith from the clutches of patriarchal theology, they have often reached right back to Scripture itself to shine a light on the radical and liberatory teachings of Jesus. In the New Testament we find Jesus turning the world on its head in the very act of speaking to women publicly, and doing so openly in a society in which women's voices had no place. Jesus noticed women the world had forgotten or cast out. He healed women, including those with afflictions considered taboo – those tainted by blood or possessed by evil spirits. A resurrected Jesus appears first to women in a society in which women's accounts were not valued. It is also in the New Testament that we find a woman, Mary, chosen to bring forth the Messiah, and that same woman is the first to announce that God's kingdom – a new world order – is at hand, through her song, the Magnificat. Women – including Jesus' mother – played key roles in Jesus' ministry, as well as in leading the community of believers after his death. For example, Mary Magdalene was the first witness to his resurrection, Joanna supported him financially, and Salome accompanied Jesus and his disciples in their ministry. Historians of early Christianity have suggested that there existed within the early Church a belief that Mary was the new Abraham. The Gospel accounts of both Luke and John contain rich symbolism that alludes to this, including the announcement to Mary by a messenger of God that she would conceive a firstborn son, just as happened to Abraham (Genesis 18:10). In John's Gospel, Jesus – Mary's son – carries the wood for his own sacrifice up the mountain towards his crucifixion, just as Abraham did when God told him to sacrifice his son Isaac. Just as Mary stood atop Golgotha at her son's sacrifice, so Abraham stood on top of Mount Moriah. Ally Kateusz summarises: 'The authors of Luke and John, thus, appear to have believed that a Judean woman could be both a mother and a leader.'[7]

The earliest examples of Marian theology date from around the fourth century. It is easy to see how, in an age without the printing press, ideas about the nature and personhood of Jesus and God, and in turn Mary, might have been disparate, wild and uncontainable. All sorts of ideas sprang up, many of which are documented in historic writings from the earliest centuries. It was during the

Council of Ephesus in 431 – when a gathering of clergy sought to nail down once and for all a few of the main ideas of Christianity that had been in circulation for decades – that a high view of Mary was confirmed, sifting through the disparate ideas about Mary that had circulated over the previous century to arrive at a more defined Marian theology. During the Council, they discussed the relationship between Jesus' human nature and his divinity, and therefore had to discuss the circumstances of his birth. Poring over scriptural references and logic, these early church Fathers settled on the following: 'If anyone does not confess that Emmanuel is God in truth, and therefore that the holy virgin is the mother of God (for she bore in a fleshly way the Word of God become flesh), let him be anathema.'[8]

Catholic theologian Tina Beattie marks this moment as the start of a high view of Mary, writing that her 'motherhood begins to acquire power not just through her historical privilege in being the mother of the incarnate Christ and her womanly significance as the new Eve, but predominantly through her transcendent personal glory as the Mother of God'.[9] Consistent with the patriarchy of the world and the Church at the time, there were of course no women in attendance at the Council of Ephesus – not even just to take the notes or make the tea. The bishops had, however, recognised the importance of motherhood in bringing about the birth of God and the salvation of all humankind. They had dared to place Mary at the heart of the story, through being true to what they understood the Scriptures to be saying. They had a high view of Mary because of their beliefs about the nature of Jesus' fully divine and fully human status. To this end, as Atkinson writes, 'Mariology conformed to Christology'.[10] Although the early church Fathers thought Mary was holy, they did not think she was immaculate.[11] This doctrine came later. Mary's Immaculate Conception – the belief that she herself was born without sin, not, as it is often confused with, the belief that she became pregnant and gave birth as a virgin – was officially declared dogma by Pope Pius IX in 1854. Although this doctrine was confirmed more than a thousand years after the early church Fathers first put it into words, it is thought that beliefs about Mary's sinlessness had existed for centuries.

This high view of Mary is important, and shows us something of the nature of who God is; but the flip side is that it has contributed to setting a high, even impossible, standard for all other women. As Beattie writes, this 'may have worked to the detriment of real women in the Church, marking the beginnings of a widening gulf between Marian symbolism and women's experience'.[12] The doctrine of the Immaculate Conception further widened the gap between Mary and ordinary women, who of course could never be perfect.

A medieval Mary

In the eleventh century, significant changes took place in the personal, political and cultural lives of Europeans. Increased trade, the development of towns and cities, and agricultural and techno-logical developments led to – among other things – better food and nutrition, better fertility rates and a decrease in child mortality. Alongside this came increased opportunity, including better educa-tion and more literacy, which previously had only existed within monasteries. Where once the only resources people had to form their theological understanding were sermons and pictures, they now had words. The implications were profound, including 'the construction and circulation of new literary representations of the Virgin Mary', writes Atkinson.[13]

But it is important to note that until the modern era, most Christians could not read. For them, 'the walls of the churches were their Bible',[14] and it was on these walls that, through vivid imagery and iconography rather than words, Mary was constructed and portrayed. So it has often been artists who have been those communicating profound truths – both about what society tells us about Mary and motherhood, and about the deeper divine truths that can often lie beneath the surface. From cave drawings to Renaissance paintings to today's artworks, artists have either made evident the overarching narratives about what it is to be human through their work, or challenged these dominant narratives through subversive images.

While writing this book, I have been struck again by the power of art to both reflect and shape our cultural narratives. Ally Kateusz charts the ways in which iconography tells us a lot about society's ideas about the role of women and mothers – for example, by analysing how women sit or kneel or stand within imagery, and whether they are outside the home or confined to it. She writes:

> Religious authorities as well as women themselves have used, and continue to use, Mary's gendered behavior to validate similar behavior in women and girls. Mary's body performs as a model for Christian women. When scribes and artists gradually changed their portrayal of Mary from an arms-raised liturgical leader to a silent woman who physically expressed her submission by looking at the floor, we may conclude that at least metaphorically, something dramatic had changed with respect to this feminine cultural ideal for women.[15]

Mary's making and unmaking through the centuries have seen her portrayal as a feminine cultural ideal changed and developed depending on the wider socio-political context of the time. It is in the stained-glass windows of medieval churches and the artistic retellings of Mary's story through paintings and sculptures and plaques that we see the democratisation of the Christian story, as well as the ways in which certain narratives about Mary and mother, anchored in the Church's theology, impacted the lives of those who could not read the Bible, but could understand its truths through imagery.

One of the dominant portrayals within Marian devotion and art in the early Middle Ages was the depiction of Mary as the Queen of Heaven. Her royal title and subsequent portrayal reflected the idea that she was the mother of the King of Israel, and also the Catholic teaching that Mary was assumed into heaven at the end of her life, where she then reigned alongside her son as heaven's queen.

It was during the Middle Ages – when there was also a massive explosion of Marian devotion alongside these visual representations – that a number of powerful representations of Mary were created to communicate who she was, what she represented, and the message being sent to other mothers, and other women more widely. This explosion of Marian devotion occurred around the time of the Crusades in the twelfth century, which signalled the arrival of a 'new

Christendom'. Rome needed unifying symbols for military success, and so 'Mary gradually took the place of old, familiar, and beloved local saints and acquired some of their characteristics – intimacy, immediacy, and parental concern for the affairs of her children'.[16]

In his iconic 1969 BBC TV history series *Civilisation*, Sir Kenneth Clark said that one of the greatest achievements of the Catholic Church over this bloody and brutal period in history had been in 'harmonising, humanising, civilising the deepest impulses of ordinary people'.[17] What made this possible, in his view, was the maternal influence of Mary. 'In the early twelfth century,' Clark says, 'the virgin had been the supreme protectress of civilisation. She had taught a race of tough and ruthless barbarians the virtues of tenderness and compassion.'[18]

Motherhood and the Reformation

Whereas once it was Mary's virginity that needed to be protected at all costs, because it was that which symbolised her holiness, Mary as Mother grew in popularity and influence following the Reformation, as did the idea of the family, and a woman's role as mother within the family. Medieval historian Dr Beth Allison Barr writes in *The Making of Biblical Womanhood* that, while the Reformation's ultimate aims – to highlight God's saving grace – were good, it had negative side effects when it came to the place and role of women within society. 'Women have always been wives and mothers, but it wasn't until the Protestant Reformation that being a wife and a mother became the "ideological touchstone of holiness"[19] for women.' In prior centuries, it had been asceticism, set-apartness and abstinence from worldly pleasures such as sex that had symbolised holiness, but now the opposite was required.

Barr writes: 'The further removed medieval women were from the married state, the closer they were to God. After the Reformation, the opposite became true for Protestant women. The more closely they identified with being wives and mothers, the godlier they became.'[20] In his lengthy treatise of 1522, *The Estate of Marriage*, German theologian and priest Martin Luther, a seminal figure of the

Reformation, extolled the virtues of parenthood and said that it was women's sole purpose to be a mother. 'If you were not a woman you should now wish to be one for the sake of this very work alone, that you might thus gloriously suffer and even die in the performance of God's work and will.'[21]

Alongside the Reformation's challenge to the authority of the Pope and what it perceived as an undue focus on saints and relics, there also came a strong critique of Catholic devotion to Mary. Sir Kenneth Clark highlights the psychological and spiritual repercussions for everyday Catholic devotees of Mary following the impact of the Reformation. While remaining the Queen of Heaven, Mary had – before the Reformation – 'become also the human mother in whom everybody could recognise those qualities of warmth and love and approachability'.

The Holy Family

While the Queen of Heaven imagery had represented an unattainable ideal – a supernatural and divine mother who stood above all other women – medieval imagery at other times emphasised Mary's humanity, so that she might serve as an example to other mothers. The cult of the Holy Family (Joseph, Mary and Jesus) created a template for other human families at a time when the construction of the family as providing stability hinged on the authority of a father. Whereas once Joseph was most commonly portrayed as feeble, elderly and an unimportant extra in the scenes telling the stories of Jesus' childhood, the late Middle Ages saw him begin to play a more central role in the imagery, as marriage became a more important state within Christian ideology. For the Holy Family to shape societal attitudes, they needed to be relatable. Late medieval European imagery of Mary and Joseph, writes Atkinson, included Jesus' parents carrying out 'domestic roles and relationships that might be emulated by ordinary people'.[22] Artists started to depict Mary as the Queen of Heaven less often, and more often to portray her 'as the humble young woman nursing her baby or the tortured old woman at the Cross'.[23]

Joseph's movement from the periphery to centre stage within this period is a stark demonstration of the symbiosis between theology and culture and social norms. If the powers-that-were wanted to highlight the importance of male authority and female submissiveness within the home, then Joseph became a prop – in reality, a form of propaganda – to help get their message across. During the Catholic revival in France, which took place in the seventeenth century, books and devotional material centring on the Holy Family were created that further emphasised domestic roles. In these, as Marina Warner writes, young women were encouraged to imitate the Virgin Mary, and know their place. In this time, she was portrayed less as a regal monarch, no longer embodying the female power of deities or of characters such as *Game of Thrones'* Daenerys Targaryen, and more like the helpmate of St Joseph: 'Her purity and submissiveness and poverty became quintessential motherliness. Joseph protects her and works to keep her and the child; she is obedient, respectful, humble, quiet, and modest, simple in her tastes and demeanour, compliant, and gentle. Even her silence in the Gospels is turned to good account, becoming an example to all women to hold their tongues.'[24] It is not hard to see the potential pitfalls of this messaging. As feminist theologians from the Asia–Pacific region noted in 1994: 'The idea of Mary's perpetual virginity has . . . given us Mary, Joseph and Jesus as the example of the "ideal family". In this family, the two adults have no sexual relationship, and there is only one child, who is not the son of Mary's husband. It is not surprising then that Catholics have inherited a marked sexual neurosis.'[25]

The Madonna complex

Mary is the most prominent woman in the Bible, but her foremother Eve comes a close second. Just as Jesus has symbolically been described as the 'new Adam' in theological thought, so Mary has been described as the 'new Eve' in whom the renewal and redemption of the earth is completed, following the transgressions of her foremother, Eve, in the Fall. The Madonna–whore complex is a construct that speaks to this categorisation of women into two distinct identities. The complex, which was first identified by the founder of psychoanalysis, Sigmund Freud, describes the male psychological categorisation of women into either 'Madonnas' or 'whores': perfect mothers or fallen women; Mary or Eve. Some of the earliest teachings about Mary pertain to her as this second Eve, with early church Fathers such as Tertullian and St Irenaeus sharing their belief in this doctrine. In the second century, St Justin Martyr wrote that Eve 'brought forth disobedience and death', while Mary acted in 'faith and joy' when she was told by the angel that she would bear God's son.[26] In the Second Vatican Council, which took place between 1962 and 1965, Pope John XXIII continued the tradition, citing the early Fathers' views about the two matriarchs: 'Hence in their preaching not a few of the early Fathers gladly assert . . . "The knot of Eve's disobedience was untied by Mary's obedience. What the virgin Eve bound through her unbelief, Mary loosened by her faith." Comparing Mary with Eve, they call her "the mother of the living," and still more often they say: "death through Eve, life through Mary".'[27]

Together, these two matriarchs of the faith symbolically represent the binaries by which women throughout the ages have been labelled. Their treatment within early patriarchal Christianity, the vestiges of which remain today, also pertains to all women. Gloria Thurmond writes: 'The sharp parallelism between Eve and the Virgin Mary has served to fragment and objectify all women, and to project onto their lives an overlay that lacks the depth, the complexity, and the reality of all that it means to be fully human.'[28]

Eve has been blamed for sin entering the world, the Fall ushering in an irreparable brokenness. 'Because of her actions,' Elina Vuola writes, 'Eve proved to be not the mother of life but rather the "mother of death"'.[29] Sin, guilt, shame, death – only here because of this womanly temptress's actions. *The woman you put here with me*, Adam tells God, *she made me do it*. The blame lies solely at her feet, we have been made to believe, and men cannot be held responsible for their actions. Women in many ways have been blamed for the sexual violence and assault that has been wrought upon them, because men have not been able to resist the temptations of the female body. Adrienne Rich, in *Of Woman Born*, outlines this idea well:

> Throughout patriarchal mythology, dream symbolism, theology, language, two ideas flow side by side. One, that the female body is impure, corrupt, a site of discharges, bleedings, dangerous to masculinity, a source of moral and physical contamination, the devil's gateway. On the other hand, as mother, the woman is beneficent, sacred, pure, asexual, nourishing, and the physical potential for motherhood – that same body with its bleedings and mysteries – is her single destiny and justification in life. These two ideas have become deeply internalized in women. Even in the most independent of us, those who seem to lead the freest lives.[30]

We see this polarisation not just in descriptions of Eve and Mary, but with Mary Magdalene and Mary, Jesus' mother. As Kateusz describes it, though both played leading roles in Jesus' ministry and the formation of Christianity, both have been 'recast as caricatures . . . one as a sinful whore and the other as a submissive virgin'.[31]

Rich goes on to explain: 'In order to maintain such notions, each in its contradictory purity, the masculine imagination has had to divide women, to see us, and force us to see ourselves, as polarized into good or evil, fertile or barren, pure or impure . . . The asexual Victorian angel-wife and the Victorian prostitute were institutions created by this double thinking, which had nothing to do with women's actual sexuality and everything to do with the male subjective experience of women.'[32]

For Katharine Bushnell, who, among many other things, worked as a global anti-trafficking activist, and committed herself to highlighting the plight of sex workers in the nineteenth century, it was Christian men – and a bad theology that saw women as lesser – who were the culprits of these heinous trades of trafficking and prostitution. When she travelled to India, she uncovered the abusive practices of the British army, who put local women in military brothels. She was outraged by this sexual double standard. Writing about Bushnell, Kristin Kobes Du Mez states: 'Bushnell was shocked to discover that the men guilty of abusing women were more often than not Christian men. Ultimately, she concluded that patriarchal theology must be to blame.'[33]

The paradox that has long persisted within patriarchal Christianity is that women have traditionally been seen as less than men in most spheres: morally deficient, lacking in intellectual capabilities, full of vices that would cause them to be the instigators of sin entering into the perfect Garden of Eden. And yet it is these fallen, unclever women who have been trusted with the greatest task there is: to raise the future generations.

By the later Middle Ages, the myth of perfect motherhood had found its outworking in the cult of the Virgin Mary, but it was the decision to situate the sphere of womanhood firmly within the home that coincided with a rebrand of sorts for Mary in the lead-up to the Victorian period. From the sixteenth century, women were no longer seen as morally deficient, but as innocent – and as those who needed to be protected from the sin and avarice of the rational outside worlds of business, science and church leadership.

In the shadow of the Enlightenment, in which the West loosened the grip of religious institutions in favour of belief in science and reason, the Virgin Mary continued to shape consciousness about women and family, albeit now in a more secularised form. The idea of Mary's virtue and purity became less about religious ideas and more about 'sentimental heroines, such as the beneficent domestic "Angel in the House"',[34] which will be explored more in the following chapter. In the UK, it could perhaps also be argued that Queen Victoria, with her husband, Albert, and their nine children, was more prevalent in the minds of Victorians as a paragon of motherhood to which all women should aspire.

A millennial Mary

The Second Ecumenical Council of the Vatican, or Vatican II, took place between 1962 and 1965, and marked a moment in which the Catholic Church considered again the nature of Marian devotion. The Council resisted the call from some quarters to elevate Mary to a higher status by introducing new dogma about her relationship to divinity, but maintained that she was to be honoured and venerated. But the Church was wrestling with how to modernise and appeal to an ever-changing world where both the role of women and the role of religion were changing.

In the preceding pages we have seen the fruits of two millennia of this creative imagination, and the ways in which the Mary myth has constantly reinvented itself. A decade after Vatican II, Pope Paul VI addressed this, and recognised that Mary had to be remade – as she had always been – in the light of the social, political and cultural context of the day. As feminist theologian Elizabeth A. Johnson would say three decades after this in an address in 2000: 'The image of Mary has allowed the Christian imagination to think very creatively and very differently about understanding Mary.'[35] Pope Paul VI's *Marialis Cultus* said that Mary continued to be the perfect example of Christian devotion which all – including women – should aim to imitate, but not necessarily in the restrictive ways that preceding patriarchal cultures had suggested. He wrote:

> It should be considered quite normal for succeeding generations of Christians in differing sociocultural contexts to have expressed their sentiments about the Mother of Jesus in a way and manner which reflected their own age. In contemplating Mary and her mission these different generations of Christians, looking on her as the New Woman and perfect Christian, found in her as a virgin, wife and mother the outstanding type of womanhood and the preeminent exemplar of life lived in accordance with the Gospels and summing up the most characteristic situations in the life of a woman.[36]

He added that while the Church's long history of devotion to Mary was to be celebrated, it should not be bound to any 'particular expression of an individual cultural epoch or to the particular anthropological ideas underlying such expressions' and said that some ways of expressing religious devotion to Mary might just not work for the culture of the day. The myth of perfect motherhood, just like the portrayal of Mary, has shapeshifted through the centuries. As Nadia Maria Filippini writes: 'Over time, representations of motherhood in its various facets have constantly changed, albeit in anything but linear and progressive ways, with periods of sudden acceleration and long continuities, alongside innovations and changes. These cultural representations are at the root of the rituals that accompany mother-hood and birth.'[37] Though it is ever-changing, what I've come to understand is that no matter what maternal ideal is presented, most mothers are convinced that we fall far short of the standard, leaving us feeling constantly inadequate.

Chapter 2

Mother Superior

Dispatches from Maternal Inadequacy

'Many women have done excellently, but you surpass them all.'

—Proverbs 31:29 (ESV)

'If I had been able to let go instead of wanting everything
to be perfect, maybe I would not have gone crazy.'

—Sarah Hubert and Isabelle Aujoulat, 'Parental
Burnout: When Exhausted Mothers Open Up'[1]

To be a good mother, all you need to do is to be perfect. I was
alarmed at how quickly I felt the pressure to be just that – a perfect
mother; or at least seen to be one. In the days and weeks after I
found out I was pregnant, the weight of responsibility and expectation grew with my baby bump. In truth, it grew much faster. My
bump took its time. But once the pregnancy test confirmed our
hopes, I started to feel self-conscious about every action I took. Was
my posture correct? Was I attempting to eat a balanced diet? Was I
staying away from too much caffeine, the wrong types of cheese, too
much tuna? I was taken aback at my booking appointment – when
you become pregnant, it's the first time you go to your GP to
confirm the estimated due date (EDD), and it sets off a series of
appointments that see you through till the baby's arrival – when the
nurse practitioner reeled off information and advice as she handed
me my pregnancy book and leaflets all stored in a shiny, colourful
folder. 'Remember not to stretch your hands above your head. It's
dangerous for the baby.' Really? I'd not heard that one before. But

she insisted that this was true. I walked home with my hands at my sides.

Margaret Hebblethwaite describes the pressures placed on mothers to make perfect choices to ensure we do no harm to our babies. She writes in *Motherhood and God* of the methods parents employ to get their babies to sleep, because sleep deprivation is the root of so many maternal challenges, or at the very least, it exacerbates them. Writing in 1984, she described parents playing classical music, or driving around the ring road at 50 mph, or playing tapes of the mother's heartbeat to soothe the baby, or turning on the vacuum cleaner. 'Not feeling guilty is possibly even harder today than it used to be,' she writes. 'Now that there are so many schools of advice, so many idealistic words poured into baby books, such high maternal hopes.'[2] Forty years after these words were written, high maternal hopes are now in overdrive, with technological advancements, internet forums and social media placing even more pressure on mothers to live up to unrealistic expectations. Parenting manuals abound. The book *What to Expect When You're Expecting* – known as the 'pregnancy bible' – is now in its fifth edition, and has sold more than 22 million copies. Written by Heidi Murkoff, it has been named one of the most influential books of the past twenty-five years by *USA Today*. Advice and guidance aimed at helping us achieve the status of perfect motherhood are now legion. It is thought the parenting advice industry, dubbed the 'new mom economy' in the USA, is worth $46 billion in the States alone.[3] Just as the beauty industry thrives on our imperfections with the promise of flawless skin, perfect eyebrows and defined cheekbones, so too the parenting industry exists to play on our insecurities about how we are mothering. Although these products are described as offering advice on 'parenting', the reality is the vast majority of people who buy the books, listen to the podcasts and subscribe to the courses are women. I remember soon after finding out we were pregnant the first time buying a pile of books so I could read up on it all. I had thought that arming myself with knowledge was what would get me through; that I would be prepared. It was as if all those subtle messages that had entered into my subconscious through various media and societal pressures my whole life were channelled into this drive to devour all the knowledge I could – to equip myself to be the perfect mother. I scrabbled around for books for Mark to read too, aimed at the father's experience. But there were fewer dad-oriented resources around. It was as if no one was expecting anything of men. And the books that there were played on lazy stereotypes about men, with swear words on the covers and advice about the 'practical' knowledge required, and were littered with terms like 'survival' and 'mastery' and references to warfare.

Hail Mary, full of grace

Catholics around the world will be familiar with the prayer that begins: *Hail Mary, full of grace*. The words echo the proclamation in Luke's Gospel by the Angel Gabriel to Mary as he announces that she will be the mother of God. Catholic theological tradition affirms that being full of grace equates to being without sin; and that it was fitting for her – as the mother of God – to herself be immaculately conceived. It follows that a sinless Saviour would be born of a sinless mother. Unlike the rest of humanity, so this tradition states, Mary was not born with original sin and never sinned at all.

The construction of this Mary – the perfect ideal of both mother-hood and womanhood – would not be a problem if every other mother was not expected to resemble her in some way. The Council of Nicaea in 325 held her up as the example for women to follow, declaring: 'The Lord looked upon the whole of creation, and he saw no one to equal Mary. Therefore he chose her for his mother. If therefore a girl wants to be called a virgin, she should resemble Mary.'[4] It is not, however, the call to resemble a 'perfect' person that is in itself problematic; Christian discipleship at its heart is about resembling Jesus, who himself was a perfect incarnation of God. What is problematic, though, is when our *idea* of what we are trying to resemble – this constructed, 'perfect' Mary – is shaped by sexist or imbalanced expectations. 'Mary' must be unmade in order to free other women from the pressure to be perfect mothers, which is a futile ambition if this perfection means poise, aesthetic beauty and everlasting serenity and submission. In fact, motherhood might be beautifully demonstrated in feeling at the end of your tether, exhausted and covered in your own breast milk, shouting at your baby because they take too long to go to sleep, and then *still* waking up to comfort them an hour later. There is beauty there, in this divine motherhood; this more textured construction of motherhood could help to free us all.

There is an unwelcome drive in me to become a mother – a woman – like Mary. Or at least to become the venerated ideal of motherhood she has come to represent: a perfect mother. Blameless, without sin. Forever loving, ever-faithful, always sacrificial. For some Christian thinkers, this is exactly the ideal that I as a woman and a mother should be striving towards – doing my utmost to try to be like the mother of God. For some, men should imitate Christ, while women should imitate Mary.

'Just as the goal of all human education is presented to us in a concrete, vital and personal way through Christ,' writes Saint Edith Stein, 'so also the goal of all women's education is presented to us through Mary . . . God chose as the instrument of His incarnation a human mother, and in her He presented the perfect image of a mother.'[5] But the idea of the immaculate conception drives her further away from everyday women's experiences. Where we are ordinary, she is extraordinary. Where we are fallible humans, she is a human whose perfection bestows on her a divine-like status.

Of course, Mary is not ever-present in my mind, but what she represents – the image of a perfect mother – is. This institution of motherhood that has been both subtly and unsubtly represented in art, music, entertainment, literature and theology for many centuries is the ideal against which I measure my motherhood. There are times when I might resemble this perfect mother. A freeze-frame in which my children are being well-behaved and I seem to have it together: all of us dressed, fed, watered and happy. These moments are rare. For most of the time, I feel that I am drowning under the weight of imperfection. As if the goal of being a good mother will forever remain just beyond my grasp. As writer Elise Loehnen puts it: 'Nobody can quantify what a "good mother" even looks like these days; most of us just swim in the shame of certainty that we wouldn't qualify.'[6]

In her fascinating exploration of the depiction of women in art through the male gaze, art historian Catherine McCormack describes the ways in which depictions of Mary exacerbate the unachievable ideal. Writing in *Women in the Picture: Women, Art and the Power of Looking*, McCormack says:

> If ever we doubted how much motherhood is asked to contain, we need only look to images of the archetypal Madonna of Christian images who bears the burden of a schizophrenic number of responsibilities. Mary is a teenage mother to a son who is later murdered as an adult. She is comforter to the desperate and the humble, and is a meek girl from Galilee but also wears the mantle of queen of the court of heaven. Mary is a personification of the Church, intercessor between the human and spiritual realm, and bride of Christ; all the while remaining uncomplaining, pliant, accepting, and silent.[7]

This is an insightful description of the competing identities and juxtaposed responsibilities and pressures placed on women as mothers. While only Mary herself faced the unique realities of being the mother of God, the rest of us can understand the ways in which we are called to be everything – beautiful, calm, patient, doting domestic goddesses. The pictures of motherhood painted over time still have an impact on us today.

A portrait of a mother

When I think of a good mother, I think of a mother who prepares fresh meals for her family, and who is able to do so through meticulous planning and meal preparation. Her children always eat what's on their plates, even if that includes broccoli. She is such a success as a mother that there is not a fussy eater among her brood. After her children have finished their food, they clear up the table and wrap their arms around their mother's legs and bury their heads in her apron (she actually has an apron), and she lovingly strokes their heads before they run off to their playroom. The

playroom is pristine. It looks like one I've seen in an IKEA catalogue, with a child-sized wigwam and fairy lights and wall art. The
good mother is able to keep it pristine because she has a strict
system of toy rotation – choosing small selections of toys at a time
that the children can play with until they are bored with them, at
which point they are switched for other toys. If they are not playing, her children willingly do their homework. They do not beg
for the iPad, and their mother definitely does not just give in after
an eternity of whining and let them sit in front of the screen up
until (and including) bedtime. Her children play together nicely
because of her good mothering. Back in the kitchen, the good
mother tidies away the dinner plates, washes up the pans and stacks
the dishwasher. The good mother never leaves the clearing up until
the morning. Once this is done, she sits down at the kitchen table
and looks at her to-do list. A few things still to do: iron her
husband's shirts for tomorrow; make up the children's lunch boxes
(there is no chocolate in these lunch boxes, but there is both fruit
and a flapjack – homemade, of course); let the school know she
will be able to attend the reading morning later that week. Because
where else would she rather be? A good mother does not go to
work because what more fulfilling role is there than raising her
children? She does it out of choice, not because she has no other
option. Not because her income would not cover the cost of childcare. This mother can choose to stay at home because she has a
partner who can take care of the finances and who supports her
decision to stay at home because it means his wife can do what
good mothers are supposed to do. And not because it means he no
longer has to iron his own shirts. Because of course being a good
mother means being a spectacular wife.

Societal ideas about being a good mother – indeed, a perfect
mother – in the end boil down to how our society expects all women
to be, whether or not they are mothers. Mothers – and all women
– are expected to be caring. Mothers – and all women – are expected
to be domesticated. Mothers – and all women – are expected to be
kind. Mothers – and all women – are expected to be beautiful.
Mothers – and all women – are expected to be only truly fulfilled by
motherhood alone. One writer suggests: 'The ideology of good

mother is a patriarchal construct traditionally defining the mother as "white, middle-class, married, stay-at-home".[8]

Often added to societal expectations are narratives about women as mothers that come from the Church. I used to believe that my greatest and most important role in life was to be a mother, and that any other achievements paled into insignificance if I were not fulfilling the divine mandate to go forth and multiply, and, having multiplied, if I did not then devote my energies to the pursuit of perfect motherhood. Although it is something that we have to work towards, it is also implied that perfect motherhood is *natural* for women. *God made women to be mothers. The Bible tells us so.*

But for many women, motherhood does not come easily. This unnaturalness can sometimes be made evident in the process of becoming a mother, where fertility journeys are fraught and heartbreaking and difficult and dark. When the body does not do what we have been told it should do 'naturally'. For those who do have children, part of the fissure brought about by first-time motherhood is that we believed that it would be natural, that God made us for this. The effortless ease presented to us in maternal portrayals of Mary jar against our daily experience that being a good mother is in fact something that feels like really, really hard work. As Elina Vuola states: 'Picturing Mary as the most perfect woman, the patriarchal tradition functions paradoxically to disparage the rest of her gender. Mary as the great exception among all women makes all the other women daughters of Eve, tied to flesh and sin.'[9] Because of this ideal, mothers are required to be perfect even in our thought life, and this has always been the case. A 1920 book by a team of eugenicists advised pregnant women to 'avoid thinking of ugly people, or those marked by any deformity or disease'.[10]

Instinctively, we know what we mean by a good mother. We recognise the messages in art, TV, literature and entertainment. We know that a good mother is self-sacrificial; a good mother is always calm and kind; a good mother bounces back; and a good mother just keeps going, even in the face of her own psychological, physical and spiritual pain or discomfort.

A good milky mother

One night in the days following my return to work after having my second son, I was up for a feed. As I sat in our feeding chair, with him cradled in the crook of my arm, feeding, guzzling, I was overcome by an overwhelming sense of revulsion. I gritted my teeth and clenched my fists until I could take it no longer, and unlatched him from me. All of a sudden, I felt repelled by the thought of ever doing that again. That was to be the last time I breastfed. He was about nine months old.

Some people experience a deep sense of mourning as they gradually stop breastfeeding their child, or when they choose to stop cold turkey. They feel a sense of loss, perhaps at crossing a threshold from complete interdependence and connection with their child to enforced separation. I can understand the grief at knowing you might no longer be the only person who can immediately provide them with comfort; to fear that other things will take one's place. I look back now – years after that last feed – and see myself in that maternal pose, etched in my mind because of the countless images I have seen of Mary feeding the infant Jesus.

There are fewer places in which the pressure to be a perfect mother is felt more than when breastfeeding. Cultural historian Joanna Wolfarth describes the 'social, economic and cultural detritus' that, for her, intermingled to create this association of breastfeeding with good mothering in the run-up to having her first child. 'All I knew', she writes, 'was that I associated babies with milk and milk with my body, because this, in my mind, was what "good mothers" did. And, when I had a baby, I would try to be a good milky mother too.'[11]

Etched into our subconscious are the images of the Madonna lactans – iconography of the nursing Mary of Nazareth, feeding the infant Jesus. On display in the Louvre in Paris are images including *La Vierge au coussin vert* – Madonna with the Green Cushion. Painted by Italian artist Andrea Solari in around 1507, this Madonna represents the most perfect of good mothers. Her skin is porcelain-white, without blemish or stretch mark; her eyes are fixed solely on her child. She has that motherly glow that people talk about, and she is bent over protectively, consumed by the act of nourishing her child. It is a stunning image.

The green cushion upon which this Mary places her naked baby and stands feeding him from her breast is so familiar to me, not least because throughout nursing my children, I could not be without my own feeding cushion. It was soft and firm and provided me with the support I needed to feed my baby. In our prenatal classes, I had imagined myself as just such a serene Madonna lactans, cradling my baby in one arm and looking starstruck into my infant's eyes. I tried to suppress the ickiness I felt about feeding a tiny human from my boobs – which for all of my life I had been encouraged to pretend did not exist. I anticipated feeling ashamed about my body, and baring too much flesh in the act of trying to feed my future baby. But I assumed that the maternal feeling would overwhelm me once the baby was born, and I would not be so self-conscious. This turned out not to be true. When my elder son made his entrance into the world following a labour that lasted nearly three days, during which I had gone through every possible emotion, only to end up at exhaustion-verging-on-delirium, I felt ill-prepared for the midwife to place him at my chest, ready for his first meal. It immediately felt alien. Rather than the rush of maternal love that I had expected to feel, I wanted to escape, my toes curling, my teeth grinding at the strangeness of it. Within the first few hours in the hospital, we were visited by my closest relatives, who cooed over the baby. I felt like a ghost, floating disembodied, wanting to run from my body. When my husband and family were gone, the baby and I were left alone. Though the first hours were hazy, I remember it had already been discovered that I wasn't doing the breastfeeding thing right. The industrial pump was brought in and I was instructed on how to use it. It made a deep mooing sound and I felt like an animal – cattle being milked. Even with the help of that machine, and although I was staring intently at my baby, as was advised to aid the release of oxytocin to encourage the production of milk, it was not enough to get the required amount of milk out of me. So the midwives brought tiny bottles of formula to make sure he did not starve. Oh, the shame of maternal inadequacy!

I would realise in the days and weeks afterwards – as we continued combination feeding (using both breast and bottle) – how much judgement was involved in mothers' choices to feed their baby with formula, and how such judgement negatively impacts mothers' lives. As Rachel Cusk writes in *A Life's Work*, 'a quantity of evangelical fire is reserved for those tempted to sin with the bottle'.[12] A study by the University of Liverpool found that mothers felt both shame and guilt regardless of how they chose to feed their babies. The research, which explored the views of 1,600 new mothers, found that those who formula-fed felt guilt, stigma and the need to defend their choice. Mothers who fed their babies a combination of formula and breast milk reported negative emotional experiences too, albeit at a lower rate than those who solely formula-fed. The reality is that in the UK less than 1 per cent of mothers exclusively breastfeed until their babies are six months old, which means there is the potential for 99 per cent of mothers to feel that they have failed to live up to the perfect standard of motherhood. When the midwives suggested formula feeding while I was still in the hospital, I felt relieved. To me, the bottles represented respite from the frustration of not being able to feed correctly. In my first day as a mother, I had already failed. I was already a bad mother.

Writing about her breastfeeding ordeal after having her son in 2022, journalist Sirin Kale described her mental, along with her physical, disintegration. 'My sanity and my nipples began to corrode around day three,' she wrote. 'First they bled, staining my white nursing bra. Deep fissures appeared, like the cracked surface of a freshly baked cake. The scabs wouldn't heal and oozed a crust that stuck to my nursing pads. Breastfeeding Cyrus day and night through an open, infected wound felt like being scrubbed with wire wool and doused with battery acid.'[13]

Women are pressured to breastfeed, with little regard given to whether it causes them pain, with little regard to whether they find it challenging, and with little regard to whether, indeed, they even want to breastfeed. Both my sons turned out to be tongue-tied, which can exacerbate the challenges during feeding, but as I sought advice from professionals in the early weeks of breastfeeding agony, dragging my baby across London to breastfeeding cafés, I couldn't help but feel judged rather than supported. As experts watched me feed and offered advice about positions – themselves demonstrating how it should be done by breastfeeding vacant, lightweight dolls – no one seemed to acknowledge that maybe, for some of us, breastfeeding is just hard.

Throughout history, women have chosen not to breastfeed their children, for a variety of reasons. The practice of wet nursing dates back to 3000 BC and was used right up till the twenty-first century, beginning to fade out once the production of baby formula became safer owing to sterilisation. But previously, mothers – more often the affluent ones – employed wet nurses for convenience, while elsewhere around the world wet nurses have been employed to avoid the danger of a mother passing on diseases such as HIV to her child. As is the way with all things women-related, at certain points in history wet nursing among wealthier classes has been promoted, while at other times, the practice has been criticised. Writes Joanna Wolfarth of writings in the seventeenth and eighteenth centuries: 'Women who did not breastfeed their own babies were characterised as unnatural, sinful and vain. Breasts were maternal and utilitarian – sending a child to a wet nurse was seen as a sign of an unnatural mother and this criticism was often directed at wealthy and middle class women, who were seen to prefer socialising and maintaining a fashionable physique to the solid work of nursing.'[14] Even when women themselves started to write their own manuals in the Victorian period, much of their writing also suggested that not breastfeeding your child was either about 'fashion or frivolity' and that those women who did not breastfeed were 'somewhat unnatural, and cold-blooded'.[15] In the colloquy *The New Mother*, written by Christian humanist and Catholic theologian Erasmus in 1526, his female protagonist Fabulla, who is being visited by the pedantic Eutrapelus, is ridiculed by him when he learns that she has outsourced her breastfeeding to a wet nurse – a common practice in the Middle Ages. For him, as Clarissa Atkinson writes: 'A woman who will not nurse is only half a mother.'[16]

This idea of 'natural' motherhood, alongside the concept of 'motherly love', would be further emphasised in the centuries after Erasmus' writing, as the Industrial Revolution called for clearer definition of a woman's place. Prior to the eighteenth century, middle-class families would send their newborns to wet nurses in villages some way away. Meanwhile, those with enough money would have their wet nurses live with them. There were a number of practical reasons for outsourcing feeding: women simply did not have enough time in the day to spend half of it attached to an infant, and wealthy men also did not fancy their wives being unavailable to them sexually for the duration of their time breastfeeding. There were tragic reasons too: the high infant mortality rate meant that wet nursing allowed a mother not to get too attached to her child until that child had survived those first few precarious months.

In her book *A History of Women in 101 Objects*, journalist Annabelle Hirsch writes of the Nuremberg porcelain figurine 'The Good Mother', created by Karl Gottlieb Lück in around 1765, which features a breastfeeding mother surrounded by her children. The ornament and others like it were found in well-to-do homes and functioned 'both as a decorative object and something like a warning'[17]. For Hirsch, the figurine represented the 'pernicious' notion of motherly love, which 'pinned women down and imposed yet another new myth on them'.[18]

Breastfeeding has been portrayed for centuries not only as good for a child, but as a marker of moral virtue, as important for raising future generations, and as a profound symbol of the love of God. In wider narratives about breastfeeding, it is the self-sacrificial nature of it that seems to be being applauded, with women being praised for continuing to feed their children, foregoing sleep and their sanity in doing so. That they continue to breastfeed even when it's painful is imbued with virtue, like the self-denial of a self-flagellating monk. Inherent in this push to breastfeed are these notions of maternal sacrifice. But, as Shannon K. Evans writes in *Rewilding Motherhood*, 'When the selflessness of motherhood above all else is exalted, value is indirectly assigned to each mother based on how small she can make herself. The result is not true self-giving but needless martyrdom.'[19]

Mothers who exclusively breastfeed their children know the torture of having to wake up several times in the night to feed insatiable babies. Despite much progress in women's liberation, breastfeeding is still marketed as the most beautiful and most important thing that a mother can do for her child – even if it hurts. Even if it really, really hurts. To the point where to consider introducing just one bottle of formula a day so that a partner can feed the baby instead feels like failure. Is this liberation? Although I found breastfeeding torturous in the two sets of nine months in which I did it, many of my friends and relatives absolutely loved it. For them it provided a sense of profound connection; a deep and indescribable beauty; a closeness to God. This, however, was not my story and it was one of the main ways in which I felt I did not live up to the maternal ideal.

The nursing mother is synonymous with being a good mother. What does this mean for those women who find breastfeeding challenging? I had not heard of the term 'breastfeeding aversion' until long after I myself had experienced it. The condition can lead to a number of feelings, including an overwhelming urge to stop breastfeeding, a sensation of being trapped or like a prisoner, a desire to run away, or even an itchiness all over the body. Although not much research has been done into breastfeeding aversion, those who have studied it suggest it could be down to hormones, or sleep deprivation, or 'negative embodied emotions' projected onto the infant, or simply nature's way of telling us that it is time for our children to start weaning. Hanna, who experienced breastfeeding aversion, said in a study in 2017: 'I get so angry, like a rage when my son latches now, and I am not sure why. I used to LOVE breastfeeding and we had such a good relationship. All I think about now is leaving, running away when he suckles. Then I feel so guilty it hurts.' Meanwhile, Preena said it made her 'want to scream'.[20] Despite the variations in how they respond to their aversion, a running theme is the feeling of guilt and shame at experiencing these negative emotions at all. The rage and the disgust that these women feel show them up for what they really are: bad mothers. Because a perfect mother always sacrifices herself for the needs of her child.

The rage of imperfect motherhood

Growing up in a house full of women, and with a mother who loved to read us classic books that taught us about love, life and adventure, my sisters and I adored *Little Women*. Nestled in the pages of this Louisa May Alcott coming-of-age tale was the story of the four March sisters, Meg, Jo, Beth and Amy, growing up in Massachusetts in the nineteenth century. Each of them comes face to face with situations that challenge their sense of self and what it is to be a woman. For these little women, it is the particularity of their woman-hood that in the end is what matters, even though some of them – Jo in particular – might wrestle with and rail against these ideals and pressures. As a child, and early into adulthood, as I read the book again and watched every screen adaptation, I began to pay less and less attention to the daughters, and more and more to their mother, nicknamed Marmee. Quiet, stoic and wise; the picture of grace. The one who wanted more than anything for her daughters to be safe, to be loved; to be kind and to be generous. I start to wonder how it is that she was able to hold it together. We meet the March women during their first Christmas without their father, who, having lost all his money, is working as a chaplain for the Union Army during America's Civil War.

Little Women is a tale of strong women, and yet the saccharine nickname Alcott gives to the March matriarch represents how we so often view mother figures. Indeed, it is thought to be what the author herself called her own mother. I could not tell you Mrs March's actual first name. Instead, this mother's identity is consumed by her maternal role, referred to simply as 'Marmee'. As one commentator describes the name: 'The word occasions a shudder. It's sentimental, sexless, without drive. It's sticky and cloying.'[21]

A simple reading of *Little Women* as being solely about the daughters' coming of age fails to see the profound message about mother-hood that is lurking in the shadows of the pages. When feminist director Greta Gerwig created another big-screen adaptation of *Little Women* in 2019, she included a line that had often been left out of film versions of Alcott's book. Gerwig described being inspired by a simple yet shocking line uttered by Marmee: 'I am angry every day of my life.' Marmee – played by Laura Dern in Gerwig's film – makes this revelation to her daughter Jo, after Jo almost lets her younger sister Amy drown in an icy pond.

Throughout the books and films, Marmee is the epitome of a Good Mother. I am now struck by the similarity between the sounds of the names Marmee and Mary, the name of Jesus' mother – soft, unassuming sounds, befitting of perfect mothers. And yet this insight into her inner life, the rage seething underneath the surface, at once makes Marmee feel threatening, yet also, to me, relatable. What is she angry about? Perhaps the realisation that her daughters' futures are uncertain and at the same time restricted, their womanhood predestined to fit into predefined boxes that pinch her vivacious girls in all the wrong places. Perhaps she is angry every day of her life about the precarity of her family's lives; the poverty, the sickness and the requirement to stay cheerful despite it all. Perhaps she is angry that if her children survive into adulthood, their fate is to become a Marmee, just like her. Soft, unassuming, endlessly caring, patiently nurturing.

For many mothers, there is a fear of letting anyone glimpse the maternal rage that can fester just underneath the surface. Anne Lamott writes candidly of her experience of nursing a colicky baby, as well as of the sheer tedium of motherhood. A tedium that can lead to rage. She writes:

> One of the worst things about being a parent, for me, is the self-discovery, the being face to face with one's secret insanity and brokenness and rage . . . I have always known . . . that way down deep, way past being kind and religious and trying to take care of everyone, I was seething. Now it's close to the surface. I feel it racing from my center up into my arms and down into my hands, and it scares the shit out of me.[22]

For many women, to speak honestly about this rage would mean we have failed. Failed to play along with the idea that a perfect, ethereal motherhood is the only acceptable kind of motherhood. 'The Good Mother,' as Adrienne Rich wrote, is 'linked implicitly with suffering and with a repression of anger.'[23] Although Marmee's explanation for why her anger might surprise her daughters is not included in Gerwig's film adaptation, it is laid out in Alcott's book, when Marmee explains: 'I've learned to check the hasty words that rise to my lips, and when I feel that they mean to break out against my will, I just go away for a minute, and give myself a little shake for being so weak and wicked.' As *The New Yorker* describes it: 'The scene is not just about the expression, or existence, of righteous anger; it's about the depressing processes through which mothers suppress that anger.'[24]

A good mother never shows her anger; perhaps a good mother is never supposed to feel angry at all, but to live a life devoted to loving others. As Adrienne Rich writes: 'Mother-love is supposed to be continuous, unconditional. Love and anger cannot coexist. Female anger threatens the institution of motherhood.'[25]

The Angel in the House

Louisa May Alcott was writing about Marmee and the March girls during a period in history when ideas about the maternal ideal were being cemented within society on both sides of the Atlantic. In many ways, Marmee is a perfect example of the Victorian 'Angel in the House' trope – which takes its name from a narrative poem by Coventry Patmore. Written between 1854 and 1862, the poem, 'The Angel in the House', expounded the virtues of Patmore's own wife, who he believed was the greatest example of a wife and mother, and whom all other women should emulate. In the late nineteenth century, Patmore's poem became a very popular depiction of womanhood in America, and then in Britain. Rebecca Etherington writes that the poem and the subsequent attention it received as a model for how women should be 'not only romanticised but also contributed to society's constricting expectations; that women should be submissive, passive beings whose only role was as a devoted, perfect mother and wife'.[26]

Queen Victoria herself embodied this ideal, becoming an emblem for domesticity, motherhood and female virtue. She had nine children, forty-two grandchildren and eighty-seven great-grandchildren, and came to symbolise the ideal of a devoted mother, although some have noted the contradiction that, as queen, she was far from an ordinary mother. Author Adrienne Auslander Munich notes the 'cultural paradox of Queen Victoria's specific kind of monarchy – the apparent contradiction of a devoted wife, prolific mother, and extravagant widow who is also Queen of an Empire upon which the sun never sets'.[27] It seemed to fall to mothers to protect the home from the terrors of the outside world, the uncertainty and the danger, by providing a safe home in which they cared for their husbands and their children, denying themselves.

Writing around seventy years after Patmore's poem, feminist and author Virginia Woolf attempted to unmake this ideal of Victorian respectability and motherhood by 'killing the Angel in the House'. For Woolf, this phantom of perfection hovers over her as she attempts to write, coaxing her to conform to, rather than reject, feminine ideals of the era. Woolf writes of the Angel:

> She was intensely sympathetic. She was immensely charming. She was utterly unselfish. She excelled in the difficult arts of the family life. She sacrificed herself daily. If there was a chicken, she took the leg; if there was a draught she sat in it – in short she was so constituted that she never had a mind or a wish of her own, but preferred to sympathise always with the minds and wishes of others. Above all – I need to say it – she was pure. Her purity was supposed to be her chief beauty – her blushes, her great grace. In those days – the last of Queen Victoria – every house had its Angel.[28]

In her study of how Mary was seen within Victorian feminism, Kimberly VanEsveld Adams describes the many Madonna-like characters that found their ways into literature of the era. These characters would be so identified 'because of their looks and their love and purity'. Examples include Little Nell in *The Old Curiosity Shop*, Agnes in *David Copperfield*, and 'purified fallen mothers' like Thomas Hardy's Tess. Citing other scholars, she writes that 'there is a "clear line of literary descent"[29] from the Madonna in heaven to the Angel in the House, but the angel is the preferred representation of female purity in a more secular age'.[30]

There were also more progressive views of Mary, with some seeing her as a paragon for women's liberation. Victorian writers such as George Eliot and others, writes VanEsveld Adams, 'rediscovered and to some extent reconstructed a religious tradition that harmonized with their feminist principles and promised the elevation and empowerment of women'. For them, 'the figure they used most often to represent these hopes was the Virgin Mother of Christianity, who became their Lady of Victorian Feminism'.[31]

Art and culture have ways of manifesting those things that we all feel or sense, but which are unsaid. While this may not have been Patmore's intention in writing his ode to his perfect wife, it named an unnamed spirit of a maternal ideal. That this ideal comes in an angelic form continues the religious imagery that so often surrounds how we speak about women: saints, sinners, angels. This angel hovers over the Church, too. She is present in the bring-and-share lunches and bake sales; she hovers over those women who are called to speak – female clergy, ministers and preachers; her presence puts pressure on women theologians: don't say too much, don't say it too loudly, don't sound ungrateful or aggressive. She is present right now in my own home, as I attempt to give voice to the pressures on me and the women I see around me. In the same way that Virginia Woolf writes of killing this maternal ideal that invaded her thought life, I too want to unmake Mary. Not to kill the mother of God, but to strip her of the trappings society has loaded on her that say more about how the world wants women to be – sat daintily inside the box of so-called perfect mother – than they say about the radical and too often overlooked truth of what is portrayed in Mary's story and what that says about God, and how God sees us.

The Church's scorecard on providing a template for liberating, godly motherhood is mixed. Inspired by Jesus' open-armed welcome to women he encounters in the New Testament, some churches have found ways to free mothers from sexist and restrictive ideas about who they ought to be. But too often the Church has consumed the worldly patriarchal blueprint for motherhood, and at times has in fact been the driver of it. The Church needs to do better, not least because the Christian understanding that God chose to redeem the world through the incarnation necessitated Jesus being born of a woman, which gives us a glimpse into how God values women and mothers, even in a world that might suggest they are in some way less. The Church should be moved to lift mothers' eyes to the fact that, as Amy Peeler puts it, 'God chose to have a mother.'[32]

The Angel in the House image still pervades our collective cultural consciousness. She is the Angel in *Good Housekeeping* magazine, the Angel of Instagram. But nowhere is her presence more felt than in conservative complementarian evangelical spaces, where men lead in the family and the church, and women's role is to help and support. We can draw a line directly from the misogyny we see in churches today right back to the denigration of women by the early church Fathers. Their views seem abhorrent yet also somewhat comical when read back. Second-century theologian Tertullian, for example, described woman as 'a temple built over a sewer, the gateway to the devil'.[33]

I spent a large part of my childhood and teenage years within the complementarian movement, but failed to be convinced by the suggestion that the Bible required women to submit to their husbands – the assumption being that they had one – and confine themselves to the hearth. My faith was formed in an environment in which men – kindly and reluctantly, of course – put forward teachings about male headship. Accompanying these teachings was the belief that the Bible called us to live counterculturally; to be salt and light in a world tainted by the poisonous ideas of feminism, which sought to tear women away from the home and challenge the authority and purpose of the male as provider and breadwinner. To live differently and stand tall against the prevailing narratives of the day was part of my identity as a young Christian. But the truth is that, for much of history, the Church has simply echoed the patriarchal structures of the day. As Beth Allison Barr writes in *The Making of Biblical Womanhood*, 'Once I finally came face to face with the ugliness and pervasiveness of historical patriarchy, I realized that rather than being different from the world, Christians were just like everyone else in their treatment of women.'[34] As she puts it: 'Christian patriarchy is just patriarchy.'[35]

John Piper – the theologian and preacher who is one of the most prominent voices in the complementarian movement in the USA

– has said much over the years about 'biblical manhood' and 'biblical womanhood'. Piper and his friends warn against the Catholic devotion to Mary and see her only as a one-dimensional character in the drama of God's great big story. She is a plot device to demonstrate that a woman's virtue is found in her subservience and obedience to authority. In Piper's world, motherhood is the pinnacle of a woman's calling in the kingdom of God. Biblical womanhood must entail motherhood. In his 2005 sermon entitled 'Honoring the Biblical Call of Motherhood', he said:

> What I want to honor in this message is the biblical calling on a woman's life to weave a fabric of family life out of commitment to a husband and his calling, and commitment to her children and their training, and commitment to Christ and his glory. In other words, I want to honor the biblical calling that makes marriage, motherhood, and home-management, in the context of radical Christian discipleship, the central, core, dominant commitments of a woman's life.[36]

Piper sought to encourage the faithful Christian women who believed this, knowing that they would not get validation from the secular world for this devotion to marriage and family. While complementarian Christianity does not permit women to have authority over a man in the home or in the Church, Piper is regretful that women do choose to work outside the home, and sometimes lead men. For him, this is all well and good as long as the mothers 'have found creative ways to interlace schedules so as not to compromise their core commitments at home'. But mothers who do not support their husband's calling, who do not manage the family home, and who do not pour their lives into their children – the mothers who do not conform to the Angel of the House symbol – are to be critiqued. 'They've simply absorbed the values of the world from television, media, friends with no biblical framework,' he writes. John Piper's own father, Bill's, tribute to his late wife, Ruth, extols her virtues in a remarkably similar way to that of Coventry Patmore expounding the qualities of his perfect wife in the nineteenth-century 'Angel in the House'. Eulogies often idealise the person who has died, and in many ways that is the point of them, but what I note here is the striking way in which the celebration of the mother's goodness is intertwined with ideas about perfect motherhood. 'She was a priceless gem, rarer by far than sapphire, ruby or diamond,' says Bill Piper of his wife, in the spirit of the Proverbs 31 woman. He writes of Ruth:

> The dancing sparkle of her life resulted not from material stimuli. It came from a heart that gave and gave and gave again with never a thought of receiving. It reflected a life that loved and loved until there was just no more love. Her beauty was that of expanded unselfishness. Her whole life was others, her loved ones, her friends, her neighbors and her church. She knew no resting place. The needs were endless and her devotion always equaled the demands. Deep weariness of mind and body never deterred her.[37]

I would have loved to get Ruth's perspective – to hear her thoughts on this drive to be the Angel of the House; whether it came naturally to her, or whether she had to summon the strength to suppress her own wants and desires for the needs of those around her.

Marina Warner's cultural history of the Virgin Mary, *Alone of All Her Sex*, suggests that this idea of the good mother as one who sacrifices or denies herself is a vestige of the martyrdom of centuries ago. 'For in times of persecution,' she writes, 'martyrdom made amends for nature's wrongs, and proved the faith of the victim . . . Through virginity and self-inflicted hardship, the faults of female nature could be corrected.'[38]

Saints such as Perpetua and Felicity – who were both mothers of infants – are venerated because of their willingness – or even desire – to be martyred. They were killed in Carthage around AD 203 for refusing to recant their Christian faith. Perpetua was a noblewoman who was recently married and had a baby son she was still nursing. In her written account of her ordeal, *The Passion of Saints Perpetua and Felicity*, Perpetua describes the horrific circumstances of her imprisonment, and the suffering she endured, including the torture of having to stop breastfeeding. When she bribes the prison guards, they move her and her fellow soon-to-be martyrs, including her

slave Felicity, who is also pregnant at the time of her imprisonment, to better conditions, and she is able to feed her child again.
Any mother who has breastfed her baby will know the feeling of
physical release – the relief of overfull and painful breasts being
drained – when nursing after too long away from her child. Felicity
was said to have been delighted to have given birth prematurely in
the prison, because this meant that she would still get to be
martyred. Warner writes: 'For even the Romans drew the line at
throwing expectant mothers to the beasts, and Felicity yearned for
martyrdom.'[39]

The accounts of Perpetua and Felicity describe the suffering of
mothers martyred *despite* being mothers. However, the Victorian
Angel in the House and the thread of maternal martyrdom that
lingers today subtly imply that women should be martyrs *because* we
are mothers – we suffer for the sake of our children and families, and
that is what is to be expected of us. A perfect mother sacrifices
herself for her children. Here there is, again, a tension. The Christian
faith on the whole is positive about thinking less of oneself and more
of others. It hinges on a cosmic act of self-sacrifice. How do we
balance the beauty of self-forgetting with the recognition that each
mother is worthy of inherent dignity, value and respect? Maybe it is
a matter of motive: sacrifice must be fuelled by love, rather than by
a fear of failing to live up to an arbitrary and damaging perfect
standard.

There are reported to have been two thousand sightings[40] of Mary
around the world since AD 40. Perhaps like the Angel in the House,
she hovers, emerging in homes where tired mothers are giving and
giving and giving of themselves and yet failing to measure up to the
myth of perfect motherhood.

In two minds: maternal ambivalence

When I became a mother, I never expected to feel anything other
than pure love towards my child. The idea of perfect motherhood so
imprinted in my mind did not prepare me for the shocking moments
in which I felt the opposite. I was not ready for the ways in which

impulses towards hatred and violent thoughts occasionally intruded into those feelings of profound love.

I love my children. There are times when I am so overcome with love for them that I can barely contain it. It is a love so all-consuming, so overwhelming, that it pours out of me. I feel it in the pride filling up my grinning cheeks as I witness their achievements: the first smile, the first roll, the first step; the first word, the first day at school, the first time they say 'I love you' unprompted. Loving my children is a front-row seat to the wonder and beauty of the world. Through loving them I bear witness to the spirit at work – moving and creating and doing and being.

Mother-love is like obsession. For me, it sparks strange desires like wanting to eat my baby; the overwhelming need to nibble his cheeks or bite his thighs or pinch his toes. Scientists say that this pseudo-biting response is a negative action to counterbalance the overwhelming love sensation a mother might feel. 'Motherhood makes you obscene,'[41] confesses the French writer Marguerite Duras. In the early days and weeks and months after my children burst into the world, I was always watching them. I craved them – every part of them. Seven years into my motherhood journey, and the feeling has not waned. I now have two objects of my affection. My elder son is no longer a baby; no longer soft and squidgy, but long-limbed and growing taller by the minute. He still curls up on my lap and I breathe him in. He is funny and bossy and inquisitive, and helps me see the world through the wonder of childlike eyes. As I write, my younger son is two years old. He is the perfect size for cuddles. I never feel more loved than when he sees me at nursery pick-up, or when I walk through the door and he runs to his Prodigal Mum, arms outstretched, knowing that I will scoop him up and kiss his cheeks as he squeals, euphoric. This mother-love evokes the intense butterflies of a teenage crush. And it terrifies me, too. To love something – someone – so much that the thought of living without them is unthinkable.

In church, I have heard much about the all-consuming love of motherhood. I have seen women lay down their jobs and lives, sacrificing careers and ambitions and hopes and dreams in the service of the family. The nuclear family: one leading man, one supporting lady and a cast of picture-perfect children – that was the standard to which we were all to aspire. I spent the first thirty years of my church life single, and wanting more than anything not to be. Some of my church girlfriends had long been wed and I watched with envy as they became mothers. I held their newborns after church, breathing in the intoxicating baby scent that emanated from their chubby cheeks and folds of skin. I longed for a husband and babies of my own but felt terribly behind, as if I would never catch up. In many other areas of my life, I was seemingly doing well. I had graduated from a top university with a good degree; I was progressing in an exciting career; I was being given new opportunities to lead things; I had a wide circle of friends; I travelled all over the world; I had the time and freedom to do whatever I wanted. But despite these great things, I felt inadequate when I compared myself with women at church who had attained the prize of being Wife and Mother. I felt judged – whether or not this was the reality – and looked down upon; as if everything else I was doing was merely filling up the void of not being a mum. The myth of perfect motherhood encompasses the trope of perfect womanhood, and perpetuates the lie that to be a woman must include being a mother.

I adore my children, but motherhood – or at least motherhood as an institution – can be suffocating. It is this institution of motherhood that I think has also wrapped itself around the mother of God. It attempts to squeeze women into the box of Perfect Mother, the standard that so many of us beat ourselves up in trying to achieve. We think everyone else is coming close to achieving that standard when, in reality, we are all falling short. Of course, it's not all bad. Motherhood is so discombobulating precisely because it is a roller coaster with ups and downs. At times we feel so burdened by the stress and the strain of it all that we consider running out of the door, never to return again. At other times we experience the all-consuming feeling of not wanting to – not being able to – breathe without our children. We can feel these things all at the same time.

This is the nature of maternal ambivalence. The obsession sits alongside the rage, the need to nurture alongside the apathy, the wonder alongside the utter boredom. Psychotherapist Rozsika Parker, who wrote extensively about maternal ambivalence, described it as the phenomenon in which a mother's loving feelings and hating feelings sit side by side.[42] Women have not been able to express this ambivalence – the light and shade of maternity. It is, as Parker describes it, 'the unacceptable face of motherhood'.[43] Where there should have been honesty and vulnerability, there has been silence. The picture painted of motherhood has been in one shade, leaving no room for the shadows that form part of the reality of the maternal experience.

Keeping up appearances

I've never been to confession. Instead, in my tradition, we bring to mind all of the things we have done that week, how we've sinned against our neighbours and against God, in thought and word and deed. Privately and quietly, we confess, before heading to the Communion table and taking the bread and wine. We do not mention our sins out loud; we do not whisper our misdemeanours to a priest. Yet perhaps there is a profound power in doing so. 'Confession heals, confession justifies, confession grants pardon of sin,' St Isidore of Seville, a seventh-century theologian and archbishop, once said. 'All hope consists in confession; in confession there is a chance for mercy.' Perhaps the Catholic tradition of confession can provide a sense of comfort – perhaps an exhale – in knowing that others regularly confess too; that each of us has fallen short of the perfect ideal.

I find power, too, in confessing the ways in which I think I have failed as a mother because of the standard to which I'm – wrongly – holding myself, and being met with another mother's quiet: 'Me too.' There is a vulnerability that comes in confessing to another mother, and not knowing whether she will step into that sacred meeting place in which we see each other's brokenness through the drooping eyes of sleep deprivation. For psychotherapist Daphne de Marneffe, it is in the dark side of motherhood that the beauty is found. For her, the negative feelings mothers might have are 'where the real human work gets done, where the emotional action is'.[44] Confession does not end here, though. In the Christian tradition, we confess first, so that we might then receive the grace and mercy of God. God who loves us totally and completely, no matter what it is that we have done. This profound grace lightens our burdens and – if we really believe it is there, freely given – releases us from the grip of striving for perfection, especially a perfection that is based in a false image of what a mother should be. Hebblethwaite writes in *Motherhood and God*: 'In mothering, as in Christianity, we mess things up by striving too earnestly, obeying too literally, working too scrupulously: we cannot replace grace by effort.'[45]

Perhaps the key to living the good motherly life is grace. The Christian story tells us that we cannot live up to an impossible standard and that no one is expecting us to. Much of the pressure on mothers today is akin to the Protestant work ethic, which suggests that we can do more and more stuff in order to achieve our salvation. Motherhood seems to require a lot of doing, and very little resting in God's profound grace. Maybe there is a freedom that comes when we choose to exhale in the presence of divine love, and not take on the task of attempting to be that divine love ourselves – another task on the eternal to-do list. Perhaps we might find solace in the truth that 'God is more of a mother than any human mother can be.'[46]

Chapter 3

Mother God

Gender and Divine Revelation

'So you, Lord God, are the great mother.'

—St Anselm[1]

A slow, quiet yet significant revival has been happening in recent years: public intellectuals have been turning to God. People like historian Tom Holland, former arch-atheist Ayaan Hirsi Ali and Tammy Peterson – wife of psychologist Jordan Peterson. What is fascinating in some of these thinkers' testimonies of their attraction to Christianity is that it is the Blessed Virgin Mary who has enticed them.

Despite having moved away from the Anglican faith in which he was raised, Tom Holland began attending Christmas services at St Bartholomew the Great after receiving a cancer diagnosis. The church is the only place in London where the Blessed Virgin is reported to have been sighted. Aware of St Bart's history of Marian apparitions, Holland knelt on the spot in the Lady Chapel where the Mary is believed to have appeared, and prayed for the first time since childhood. 'I gave this huge heartfelt prayer. *Come on. Please.* And all kinds of things went right from that point on.'[2] Soon after, his bowel cancer receded, and he no longer needed the surgery that he had been due to have to remove it. Likewise, Jordan Peterson, the Canadian psychologist with a mass following, particularly among men, has spoken of his wife, Tammy's, conversion to Christianity, and in particular, Catholicism. Tammy, a podcaster who had survived cancer, was baptised into the Catholic Church in 2024, at the age of sixty-three. Her husband told the media that it was Mary – and in particular, Mary's motherhood – that attracted his wife to the faith: 'Tammy loved being a mother . . . and certainly that was the best part of your life, especially when you had little kids . . . I think the best part of [Tammy] came out [with] them.' It is, Dr Peterson said, the Catholic Church's 'insistence upon the Divine nature of the mother' that 'the West desperately needs'.[3]

Tom Holland and Tammy Peterson are among the latest in a centuries-long tradition of seekers being drawn to God through Jesus' mother. The Reformation famously sought to reduce the level of Marian piety that had built up in the Church by the sixteenth century, claiming that the medieval cult of Mary had obscured the foundational truth of the Christian story – that Jesus Christ was the only way to God, and did not need a mediator. But there is something about Mary that continues to draw many men and women towards her. Even Martin Luther himself, despite being critical of over-the-top Marian worship, maintained a devotion to Mary, albeit the domesticated, obedient, maternal version, rather than the glorious Queen of Heaven. What is it that keeps people coming back to Mary? Some have suggested that, as with Tammy Peterson, it is her motherhood that appeals most, and in particular, the perfect ideal of motherhood that she has come to represent. As *The Economist* noted in 2003: 'A psychotherapist in the school of Carl Jung might say that motherhood, as a force that feeds and protects all humans, is the most important of all the "archetypes" that lurk in humanity's collective unconscious.'[4]

American priest and writer Richard Rohr suggests his Catholic tradition has 'divinized Mary', and says that though some might have a 'poor theology of Mary', they have an 'excellent psychology': 'Humans like, need, and trust our mothers to give us gifts, to nurture us, and always to forgive us, which is what we want from God. My years of work with men's groups have convinced me of it. In fact, the more macho and patriarchal a culture, the greater its devotion to Mary.'[5] Perhaps people *think* they need Mary – because they wrongly believe that God is a man, and all the negative stereotypes that have been used to describe men in recent years have made a masculine God less attractive. 'Much of the human race can more easily imagine unconditional love coming from the feminine and the maternal from than from a man,' writes Rohr.[6]

I believe that by exploring the beauty of motherhood through Mary, we are presented with two profound truths: first, that motherhood itself is a demonstration of the nature and love of God; and second, that God's love for us is best understood maternally. The first adjective used about God's character is found in Exodus 34:6, where God is described as compassionate. The Hebrew word is *rahûm* or *rechamim*, which is derived from the term for womb, and paints a picture of a love that envelops, nurtures, encircles and protects – a fierce and all-consuming love for another person that is both distinct from you and part of you.

A mother's love has become the archetypal expression of self-sacrificial, unconditional love, and I believe mother-love can help us grasp what theology professor Frederick Bauerschmidt describes as 'the love that is God'. As Julian of Norwich once wrote, as one translation puts it: 'To the property of motherhood belong nature, love, wisdom and knowledge, and this is God.'[7]

Motherhood provides a way into understanding God's love – whether we ourselves are mothers, or have simply experienced the love of a mother, or have suffered because of a lack of this mother-love in our own lives.

Whitemalegod

Because of the predominant theological and Christian voices that have shaped me, I had always imagined God to be white and male. Of course, I didn't really, when I thought about it. But this God was the one that had been ingrained in my mind, whose image I recalled when I thought about God. When it came to the physical depiction of God, I couldn't help but be influenced by the centuries of artworks and the ways in which God was portrayed on film and TV. But beyond the physical, 'whitemalegod',[8] as theologian Christena Cleveland describes it, represents more than just white skin, blue eyes and blond hair. Whitemalegod represents brute strength and binaries and triumphalism and power. It leaves no room for the shadow side of being; no space for the fluidity and the grey and the movement as symbolised in the description of the (feminine) Spirit of God as she hovered over the waters in the creation story in Genesis. To conceive of God as male alone, or even as a father alone, is to have an incomplete picture of who God is.

The static stereotyping of what it is to be male does a disservice to the diversity of characteristics that we find in men, and in men who are fathers, too. Fathers can be strong, yes; and they can be protective and have manual dexterity; but they can also be gentle and creative and loving and kind. Whichever side of the conversation you lean towards about divine pronouns, what is clear is that 'language is . . . where theology begins'.[9]

There is in me what seems like very real biological wiring that, at least in my own experience, I sense that my husband does not have or experience in the same way. The idea of sleeping through my children's cries during the night was simply an impossibility for me – especially in the early days and weeks, when I leaked milk at the smallest hint of separation from them while they were in distress. I noticed, too, the anxious pull in me as they went from being tiny newborns to older toddlers who experienced separation anxiety and cried out 'Mummy!' every time I left the room, and then the shift as they increasingly wanted to spend much more time with their daddy. In the early days, Mark would sometimes feel invisible to our babies, as if their bodies knew and my body knew that we needed each other and were still feeling the rupture of moving from our oneness to the reality of twoness. I am obsessed with my children. Mark adores them, and loves them fiercely. But he doesn't lie in bed looking at photos of them after having just put them to bed. He doesn't cry at the thought of being away from them. His relationship to them, and theirs to him, is just . . . different. While mothers and fathers may interact with their children in different ways, sometimes I wonder whether the differences are overplayed. Maybe some of the varying ways in which we interact can be explained by the simple fact that we are different people. Mark is much more outdoorsy than I am, so loves taking our boys to the park or for walks in the woods; I would much rather stay at home with them and bake. These differences are as much based on personality and interest as they are on gender. I understand this most vividly when I look at the ways in which friends in same-sex relationships, or single parents – whether

male or female – parent differently. The interactions with their children are less gendered.

In *Matrescence*, Lucy Jones writes powerfully of the physiological,
biological, psychological and spiritual changes that take place in the
weeks and months after having a baby. But she also notes new neuro-
scientific research that demonstrates the ways in which fathers' brains,
as well as the brains of non-birthing parents, including adoptive
parents, can change in response to caring for an infant, alongside
changes in their hormones too.

None of this surprises me, as I have had a front-row seat to witness
how Mark has become more nurturing – more stereotypically
maternal – since becoming a dad. My heart melts when I watch him
soothe our babies after they have hurt their head; or when he blows
raspberries on their bellies or kisses their cheeks. Just as God is
Father, Mother and Other, so earthly fathers do not only behave in
stereotypically male-gendered ways. God – and men – are more
interesting than that. To split parenting along rigid gender lines is
bad for both women and men, especially when the pressure falls
mainly on women to be perfect in their parenting role. If I'm honest,
despite my frustration with patriarchal societies that have subjugated
women and confined women's role to motherhood and the home, I
am still a product of that society. Despite my fight for women's liberation, I can't shake the niggling feeling that the important tasks of
parenting and domestic life are *my* responsibility rather than my
husband's. My friend Maddy describes how being a twenty-first-
century mother can pull you into stereotypically 'female' tasks that it
was easier to avoid before becoming a parent:

> Once I was on maternity leave, I felt that of course it made more
> sense for me to do the washing because I was at home and could
> hang it when it finished. Of course it makes sense for me to decide
> on dinner because I'm weaning the baby so I know what's around/
> what she can eat. Of course I remember the NCT babies' birth-
> days because I'm in touch with the other mums all the time. And
> so on. Before you know it, mum is washing, cooking, cleaning,
> buying presents, etc. Before we had children, we would have had
> equal pulls and ties.

Some feminist theories fall into the trap of assuming that a father who parents 'well' is exceptional because he is choosing to engage in maternal work. This assumption in fact highlights the idea that nurture, care and housekeeping are the domain of mothers – and women – alone; that it is not natural for men to behave in this way; and that when men *parent*, they are actually mothering. Similarly, some feminists dream of a future in which there is no gender distinction at all, thinking that when it comes to parenting, it is only when men take on the full task of mothering that there would be true equality.[10] But bell hooks[11] says such an approach is unrealistic and potentially damaging, to men and to us all. 'Seeing men who do effective parenting as "maternal" reinforces the stereotypical sexist notion that women are inherently better suited to parent,' hooks suggests, '[and] that men who parent in the same way as women are imitating the real thing rather than acting as a parent should act.'[12] It would be better for us all – men and women, boys and girls alike – if good fatherhood also became associated with being caring, nurturing and loving, rather than men who behave in these ways towards their children being described as 'maternal'. There is also the reality that some mothering tasks are inescapably tied to the maternal body, including, for most mothers, pregnancy, giving birth and feeding. Nevertheless, neither the Church nor society as a whole seems to propagate an idea of perfect fatherhood. We praise men when they do what, for mothers, is considered the bare minimum – things like 'babysitting' their children, or feeding them, or taking time out of work to look after them. Perhaps we need to increase expectations on fathers to rebalance the burden on mothers, and shatter the myth of perfect motherhood.

Part of what has perhaps driven the need for a myth of perfect motherhood, as demonstrated in Mary as the ideal, perfect mother, is the idea that we need a female deity to fill the hole in the perception of a male God that many of us have, shaped by the patriarchal societies in which we live. I know I am guilty of this. As a Protestant, my interest in Mary has grown alongside my disillusionment with male representations of God. But rather than the binary choice of making God either male or female, mother or father, it could be argued that the reading most consistent with Scripture is that God is both, and neither. To claim, as John Piper does, that: 'God has made Christianity to have a masculine feel . . . [and] has ordained for the church a masculine ministry'[13] limits God to maleness and likens God only to an earthly father, and therefore diminishes who God is.

Indonesian novelist and theologian Marianne Katoppo writes: 'When God is called "Father", this is not to be taken in an ontic sense, i.e. it does not necessarily limit God to being male. "Father" is intended to express the loving concern of God who takes care of us. Here the category "father" is a symbol of divine fecundity and creativity.'[14] Maybe the patriarchal societies in which the Bible has been translated and retranslated have left us with only part of the story – or at least many interpretations of this Bible have. I have spoken many times about my decision to no longer use male pronouns when talking about God. In doing so, I have often been met with the question of what to do about Jesus' references to God as father, as seen in the Lord's Prayer and throughout the New Testament. For some, the exclusion of male pronouns for God is just a marker of 'woke' feminist theology rather than a considered response to theological and biblical interpretation. Such a reading of Jesus' reference to his heavenly father deliberately fails to notice all the other ways that Scripture points to non-male descriptions of God. In particular, as Amy Peeler outlines in *Women and the Gender of God*, we should look not just at the relationship between God the Father and Jesus the Son, but also at how the relationship between God and the Son's siblings – us, humanity, the rest of creation – is described throughout the Bible. Peeler writes:

God treats creation – and humans in particular – in ways typically associated with both fathers and mothers. The result is that, in full alignment with the biblical text, God may be called upon metaphorically as Father, just as God may be addressed metaphorically as Mother. God is the source of life, but neither in relationship with creation, nor with the Son and the Son's siblings, are God's actions more like those of men rather than women. With regard to creation, God is God, and not human.[15]

She adds: 'God acts towards the Son's community – the many sons and daughters – in ways described as both fatherly and motherly.'[16] There are several examples of God acting in motherly ways towards Israel. God is described as a nursing mother in Isaiah 49; as comforting Israel as a mother comforts her child in Isaiah 66:13; in Isaiah 42:14 God cries out like a woman in labour; and in Deuteronomy God laments how people have forgotten who bore/gave birth to them. In the New Testament, God is the woman in the parable of the lost coin (Luke 15:8–10), and the woman who puts leaven into the dough (Matthew 13:33). And Jesus describes himself as being like a mother hen (Luke 13:34).

Dr Malka Z. Simkovich, chair of Jewish Studies and director of Catholic–Jewish Studies at the Catholic Theological Union, describes God as 'the mother of Israel'. During the time in which the Torah was written, thousands of years ago, the idea of feminine deities would not have seemed as countercultural as it does today. The Old Testament was written when there was a proliferation of pagan pantheons and when goddess worship was common; and so, as conservative commentators have argued, it is in fact the Old Testament's use of *male* imagery that made it radical, and it was also a way to distinguish Yahweh from all other lesser deities.[17] Though not necessarily countercultural, the Bible and Jewish religious tradition are nevertheless rife with metaphors about God's motherhood. This metaphorical motherhood extends to the rabbinic tradition too, and also to what it meant to be a Jew. In Judaism, true motherhood is that which gives life to others. In the early Common Era, rabbis started to describe themselves as mother figures to Jewish people, because they taught the Scriptures, and therefore gave life:

Whence do we learn that whoever teaches one chapter [of Mishnah] to his friend, the scriptures praise him as if he conceived him, formed him, and brought him into the world [olam]? . . . Just as that same mouth that infused the soul into the first man, so all those who bring even one creature under the wings of the Divine Presence, we praise him as if he conceived him, formed him, and brought him into the world. (*Tosefta Horayot* 2:7)[18]

In her forensic dissection of modern evangelical patriarchy, Dr Beth Allison Barr highlights the blind spots within the complementarian movement, which holds to a gender hierarchy that places men at the top and women under their submission, in a bid to be countercultural. For Barr, the complementarian movement that has responded to the rise of feminism since the later decades of the twentieth century, and perceived that to be the dominant culture, fails to recognise the centuries of patriarchy that have come before that, and that still persist today. The places in which the Bible highlights the value of women are the ones that are truly countercultural, when held up against the light of first-century patriarchy. Barr highlights how medieval mystics were able to glimpse God's maternity and how some of the most renowned of them dared to peek behind the patriarchal curtain to see God. As Julian of Norwich writes in her *Revelations of Divine Love*: 'As truly as God is our father, so truly is God our mother.'[19] For Julian, seeing God as mother was not just a gimmick, but a profound tool to understand the very nature of God. She did not deny that God is Father. God is indeed Father. But for her, God is Mother, too. Mystics before her often employed maternal language to describe God, while insisting God was primarily Father. But, as English and medieval studies expert Sarah McNamer writes of Julian, 'This is what makes her stand out with peculiar distinctness among the mystics, for it enables her to explore maternal concepts which remain relatively undeveloped by her contemporaries: immanence, unconditional love, and mercy.'[20]

Whereas the contemplation of Mary's motherhood has been used by some to fill a gap in conceptions of the God of the Abrahamic faiths as male, for Julian of Norwich, Mary does not need to play this role because God is already Mother. So therefore Mary is not there merely to make up for perceived inadequacies of God – she in fact points us towards who God truly is. Andrew Greeley puts it well when he writes: 'Mary reveals the tender, gentle, comforting, reassuring, "feminine" dimension of God.'[21] Mary is not a goddess.

What difference might it make for those of us who sometimes find ourselves drowning under the weight of expectations to be perfect mothers? I think that lurking beneath the surface of male depictions of God is the idea that maleness is closer to godliness, that men are better than women; the dangerous idea that has existed in patriarchal theology for centuries – that women are in some way faulty. God – the divine, the most perfect – is unlike us. Likewise, the cultural representation of the maternal ideal, the perfect mother, serves to constantly remind mothers that in fact we are imperfect, that we can never live up to this standard of motherly perfection, most vividly depicted in Mary.

I wonder where the past few decades of progress have got us as women and mothers. There have indeed been great strides in enabling us to forge our way ahead in the workplace and in education and in seats of power. But I find that behind the progressive public discourse about gender there is in fact some lazy stereotyping about what it is to be a woman. For example, it is still assumed that female styles of leadership in the workplace are nurturing, caring and emotional – even if these things are seen as positives; while male leadership is assumed to be rational, strong and pioneering. It is the same lazy stereotyping of what it is to be a mother that we have seen in the dominant portrayals of Mary over the centuries. That Mary is kind and gentle and beautiful and submissive and nurturing; and that all mothers therefore are – and must be – kind and gentle and beautiful and submissive and nurturing. Added to that is the notion that all of this is natural, that it does not take love, patience and perseverance, and that there won't be times when you have to grit your teeth and love anyway.

Reflecting on who Mary is and what she has meant in the minds of believers, I have come to understand not just that the mother of God has been used as a placeholder to contain all the attributes of a female deity that are lost when all you have is a patriarchal God, but that, whether or not that is the case, Mary has been misunderstood, her femaleness reduced to a one-dimensional view of womanhood and motherhood, by 'parochial and patriarchal forces'[22], as cultural historian Joanna Wolfarth describes it. Mary has in many ways been made small and meek, despite being the same Mary who sang about a new world order in the Magnificat – something we will return to later in this book. According to Wolfarth, the earliest depictions of Mary portrayed her not solely as a mother doing things that mothers do – feeding, gazing, caressing – but also as 'a strong religious leader, arms raised, commanding attention'.[23] As we saw in an earlier chapter, the one-dimensional view of Mary developed over time.

Though we may have good intentions when we talk about embracing a more expansive understanding of the gender of God, we risk falling into the trap of reinforcing binaries if our male descriptions of God resemble stereotypes of men, and our female descriptions of God resemble stereotypes of women.

Before there was Mary

Ancient peoples recognised the power of the divine feminine and created gods in the images of mothers to demonstrate and symbolise maternal strength. The ancient Greek goddess Gaia was revered as the divine force from whom all life on earth came. The Yoruba goddess Yemọja is worshipped as the mother of all other deities (Orishas) and the mother of all life. The Hindu goddess Kali is seen as the Great Mother. Research into the history of goddess worship points to a matriarchal era in prehistory in which there existed the idea of a Great Goddess – the predecessor to the female deities highlighted above that came later.

Since the beginning of homo sapiens, humanity has found ways to worship and picture and pray to the divine feminine. As Kathryn Jezer-Morton puts it, 'Mother worship is older than monotheism.'[24] Before there was Mary, Jesus' mother, there were Isis, Gaia, Yemọja, Kali. It is widely believed that early homo sapiens worshipped divine goddesses before male divinities came on the scene. For some, these feminine deities reflect humankind's fascination with the greatest mystery of all: the bringing forth of life. Since the beginning of time, we have been obsessed with natality. In around 2300 BC, a priestess named Enheduanna penned the first ever known writings: hymns to the goddess of childbirth. As Jennifer Banks begins her book *Natality: Toward a Philosophy of Birth*:

> Humans have thought about and written about birth from the beginning of recorded history, from ancient creation stories to medieval theological tracts, from philosophic manuals to

obstetrics textbooks, and from nineteenth-century novels to twenty-first-century memoirs. Birth has been a preoccupation across cultures and eras, although its importance has waned and waxed like any other preoccupation, following the obsessions and anxieties of the day.[25]

Before there was Christianity, there were beliefs in virgin mother goddesses who gave birth in fantastical ways. According to Carl Jung, every human society holds within it the idea of the great mother archetype. Theodore Roszak writes of the myth of Mary:

> Here was the mother goddess Christianity lacked, worked up out of the most meagre historical material by the mythic imagination – a triumph of collective visionary power at times so sweeping that the virgin nearly crowded out the official trinity. Of course, the theology of the church deftly delimited Mariology: but that had little meaning at the level of popular worship or artistic creation, where the virgin rapidly occupied the psychic ground that had always been held by Isis, Cybele, Magna Mater, and their ageless sisterhood. After all, how poor and unbalanced a religion it is that does not find place for the Divine Mother.'[26]

One of the reasons for a proliferation of views and representations and articulations of the meaning of Mary arises from the nature of Christian faith, as distinct from other religions. In many of the world's religions, the gods in some ways imitate the behaviours of human beings. They procreate as humans procreate, they fall in love and trick others, and they can rage and act in ways fuelled by jealousy. They exist within family structures – they can be married and have children. These polytheistic faiths differ from the Abrahamic religions in which there is one God.

In 2022, a major exhibition on female deities took place at the British Museum. 'Feminine power: the divine to the demonic' sought to celebrate sacred artefacts, sculptures, icons and contemporary art from six continents, exploring different ways in which humans have worshipped feminine power in deities, goddesses, saints and demons for millennia. Split up into sections marked Forces of

Nature, Passion and Desire, Magic and Malice, Justice and Defiance, and Compassion and Salvation, the exhibition invited well-known commentators, including novelist, critic and broadcaster Bonnie Greer and classicist Dame Mary Beard to provide insight for each section. In the exhibition, there was a ceramic incantation bowl from Iraq dating from AD 500–800, dedicated to Lilith – known within Jewish demonology as the first wife of Adam and the consort of Satan, and for killing babies. It featured a new icon of Kali, who remains one of the most celebrated deities in India, but who is revered for her power, aggression and destruction – wearing blood-ied heads and a belt of severed arms. But where was Mary? Towards the end of the exhibition, and of course in the section on Compassion and Mercy. As one commentator writes: 'Here the Christian Virgin is put in her place . . . In fact, we get very little in the show on the female figure who was the most potent and ubiquitous in western civilisation, with the additional bonus that in acquiescing to the Incarnation she is the most important example ever of female consent.'[27]

Mary, in this exhibition, is once again sidestepped, her feminine power – the fact that she literally gave birth to God and was an authoritative figure in the Jesus movement – ignored, reduced to the 'gentler' attributes we associate with 'perfect' mothers: compassionate and merciful. In popular culture in recent years we have seen much exploration of the power of ancient goddesses. For example, in her recent albums, Beyoncé has alluded to West African goddesses, including the goddess Oshun from the Yoruba religion. Mary does not seem to have been paid the same attention among millennial spiritual-but-not-religious influencers – perhaps because of what she represents in the popular imagination. The more obvious potency of divine goddesses seems to have greater resonance in an age of feminine power, and so Mary's perceived powerlessness and passivity – shaped by the ways in which men, predominantly, have told her story for centuries – does not seem to be as attractive or relevant to young women today. But Mary has of course been misunderstood, as has the God she represents. Mary is not in fact powerless. This is the Mary who gave birth to God, and who risked societal ostracisation because of her sense of purpose and mission. This is the Mary whose song of justice has echoed throughout history.

When I was younger and less questioning, the idea that there existed other creation stories or ideas about God centuries before the Bible was written would have shaken me. So would the comparison of Mary with divine feminine predecessors. But perhaps what all of this shows is that humans have always searched for God. I have grown increasingly comfortable with this idea, but what I also believe is that the Christian story offers something truer and more qualitatively different. Mary's motherhood of God is one profound way in which Christianity achieves this.

Mary stands out for me because, unlike Gaia or Yemọja, she points not to herself, but to God. Some might be fooled into thinking that the idea of God as mother is simply a sign of the times we are living in; an outworking of political correctness and woke ideology. But beyond Mary symbolising the archetype of motherhood through her motherhood of Christ, the idea of *God as mother* is an ancient one. God's maternity is of course not just the purview of historical musings by mystics – it is found right in the heart of our sacred text, the Bible. Feminist theologian Sister Elizabeth A. Johnson writes: 'Numerous biblical texts offer potent female images of the living God: God as a woman in labor, giving birth, midwifing, nursing, and carrying a child; God as an angry mother bear robbed of her cubs; God knitting, baking, washing up, searching for her money; God as Woman Wisdom creating, ordering, and saving the world.'[28]

Womanist scholar Dr Wil Gafney speaks of the mother-love of God,[29] as described in the Hebrew Scriptures. Whether or not we have experienced this love ourselves from our own mothers, and whether or not we find ourselves as mothers constantly striving to live up to this love-without-limits in our own mothering, most of us understand what we mean by this mother-love. It is the mother-love that we see depicted in Mary's gaze towards the God-child in the images and sculptures of the Madonna. It is the mother-love displayed in the heartbreaking paintings of Christ's limp and broken body in the pietà. Perhaps this ideal of mother-love is one of the things that places yet more pressure on us as mothers when we find our children pushing us to our limits, when we snap under the weight of the cognitive load of motherhood. When we feel hatred and resentment rather than limitless love.

But it is Julian of Norwich's conception of the unconditional love of God, Our Mother, that may in fact liberate us from this myth that says that in order to love unconditionally, we must ourselves be perfect. 'Strong and marvelous is that love', writes Julian, 'which may not, nor will not, be broken by our offenses.'[30] May we remember that in the daily imperfections that make up the pieces of our mothering. May we find freedom in the knowledge that we are mothers, made in God's image, ourselves being held in the womb-like love of God, Our Mother.

What has prevented so many of us from noticing or appreciating the feminine aspects of God? The Church. A Church that has been so swayed by – and that has itself perpetuated – patriarchal ideas about power, dominance and strength and that has therefore elevated men and subordinated women. It is astonishing to see the ways in which church leaders contort themselves to avoid the reality that the God of the Bible is not a man. In fact, as Gafney notes, 'The only reproductive organ ascribed to God in the biblical text is a womb.'[31] We have to recognise that often it is through feminine characteristics that we can better understand God's nature. But so often parts of the Church have failed in this respect.

During a sermon at his church, Eleven22, Joby Martin described breastfeeding as 'gross'. He told congregants that a woman had once dared to breastfeed her child on the front row at the church. Recalling the incident, he said he had been disgusted by this woman's actions and had thought how they – the mother and her infant – should 'get a room' because 'that's gross'.[32] What was so disappointing about this clip was not just the shock-jock tactics, or the denigration of women's bodies, or the way nursing a baby was likened to a sexual act that should be kept behind closed doors and away from holy eyes. It was the irony that the topic of his sermon was supposed to be the stead-fast love of God. He was focusing on Psalm 100, in which these words are written:

> For the Lord is good and his love endures for ever;
> his faithfulness continues through all generations. (Psalm 100:5)

The Hebrew word for this love that endures for ever is *chesed*. Used more than 248 times in the Bible, it has a number of translations, one of which describes fierce maternal love. As Joby Martin says, the 'word picture' it is supposed to conjure up is that of a mother nursing her child. It is the loving-kindness and mercy that describe a mother's attentiveness to a child, the way she cannot bear to let the child suffer or be hungry – even if that means she has to breastfeed at church. These are beautiful images that tell us something about the nature of God, and so for Martin to recognise the fact that God – whom many think of as male – is described in Scripture itself as a mother makes his decision to use the passage as the basis for dissuading women from breastfeeding in church all the more puzzling. Especially when a mother nursing her child is a profound metaphor for the beauty of divine milk.

Divine milk

Both of my children have been obsessed with milk. Long after I stopped breastfeeding them, they drank cow's milk for much longer than the parenting advice suggested. I just could not break their habit. At home, they would forgo food, screwing their noses up at my courgette muffins or beetroot brownies, until they got their milk. These were my attempts to be a good mother who could disguise vegetables and be one of those mums whose children ate beetroots and courgettes. I would keep calm when they flung my creations on the floor, or miraculously seemed to gain the ability to speak in complete sentences when I offered these foods to them: 'I don't want it.' They would refuse to satiate their hunger until they finally got their bedtime bottle of the white stuff: the good stuff. Then they would shout and scream for 'more milk!' until we gave in and gave them more. Children's fascination with milk speaks beautifully of the relationship between Jesus and his mother, between us and Jesus, and between humanity and God.

Marina Warner writes:

> The milk of the Mother of God became even more highly charged with the symbolism of life, for the life of life's own source

depended on it. When the medieval mystic meditated on the Incarnation, he saw not only a mother nursing her baby – an event in historical time – but an eternal mystery whereby the Christian soul is perpetually nourished and sustained by grace, of which Mary's milk is a sublime epiphany.[33]

Christian mystics often saw visions of Our Lady, which included her baring her breast and healing ailments with her milk. There are shrines all over Europe purported to include phials containing her milk. Visitors to Bethlehem can today visit the Milk Grotto, in which a few drops of Mary's milk are believed to have spilt while she was nursing. Milk is a universal language – there is no society on earth that does not understand its importance for the nurture and growth of healthy human beings. Milk is holy; and the mother of God's milk is the holiest of all.

But it is not just the image of the Madonna lactans – Mary as a nursing mother – that portrays the theological significance of milk; this metaphor of feeding is also used to paint a picture of humanity's relationship to Christ. Julian of Norwich describes Jesus as a mother, who feeds his children:

> The mother can give her child to suck of her milk, but our precious Mother Jesus can feed us with himself, and does, most courteously and most tenderly, with the blessed sacrament, which is the precious food of true life . . . The mother can lay her child tenderly to her breast, but our tender Mother Jesus can lead us easily into his blessed breast through his sweet open side, and show us there a part of the godhead and of the joys of heaven, with inner certainty of endless bliss . . . This fair lovely word 'mother' is so sweet and so kind in itself that it cannot truly be said of anyone or to anyone except of him and to him who is the true Mother of life and of all things.[34]

As well as its being 'a deeply embedded metaphor for spiritual awakening', writes Joanna Wolfarth, many, mainly male, religious elders from the Reformation to the nineteenth century used breast milk as a symbol of divine love: 'Eternal bliss was analogous to the happy baby at his mother's breast, and weaning was symbolic of helplessness and spiritual loss.'[35] Wolfarth cites seventeenth-century Puritan Thomas Shepard, who likened eternal life to 'being laid in the bosom of Christ'.[36]

Milk is holy; and so is blood. In times gone by, people used to believe that milk was processed menstrual blood. This, it was believed, explained why women's periods only returned to normal after they stopped breastfeeding. I am fascinated by the symbolic link between a mother's milk nourishing her baby and the nourishment provided for believers in the bread and wine of the Communion table, where God feeds us with God's self.

Although the Eucharist reminds Christians of Christ's blood shed and body broken for humanity through the atonement made possible through the resurrection, when I approach the Communion table, I also come to be fed and nourished spiritually through the eating of bread and the drinking of wine. When believers say the Lord's Prayer and ask God to give us our daily bread, 'we could as easily pray for regular supplies of milk', as Hebblethwaite writes. 'Whenever we receive nourishment, be it physical food or spiritual strengthening, we should be aware of God our mother who produces it.'[37]

Taking those steps towards the Communion table has always had an otherworldly quality to it for me – a weirdness; a transcendent knowing. When I take a step back from it, it can all feel pretty strange: this idea that we eat God's body and drink God's blood. Pregnancy gave me a new insight into what this might be all about: this idea of the oneness and twoness of pregnancy, of being reconciled to God in partaking of this ritual feeding. When my babies grew in my tummy, they absorbed nutrients from me. They fed from my body through the umbilical cord that at that stage held us materially, but through which we will forever be connected, long after the cord has been cut. Wil Gafney explains how pregnancy helps us understand the complex Christian understanding of consuming the body and blood of Christ in a way that is not 'cannibalistic, vampiric, or zombie-geist'.[38]

A cataclysmic event

Reflecting on the motherhood of Mary can give us insight into the feminine attributes of God that have in recent history been down-played – whether deliberately or accidentally. But experiencing the reality of motherhood myself gave me not just a revelation of God's *feminine* nature, but new revelation about the nature of God full stop. Motherhood is an experience so earth-shattering that it can cause us to rethink all we have thought before, including what it is to be human, who God is, and, for some, whether indeed they believe in God or not.

Many mothers have written and spoken about how becoming parents has presented them with deep existential awakening. The term 'matrescence' – coined by Dana Raphael in 1975 – describes the very particular rite of passage that women go through when they become mothers. 'It is a major life crisis,' she writes, 'and should not be taken for granted.'[39] During matrescence, a woman's physiology, identity, beliefs and behaviours can change dramatically, and for some this might include a departure from their previously held theo-logical or spiritual ideas.

Writer Jennifer Fulwiler describes moving from a long-held athe-istic view that the world and everything in it was meaningless, and that there was no God, to a shift in worldview after going through the 'cataclysmic event' of becoming a mother. At first, she wrestled with an overwhelming sense of the nothingness of life, struggling with the belief that 'there was nothing transcendent about my son's life, my life, or any of the love I felt for him'. But after this realisation sank her into a deep and dark depression, rendering her almost 'cata-tonic', something changed:

> One morning, as I looked at the baby in the pre-dawn light that filtered in through the window, I felt something new within me. It was something that was not despair, some unfamiliar yet welcome feeling. I peeled back the layers to find that it was doubt: Doubt of my purely materialist worldview, doubt of the truth I had believed since childhood that there is nothing transcendent about the human life.[40]

These changes in outlook during matrescence apply not just to those who have physically given birth – it is a fundamental shift that can happen to all who take on the role of parent, including adoptive and other non-birth parents.

Blessed is she

Despite motherhood being put on a pedestal in many churches, and prized as the ultimate purpose for women, motherhood itself is not in fact to be worshipped. We see this in a particularly challenging passage in the ministry of Jesus. In Luke 11:27, a woman in the crowd calls out to him: 'Blessed is the mother who gave you birth and nursed you.' Jesus, who in that chapter is at his most provocative, responds: 'Blessed rather are those who hear the word of God and obey it.' In Jesus' eyes, what is important is relationship with God. Motherhood is not a ticket to eternal salvation. We see in the whole of Luke's Gospel the presence of Mary and her important place as mother. But what is emphasised is that she is a believer, not just that she is a mum. The message for Christian mothers is clear: that we should seek first the kingdom of God, rather than find our identity in our motherhood, hard though that may be when it is so all-consuming. We might also hear in Jesus' words a message that would have been countercultural at the time: that women are more than mothers, that we are more than women.

Though motherhood itself is not a route to salvation, as we have seen, many mothers have experienced a spiritual awakening when they have become mothers. Trudelle Thomas describes the relative lack of writing about such experiences of maternal awakening, despite the renaissance in literature describing the maternal experience. But, speaking of her own experience and noting patterns in those of other mothers, Thomas sees several themes emerging when a woman becomes a mother: a sense of breaking open and spiritual initiation; embodiment and union; major shifts in identity, emotional range, ways of relating, perspective, and therefore, ethics. 'All these have reshaped how I experience and speak of God,' Thomas writes.[41]

In some senses, a new mother could say she is 'born again', baptised into the community of mothers before her who have dealt with the disorientation and wonder of having a child. Certain words recur time and again when women describe the early minutes, hours, weeks and months of matrescence: unlocking, revealing, over-whelming; transcendence, hope, love. For me, it was the love that broke me open. The disbelief of it. The fear that I now had to carry this intense love for another around with me for-ever. That I could not be separated from it, even in death.

Women have long spoken about these spiritual awakenings. In *Natality*, Jennifer Banks tells the story of Mary Wollstonecraft, the eighteenth-century writer, philosopher and women's rights activist, who faced a serious bout of depression after the birth of her child. In 1795, a year after giving birth to her daughter Fanny, she had a failed attempt at taking her own life by overdosing on laudanum. She was in a relationship with a man who refused to commit, which, 'in addition to the social and economic precariousness she experienced as an unwed mother, and the physical demands of pregnancy, birth and the postnatal period', meant she felt she could not cope. But it was her daughter who saved her. As Wollstonecraft began to pick herself up again, to travel and write with her daughter by her side, she wrote of looking at her daughter sleeping at night, and experiencing emotions that 'trembled on the brink of extacy [*sic*] and agony . . . which made me feel more alive than usual'. Fanny, her daughter, was no 'particle broken off from the grand mass of mankind', but was instead part of a 'mighty whole'. 'Futurity,' she wrote, 'what hast thou not to give to those who know that there is such a thing as happiness!'[42]

It is not just in the big, life-altering moments that mothers can see God. We can glimpse God in the stillness of watching our children sleep, just as we can in attending to the mundane stuff of domestic life. As St Teresa of Ávila once said, 'The Lord moves amongst the pots and pans.' Motherhood – especially in the early years – comprises so much of what most of the western world would consider dull, drab and mindless. The washing, cleaning, scraping, wiping, dabbing, holding, tapping that accompanies those hazy days. Mothers who stay at home – whether by choice or by necessity – are tasked with much of the daily grind of domestic chores and child-rearing.

I confess, I have looked down on all of this for much of my life. It is why the thought of maternity leave – that seemed to stretch out like nine mindless months ahead of me – terrified me. It's why I spent far too much time in that precious liminal period before returning to work proving that I still had a mind and that I was still capable. I took my babies to meetings, I organised events, I wrote, and stayed on top of work emails. I still needed to be seen to have ambition and to be achieving things – as if these were the things that mattered, not the tender acts of care that nurture our children.

One of the things that made my first steps into motherhood so difficult was the profound challenge that it is to care for a human being. To live in a WEIRD (Western, Educated, Industrialised, Rich and Democratic) society is to be disconnected from the reality of human vulnerability. We are separated from others by screens and technologies and walls and doors. We outsource so much of our caring to others who we may feel are better equipped, despite their still being considered 'low-skilled' in our society. Motherhood thrusts you into a world in which you are confronted with the messiness of life, of what it is to be human. That the stuff of care is undervalued by our societies is because it is women's work. It is seen as less because it highlights human vulnerability – the fact that we depend on our basic needs being taken care of; that we have limits; that we need others to care for us. The beauty is that it is here, in the interdependence and mutuality that shows up in the mundane, not just in the cataclysmic, it is here too where God lives.

PART THREE
Labour

Chapter 4

This Is My Body Broken For You

'Oh, but my stomach, she is like a waterbed covered
in flannel. When I lie on my side in bed, my
stomach lies politely beside me, like a puppy.'

—*Operating Instructions: A Journal of My
Son's First Year*, Anne Lamott[1]

'"Here," she said, "in this here place, we flesh; flesh that weeps,
laughs; flesh that dances on bare feet in grass. Love it. Love it
hard. Yonder they do not love your flesh. They despise it . . .
More than your life-holding womb and your life-giving private
parts, hear me now, love your heart. For this is the prize."'

—*Beloved*, Toni Morrison[2]

Maternal incarnation

As soon as I got pregnant, I felt hyper-conscious of my body. My
body that was growing another body. My body that had until that
point been my own also became home to a vulnerable creature. My
discombobulation started when I realised how embodied I really
was. Not just a person, a soul, a mind, but a body – like any other
female of a species in the animal kingdom. The revelation was on the
one hand transcendent and ineffable – unable to be pinned down –
and at the same time completely grounded in the earthiness of bodily
existence. An embodied out-of-body experience.

No one understands the concept of incarnation – the embodiment and enfleshment upon which the heart of the Christian story

hinges – better than women. From childhood, we learn that a woman's body has a unique kind of physicality; like the phases of the moon, we wax and wane. A woman's body bleeds and cramps and doubles over in cycles of pain. From our earliest memories, we understand that we – our whole human bodies – were once housed within our mothers'; a thought grotesque yet also deeply comforting. She was our first home.

It has been suggested that in the nativity story, the angelic Annunciation to the shepherds happens not just because they represent the open-armed embrace of God by including the poor and uneducated, but also because the shepherds spent their time with God's creatures – they were closest to nature. In the same way, Jesus' first home being inside his mother, Mary, is a powerful demonstration of incarnation: God is truly embodied inside a body that – like most women in human history – cannot escape its physicality.

It was strange and surreal to find out we were pregnant the first time. We had been trying for months, and – prone to catastrophising – I had begun to harbour the growing doubt in my mind that we would never become parents. Having grown up in a Christian home, where to fall pregnant outside marriage was seen as the ultimate sin, I was relieved to get married and never have to face that particular shame. So now the attention was turned from the chastity of Christian girlhood to the Christian duty to go forth and multiply – preferably as quickly as possible. As is traditional in Nigerian wedding ceremonies, the prayers included a wish for a celebration nine months from that day, where we would mark the arrival of our first-born – ideally twins.

We waited a year before turning our attention to starting a family, deliberately trying not to put pressure on ourselves. As each month passed with no sign of pregnancy, my panic and anxiety started to increase. Would it ever happen? Cue hours and hours spent reading internet tips on how to get pregnant. A chance conversation with a friend about her own fertility journey found me following her advice and buying a book called *Taking Charge of Your Fertility* by Toni Weschler.[3] We were pregnant six weeks later. Absolute joy and utter relief followed: we had done it. Next came the fear, and the dawning realisation, that our lives would never be the same again. We were looking after precious cargo. We loved it already, tracking the apps that told us which fruit or vegetable our baby was the size of that week. The hallmark moments of my pregnancies were, however, overshadowed by the sheer discomfort I experienced. Pregnancy was not how I had imagined it to be.

When I was pregnant, I dreaded the very physical yet simple act of brushing my teeth. A thing that had seemed such a non-event every day of my thirty preceding years took on a new and torturous nature. The first time I experienced the horrific side effects of my pregnant toothbrushing was in the early weeks of my first pregnancy. Perhaps it was the sensation of saliva and toothpaste, perhaps it was the bristling of the toothbrush against my teeth and tongue, but something felt wrong. I do not know why, but it made me gag; and the gag turned into a retch and the retch turned into full-on vomiting into the adjacent toilet bowl. By this stage, I was already regularly being sick. I quickly had to get over the extreme fear of vomit that I had had my whole life – not that anyone likes it. In those early weeks, I was sick in bins on the street, in office toilets, on the train. The nausea was constant – daily life accompanied by the unpleasant feeling of being aboard an undulating cruise ship, trying to steady my gait. While the nausea was ever-present and thus predictable, the vomiting bouts were less so. I would be overcome in any place and at any time. After that first instance of toothbrushing vomit, I assumed it was just a blip; yet another strange and random incident in the chronicles of pregnancy. But no, I threw up the next time I brushed my teeth, too. And the next time and the next and just about every day until the day I gave birth. Initially, I scoured the internet and mum forums to find solace and solutions. Because surely I could not go through a whole pregnancy vomiting every time I brushed my teeth. I tried everything. One tip suggested standing on one leg while brushing; another advised turning round or moving my head in a circular motion, perhaps as a distraction technique to suppress the wave from rising up and out. Sometimes the tips provided momentary relief and I thought I had cracked it, only for the vomiting to return the next time.

The horror of toothbrushing was just one of the strange side effects of my pregnancies. As I approached the hallowed twelve-week mark during my first pregnancy, having thrown up several times a day, I said to my mother – with hope – that at least it would be over soon, because I had read that 'morning' sickness would subside after the first trimester. Her response was to tell me that she had been sick throughout the whole nine months of her pregnancy with me. In that moment, I briefly considered ending it all. Death felt an easier way out than having to continue the night-mare. Still, I hoped and prayed that the pregnancy-sickness genes that had blighted my mum and her mum and my aunts would go easy on me. They did not. I was throwing up several times a day until my baby boy eventually came out. My throwing up several times a day was a mild version of the extreme pregnancy sickness – or hyperemesis gravidarum (HG) – experienced by up to 3.6% of preg-nant women. A survey of more than five thousand women with HG published in 2021 found that 5 per cent had terminated a wanted pregnancy because of it, while 52 per cent had considered an abor-tion. A quarter of the women in the survey had considered suicide.[4]

I was so scarred by my first experience of pregnancy – and by the subsequent birth and early years – that it took me four years to be ready to try again. Even then, it felt more like a consciousness of the ticking of my biological clock than a feeling of being anywhere near 'ready'. The sickness was – unbelievably to me – worse the second time round. It felt that, in every way, I was – to quote Adrienne Rich in *Of Woman Born:* 'allergic to pregnancy'.[5]

It was while I was staring into the bottom of a toilet bowl that I saw the face of Jesus and recognised the concept of sacrifice and also what it meant for Mary to bear God in her womb – for her organs to be displaced to grow the God-child; for her body to change in irrevocable ways. Here, the theological concept of kenosis – Christ emptying himself out on the cross for the sake of humankind – began to take on new meaning for me; here, in what Laura Fabrycky describes as the 'nearly self-obliterating sacrifices' of motherhood.[6]

Those who experience extreme pregnancy sickness and vomiting know that the affliction remains taboo. It is filled with shame and guilt and the weight of social pressure to display both endless grati-tude and boundless strength while pregnant. On the occasions when I tried to explain my pregnancy-sickness anguish, I was met with a polite level of empathy. But sometimes platitudes such as *at least you know your baby's healthy*, or *this too will pass* didn't cut it. There were some women who – admittedly unknowingly – gave the impression that I was somehow weak for succumbing to the pregnancy sickness. A grandmother who had had eight children of her own once told me at a party: 'Oh, through all my pregnancies I just sucked it up. I'm not one of those people who stops when I feel a bit poorly.' In my opinion, anyone who has had eight children or who likens hyperemesis gravidarum to being 'a bit poorly' has never come close to experiencing it.

When I thought about having a baby, I never imagined some of the strange, weird and not-so-wonderful side effects I would experience in the process. On top of the trauma of toothbrushing, no one had ever warned me, for example, about the possibility of olecranon bursitis, which saw me develop a swelling the size of a golf ball on my elbow a few weeks after giving birth. Bursitis happens when one of the fluid-filled sacs – the bursae that act as cushions to reduce friction between body tissues – becomes inflamed; olecranon refers to the bony tip of the elbow where this particular type of bursitis occurs. I had developed this ailment from tensing up my arm as I breastfed my new baby. As I cradled him in the crook of my arm, I was terrified of dropping my precious bundle, so I would sit for hours on end holding my arm still in the same position. Perhaps the tensing up of my arm was also a result of the sharp pain I felt as the baby latched – like a jolt of lightning, electric shards surging through me as he drank. The first few moments were always agony for me. *Was it supposed to hurt this much?*

I wonder what Mary's pregnancy ailments were. Fatigue? Nausea? Hyperemesis? Bursitis? Food aversions? Back pain? Did she suffer from pelvic girdle pain? Constipation? Insomnia? A strange metallic taste in her mouth? Did she crave certain foods? In some Marian theology, there has existed a tradition that suggests that Mary's pregnancy and birth were supernaturally painless. The influential second-century Gospel of James is one of the main reasons theologians have suggested that when Mary gave birth to Jesus, the whole affair was over instantaneously, and without pain. In the account, the baby was in her tummy one moment and then a cloud descended, there appeared a light, and he was out of it. A totally painless, magical affair. *Meditations on the Life of Christ*, another influential work, written in about 1300 and attributed to St Bonaventure, included this account of the birth: 'The Virgin rose and stood erect against a column that was there. But Joseph remained seated . . . taking some hay from the manger, placed it at the Lady's feet and turned away. Then the Son of the eternal God came out of the womb of the mother without a murmur or lesion, in a moment . . .'[7]

To suggest that Mary gave birth in the same way as other women was regarded by these theologians as a threat to one of the most important elements in the construction of Mary: her 'intact virginity'.[8] For them, once Mary had completed the task of bringing Jesus into the world – and avoided the gruesomeness of it – she then became just like any 'natural' mother, engaging in the nurturing of the Christ-child because it was in these motherly acts that believers could get a glimpse into the nature of God's love. But in the majority of historical Christian theology, it was not Mary's *physical* motherhood that was valued; rather, it was her spiritual and emotional motherhood. As social historian Nadia Maria Filippini writes, the physical was 'not only excluded from religious representation, but confined to an animal-like dimension deemed unworthy of the Mother of God'.[9] Despite this suggestion that it is the non-physical elements of motherhood that are to be honoured, it is the human – the physical – parts of Mary's motherhood that I value most. In the story of Jesus being born of a woman, we see the beauty of the incarnation, and have a glimpse into what it meant to be inextricably linked to another, and also what it meant to suffer on behalf of something – or someone – you love. As Clarissa Atkinson puts it: 'Motherhood – true motherhood – is inseparable from suffering and pain.'[10] Despite this truth that many mothers experience, cultural and Christian representations of perfect motherhood such as those we find in portrayals of Mary suggest that non-physical, ethereal pregnancy and childbirth are the most godly, while physical, painful experiences are associated with women's sinfulness brought about by Eve's actions.

The problem with pain

There is a danger that we accept physical pain as simply part of a woman's lot – from the crippling monthly pain for those who menstruate, to the agony of miscarriage, to the overwhelming sting of childbirth itself – and that the inevitability of pain becomes attached to the image of the sacrificial 'good mother'. Mary's pain-free supernatural birth was also believed to have taken place because she was sinless. 'Since she was free of guilt and fear, she suffered no physical discomfort,' writes medieval historian Esther Cohen. 'The message was clear: pain lay in the soul; it resulted from the soul's sin and guilt, and its awareness of that guilt, of the ensuing retribution, and of the fear thereof.'[11] Therefore, Mary's perfect motherhood, her sinlessness, meant she did not experience the pain of childbirth. So it followed therefore that every other woman who experienced pain in childbirth did so because of her sinful nature. During the late Middle Ages, there was both 'a thirst for martyrdom'[12] so that people could achieve virtue by identifying with Christ's sufferings, and a belief that women were inferior to men in every way, including in their reduced ability to withstand pain. Therefore, enduring pain in childbirth – quietly – became a way in which women could demonstrate their virtue.

Before writing this book, I had not realised how much my innate belief in the inevitability of women's pain had been shaped by the creation story. The cause of humanity's sin is placed at the door of the first woman, Eve. Following the serpent's temptation of her and Adam, and their eating of the forbidden fruit in a quest for knowledge, it is the woman who receives the worst punishment. 'I will make your pains in childbearing very severe,' God tells her. 'With painful labour you will give birth to children' (Genesis 3:16). It is church theology that has been used to justify and explain the pain women experience during childbirth. It has been seen as an unfortunate, but nevertheless necessary, price that we have to pay for our sins. Women are asked to follow the example of a sinless, perfect mother, but at the same time are burdened with the weight of our foremother Eve's guilt and shame. One could start to wonder whether these two stories of the most prominent women in the Bible have been created to put women in their place.

These views have pervaded decisions about women's health for centuries. For much of human history, pregnancy and childbirth were so dangerous that they often ended in the death of the mother, or of the child, or of both. Mary Wollstonecraft died after giving birth to Mary Shelley. Fanny Waugh Hunt, the wife of artist William Holman Hunt, also died from complications resulting from childbirth, as did US president Thomas Jefferson's daughter, Mary Eppes, and Abraham Lincoln's sister, Sarah Grigsby. Many male theologians and physicians throughout history have thought that the more pain a woman went through while giving birth, the better a mother she would be. The stark reality that she could not be a good mother if she were dead did not seem to spur societies on to prioritise improvements in gynaecology and obstetrics.

The journey towards better maternal health and pain relief for women during childbirth has been much slower than other advancements in medicine or science, lagging behind owing to the enduring belief that women *should* experience pain during childbirth. It was in the middle of the eighteenth century that forceps were introduced to assist in childbirth, and it was in 1853 that Queen Victoria – who had nine children in total, but who is believed to have hated childbirth and suffered from postnatal depression – requested chloroform for the birth of her eighth child, Prince Leopold. This followed six years of debate about whether it was safe for the monarch to be administered it, following the discovery of its pain-relief qualities in 1847 by physician James Young Simpson. Following Leopold's birth, during which she inhaled the chloroform for fifty-three minutes, she described the birth as 'delightful beyond measure'.[13] At a time in which both motherhood and stable families were idealised, Victorian mothers and prospective mothers would have breathed a sigh of relief at the thought that pain relief was now fit for a queen, and would soon be fit for them, too.

The early twentieth century saw a brief trend in 'twilight sleep', in which wealthy women underwent a treatment of scopolamine and morphine, which would help them forget the pain of labour – but not get rid of the pain while it was happening. The twilight-sleep movement grew in popularity – especially in New York City – as women were understandably keen on it at a time when childbirth was a leading cause of death for women. But it dwindled when one of the leaders of the Twilight Sleep Association, Frances Carmody, died of a haemorrhage while giving birth using the method in 1915. The latter part of the twentieth century saw significant advancements, including the relocation of childbirth from home settings to hospitals (although some would argue that this has led to different issues), the use of epidurals from the 1970s onwards, and the increased use of C-sections, which now account for more than a third of births.[14]

It is extraordinary to note that it was not until the 1950s that the Catholic Church came round to accepting the use of pain relief during childbirth. In Pope Pius XII's 1956 address on the science and morality of painless childbirth, he stated that suffering came with the territory of motherhood, but that God's punishment of Eve did not rule out any subsequent human attempts to ease pain during labour. Although he welcomed scientific advancements that could help women, and permitted the use of pain relief – he warned against using it with 'exaggerated haste'. The Pope also suggested that difficult deliveries could arise out of 'an incorrect behavior, psychic or physical, on the part of those in labor', again perpetuating the idea that experiencing pain during childbirth was down to some deficiency in the woman. A good mother – the most perfect of mothers – either experiences a pain-free labour, or grins and bears it. Pope Pius XII also said that the 'intensity of pain' was 'lesser among primitive peoples than among civilized peoples'.[15] I do wonder whether in the Pope's mind this might have gone some way towards therefore explaining why Mary – both perfect and a brown woman – experienced painless childbirth. I am being deliberately provocative here, but this narrative does demonstrate one of the pervasive ideas in women's health: that brown-skinned women feel less pain. It was a popular belief at the time, espoused by influential voices in the natural childbirth movement, including the controversial Grantly Dick-Read, who, despite not being a qualified obstetrician, gained popularity among women, and in 1956 was granted an audience with the Pope, who presented him with the Silver Papal Medal. In his 1933 book *Natural Childbirth*, he wrote:

Woman, primitive, civilised or cultured, has no evidence before her which suggests that Nature ever intended pregnancy to be an illness. The primitive woman continues her work – in the harvest field, on trek, in the rubber plantation, or wherever she may be employed. The child develops while she herself lives a full and natural existence. Muscularly strong, physiologically efficient, her mechanism carries out its normal functions without discomfort, difficulty or shame.[16]

These ideas have been catastrophic for Black women in the Anglo-American Global North, who are five times more likely to die in childbirth than their white counterparts. These heartbreaking statistics were in the back of my mind during both my pregnancies. When I gave birth the first time, I did so at a hospital in south-east London at which another Black woman had died after giving birth two years before. In 2015, 26-year-old old D'Lissa Parkes went to Lewisham Hospital with crippling labour pains, only to be dismissed and sent home. She returned in the early hours of the following day, haemorrhaging severely, and bled to death during a C-section. Her baby daughter was so severely brain-damaged that doctors believed she would never walk or talk.

Such ideas about women and pain during childbirth still linger today. Both times I gave birth, I went in knowing that I would take pain relief – ideally an epidural – if I needed it. Both times I did; and yet I could not shake the slight embarrassment at having done so, or fail to recall the pride in male friends' voices as they declared their wives had bravely delivered their babies without the need for any pain relief. Why is it that there should be any pride in this, as if – long after the days of Christian martyrdom in the West – a woman's ability to withstand pain is seen as a sign of her virtue? Would we applaud someone who deliberately underwent a tooth extraction without pain relief, or a hip replacement, or a vasectomy? Historian Elinor Cleghorn states: 'I can't think of another form of human pain that is as moralised as childbirth pain.'[17]

The legend of Pope Joan

In Europe during the Middle Ages, there circulated the legendary and cautionary tale of Pope Joan. Joan was a young woman who fell in love with a travelling student and monk in England. Since monks were not permitted to marry, Joan donned male clerical clothing and joined her lover as the pair wandered through Europe, reading and learning. When her lover died, Joan carried on travelling and acquiring knowledge, rising through the ranks of the Church, but continuing to hide the fact that she was a woman. Eventually, her virtue and intellect led to her being elected to the papal throne, where she reigned for two years. But according to Giovanni Boccaccio, who told the story in the fourteenth century, her brazenness was punished when she was overcome with lust and became pregnant. Despite her erudition, she did not recognise the signs, and went into labour during a procession through the streets of Rome, subsequently dying an agonising death in front of the gathered crowds. In the 1960s, a vivid description of the scene that appeared in a nineteenth-century novelised biography was translated by Lawrence Durrell:

> Great was the consternation when a premature infant was produced from among the voluminous folds of the papal vestments. The attending archdeacons recoiled in horror while the great circle of worshippers pressed in even closer, screaming and crossing themselves. Women climbed on the backs of their menfolks for a better view, while those already mounted on horses and mules stood in the saddle until the deacons were forced to use their standards and crucifixes as clubs to hew a passage through the mob.[18]

This is a scandalous story, but commentators have suggested that it is not just the pregnancy out of wedlock that makes it so disturbing, it is also the incongruity of it all – the birth scene in particular. 'The story is about disorder,' Clarissa Atkinson remarks in *The Oldest Vocation*, 'and about the filth and chaos that ensue when objects and persons and events are out of place – a woman on the throne of Peter, a child in the belly of a pope, a birth in a public procession.'[19]

In some versions of the legend of Pope Joan, the catastrophe of a female pope and the shameful incongruency of her giving birth led to checks being done on subsequent popes to ensure that they were in fact male. It is suggested that the would-be popes would have to sit on a *sedia stercoraria* (a dung chair) that had a hole in it, through which a cardinal would reach up and establish that the man had testicles. There would then follow an announcement: '*Duos habet et bene pendentes*' ('He has two and they dangle nicely')[20] – or simply, to spare everyone's blushes, '*Habet*' ('He has them').[21]

To me, this story is all about bodies. What bodies should and shouldn't do, what bodies are capable of, the difference between men's bodies and women's bodies, what of our bodies should be seen or talked about in public, and what bodily functions fall into the category of taboo. Bodies matter. There has been much written and discussed about the nature of human bodies and how they relate to non-material elements that might comprise a person, such as the soul or the spirit. French philosopher René Descartes famously took a dualistic approach, separating the mind from the body, as illustrated in his famous quote: 'I think, therefore I am.' Most religions contain some element of asceticism – the practice of denying the physical body in order to achieve a spiritual goal. Christian thought has wrestled with the concepts of monism (the belief that the body and soul or spirit are inseparable and indistinguishable), dualism (the belief that there is a non-material mind that is distinct from the body) and trichotomism (the belief that humans are body, soul and spirit).[22] Through exploring Paul's thinking about the body in the New Testament, Paula Gooder comes to the conclusion that he has a different theory about the importance of the body in Christian thought, and flits between the above definitions. In essence, though, a right reading of Christian understanding of the body is not that it is lesser or bad in some way, but that, in Gooder's words, '[t]hrough our bodies we relate to others. Through our bodies we learn who we are. Through our bodies we live fully in the world that God created.'[23]

Despite much progress in recent decades, there are still few situations when more stringent expectations are placed upon women's bodies than when a woman is in the process of becoming a mother. Commenting on the story of Pope Joan, Atkinson writes:

The woman whose learning and virtue carried her to the heights was destroyed by motherhood. Joan was not betrayed by a lover or discovered by an enemy; she was brought down by her own body, which was inherently and catastrophically unfit for ecclesiastical dignity. The literary and artistic images that surround the birth of her child display a range of responses from hysterical laughter to horrified disgust. The notion of a female pope was scandalous; of a pregnant pope, ludicrous; of a pope giving birth, disastrous.[24]

The idea that she was 'brought down by her own body' reminds me of much of the medical terminology used about women. The incompetent cervix. The hostile uterus. The lazy ovary. The inhospitable womb. Failure to progress.[25] Such terms are both a denigration of the body, as if it were faulty, and a denigration of women's bodies themselves. Mothering bodies – or, as theologians Karen O'Donnell and Claire Williams describe them, 'un/pregnant'[26] bodies – can present us with a body theology that speaks to us about who God is and who we are. 'Un/pregnant bodies', they write, 'are places where we meet God, even as they are conceiving, gestating, and birthing new bodies, or miscarrying, aborting, or not conceiving as hoped for.'[27] Tertullian, one of the early church Fathers, wrote about the miracle of Mary's birthing of God, stating that 'there is no nativity without flesh, and no flesh without nativity'.[28] Despite the wonder of this profound story – that a woman gives birth to God – the pregnant body in public consciousness has been taboo rather than revered for its potential for theological insight and symbolism.

Pregnancy and taboo

In the summer of 1991, film star Demi Moore graced the cover of *Vanity Fair* magazine in a now iconic image. At the time, it was met with much consternation. What was so scandalous about it? She was seven months pregnant. The photograph, taken by Annie Leibovitz, featured a naked Moore, her bump in all its glory, looking radiant. Moore, who was married to Bruce Willis at the time, was expecting her second child, Scout. The cover sparked much debate and outrage.

Some supermarkets chose to cover it up with paper, calling it border-line pornographic. Staff at *Vanity Fair* were doorstepped at their office by media wanting to feed the global news machine that had been triggered by the sight of a Hollywood star's pregnant body.

The *Vanity Fair* cover marked a turning point in moving from the invisibility of women's pregnant bodies in the public consciousness to their visibility. It would still, however, take nearly thirty more years for Anglo-American society to receive the pregnant body more positively. In August 2017, Leibovitz had a new pregnant muse to photograph – this time it was tennis player Serena Williams and her bump gracing the front cover of *Vanity Fair*. In recent years, we have also seen stars take to social media, creating their own iconic photographs displaying their pregnant forms. When Beyoncé revealed in 2017 that she was pregnant with twins, she nearly broke the internet. Kneeling and adorned with a floral garland and white veil, she looked like a modern-day Mary. For Phillip Prodger, head of photographs at the National Portrait Gallery in London, the image by artist Awol Erizku – which became the most liked in Instagram's history – was a direct reference to Mary. Likening it to the famous 1473 painting *Madonna in a Rose Garden* painted by Martin Schongauer, Prodger hailed it as 'a wonderfully clever blend of references, showing Beyoncé as a Renaissance Madonna', complete with veil and roses signifying fertility and purity, but with the strong and powerful posture of someone very much in control of her body.[29] Here, Beyoncé was reimagining the perfect mother for a twenty-first-century audience.

The childbed is our battlefield

While seeing pregnant bodies in the media is now more common-place and accepted, the truth is that what we see are the pregnant bodies of supermodels and actors and singers whose bodies are airbrushed to perfection before being presented to us, again distorting the reality of what happens to a woman's body when she grows a baby. The perfect motherhood presented to us in the pages of magazines is a myth designed to make us measure ourselves against impossible standards, and spend huge amounts of money on creams and potions in a bid to resemble these maternal mirages. Held up against the smooth and sacred silhouettes of Serena, Beyoncé and Demi's bumps, our stretch marks appear sinful.

If, historically, women's pregnant bodies have been taboo, the same can be said – if anything, even more strongly – of childbirth. Childbirth itself feels uniquely carnal; it is the time in my life when I have felt most embodied. In the weeks leading up to giving birth the first time, I watched just about every available episode of the TV series *One Born Every Minute*. I can understand why some would want to bury their heads in the sand about impending labour, but I did not want any surprises. I thought that the TV show was the closest I could get to what it is really like to give birth. I watched in awe as the women panted and screamed and bore down, as they gritted their teeth and gripped their partners' hands, drenched in sweat. As they lay on their backs with their legs in stirrups while strangers worked to coax and pull and yank their babies out. As they sank into water birth pools that filled with blood as their babies made their bubbling entrances into the world. As they – numbed with anaesthesia and cut open on an operating table – went skin to skin with this new life placed on their chests. These seemed more real to me than most Hollywood depictions, including nativity films in which Mary gave birth to Jesus.

In 2022, the creators of *House of the Dragon* – a prequel to HBO's popular *Game of Thrones* series – came under fire for including a graphic depiction of a caesarean section without anaesthetic. The Targaryen family are desperately in need of a male heir. In the scene in which Queen Aemma Targaryen is giving birth, the Targaryen baby is breech, lying feet first in the womb, and the Grand Maester suggests that it might be possible to save the child through a C-section – but, of course, medieval-style, without any anaesthetic. King Viserys gives the go-ahead for the procedure that will definitely kill his wife, and may also kill his son. In the end, both die.

The show sparked much debate about whether graphic and bloody childbirth scenes should be shown, despite the programme and its sequel being known for their violent and gruesome killing scenes – usually during conflicts and wars, with hefty death tolls in each series. Before the heavily pregnant queen consort Aemma Targaryen went into labour, she had poignantly told her daughter, 'The childbed is our battlefield.' Responding to the debate surrounding the scene, director Miguel Sapochnik described how feedback had been sought about the scene before it was broadcast. 'We did make a point of showing it to as many women as possible and asked the very question, "Was this too violent for you?"' he said. 'And unanimously, the response was no.'[30] Perhaps these women would agree that part of unmaking the myth of perfect motherhood is no longer colluding in the veil of silence that surrounds the realities of the carnal brutality of pregnancy, birthing and motherhood. Continuing to do so will maintain the gap between the expectation and the reality.

Memento mori

Mary gave birth to God in a context in which, though there may have still been a squeamishness about women's bodies, they were more talked about, less murky and unsaid. The world of first-century Palestine was a highly religious one – whether it was the religion of the Christ followers, of the Jewish community or of the vast number of Roman gods worshipped – and as such, the barriers between what were seen as sacred and profane, as pure and unclean, were much more obvious in daily life. Pregnancy, and in particular, birth, were seen as particularly impure, since the whole process – from conception to labour – entailed all manner of bodily fluids and excretions, all of which were seen as unclean. First-century philosopher Plutarch's description of the grossness of birth illustrates some of the ideas that were prevalent at the time:

> For there is nothing so imperfect, so helpless, so naked, so shapeless, so foul, as man observed at birth, to whom alone, one might almost say, Nature has given not even a clean passage to the light; but, defiled with blood and covered with filth and resembling more one just slain than one just born, he is an object for none to

touch or lift up or kiss or embrace except for someone who loves with a natural affection.[31]

These ideas make all the more profound the incarnation story on which the Christian faith centres: God becomes one of us, choosing to find his home in a woman's body and enter into the world through the indignity of birth. Lurking behind the taboo surrounding pregnant women's bodies and childbirth is an existential fear of mortality. A pregnant woman's body reminds us that even though, as Christians believe, we are divine image-bearers, we are also very much earthly beings. We give birth just as cows and pigs and horses do. Though humans are described as the crown of God's creation, we are still very much part of the created order, and so we are mortal. We begin, and we end.

I've often wondered why it is so rare to see imagery of a pregnant Madonna, or of Mary in her old age; just as it has been rare until recent history to see pregnant women's bodies pictured at all. Perhaps we have feared being faced not just with the reality of mortality, but with the change and alleged 'decay' that lead us towards the grave. Suggesting why, for much of history, pregnant bodies have been seen as taboo, American political theorist Iris Marion Young explains that it may be because pregnancy embodies change: 'The dominant model of health assumes that the normal, healthy body is unchanging. Health is associated with stability, equilibrium, a steady state. Only a minority of persons, however, namely adult men who are not yet old, experience their health as a state in which there is no regular or noticeable change in body condition.'[32]

Though there appears to be more acceptance of women's bodies today, there still seems to be a veil of mystery surrounding the topic. This is perhaps because becoming a mother, together with the bodily change it signifies, brings into sharp focus our finitude. Long before we might become mothers, we hear about the danger of this rite of passage. In the stories we read as children, the shadows of dead mothers linger. In the classic Charles Dickens novel, Oliver Twist's mother dies in childbirth; the same fate befalls Snow White's mother in the Grimms' fairy tale. From Vada's mother in the 1991 film *My Girl*, to Don Draper's mother in *Mad Men*, to Lady Sybil in *Downton*

Abbey, and even Chuckie's mother in the children's cartoon *Rugrats*, all of these women sacrifice their lives bringing their children into the world. Just as women in the Middle Ages were praised for their martyr-like stoicism in enduring the pain of childbirth, so the ultimate sacrifice becomes a mark of perfect motherhood. Jane Austen mocks the trope of mothers dying in childbirth in the opening of *Northanger Abbey*:

> No one who had ever seen Catherine Morland in her infancy would have supposed her born to be a heroine. Her situation in life, the character of her father and mother . . . were all equally against her . . . Her mother was a woman of useful plain sense, with a good temper, and, what is more remarkable, with a good constitution. She had three sons before Catherine was born; and instead of dying in bringing the latter into the world, as anybody might expect, she still lived on.[33]

Childbirth and death have long gone hand in hand. In recent times, this link between the two has perhaps declined alongside improvements in maternal health and medical advancements, which in general remove us from the reality of death. But in the Middle Ages, most people recognised the profound proximity of birth and death. The influential humanist Erasmus of Rotterdam, in his colloquy *The New Mother*, has his female protagonist Fabulla make the case for mothers being braver than soldiers, who can avoid combat should they choose, 'while we,' Fabulla says, 'must engage death at close quarters'.[34] As seventeenth-century Bishop of Exeter Joseph Hall once wrote: 'Death borders upon our birth, and our cradle stands in the grave.'[35] Today, women in the poorest and most marginalised communities in the world still face poor maternal health outcomes. Despite significant improvements in maternal mortality rates globally over the past twenty years, it is still the case that every two minutes, a woman somewhere in the world dies giving birth. The vast majority of those deaths (95 per cent) take place in low- and lower-middle-income countries.[36]

While death in childbirth in western countries is now a rarity – albeit tragic when it does happen – for most of history, even in richer nations, death during pregnancy and childbirth was not just a possibility, it was a real likelihood. Until the twentieth century, women would spend the majority of their fertile years either being pregnant or giving birth. Large families were the norm, unlike today, when the average family in the UK has 1.7 children,[37] while in the USA, it's 1.94.[38] Women historically spent much more of their lives being pregnant, despite there being a high likelihood of either the mother or the child dying in the process. The taboo both around women's bodies during pregnancy and around the association of pregnancy with death explains the relative absence of depictions of pregnant bodies in art and media until the past few decades.

Karen Hearn, an art historian focusing on the sixteenth and seventeenth centuries, has explored why there had long been a reluctance to picture pregnant women in the past. Hearn, who curated a 2020 exhibition entitled *Portraying Pregnancy* at the Foundling Museum in London, suggested that these deliberate decisions to erase pregnancy from portraiture from around 1630 came as a result of changing sensibilities about women's pregnant bodies. Explaining one of the reasons for this, she said, 'It's a condition that, of course, makes it obvious that a woman has engaged in sexual activity, which was not something people wanted to think about.'[39] This avoidance of the carnal realities led artists to erase pregnancy from portraiture, even if the person sitting was in fact pregnant.

Hearn's exhibition sought to uncover some of the lost pregnancy portraiture that had been much more acceptable until the mid-seventeenth century. For some, it was the high mortality rate among both women and babies that led people to want to capture pregnancies in artworks and mementos. Husbands would commission portraits of their pregnant wives, who often would not survive the births. The exhibition featured items such as the sarafan dress worn by a pregnant Princess Charlotte in a painting by George Dawe from 1817. She tragically died giving birth later that year.

Childbirth had been so perilous that the Church of England used to include a ritual known as the 'Churching of Women', which would take place forty days after a woman had given birth and in which the priest would give thanks to God for delivering this woman from the 'great pain and peril of childbirth'. Although the rite, which is found in the Book of Common Prayer, did not contain any elements of ritual purification, it relates to the practice in Leviticus (12:2–8) of purification after having given birth, and to Mary and Joseph's presentation of Jesus at the temple (Luke 2:22–40).

As childbirth became safer, as the West became more secular, and as feminist thinkers took issue with any suggestion within the ritual that women needed to be purified following their birthing experience, the practice disappeared in the mid-twentieth century. However, despite the potentially problematic insinuation that childbirth was in some way dirty or unclean, the ritual had at least attempted to recognise the bodily and psychological trauma that women go through in the process of giving birth. Though ordinary and everyday, it can take a profound toll on our hearts, minds and bodies.

The Reverend Alice Watson has written extensively about ritual in birthing and motherhood after her own traumatic birth experience led her to wonder why there was so little done to help mothers through the physical, existential and spiritual moment. After giving birth, she found herself adrift and ill-equipped to deal with what had just happened:

> In a hospital bed . . . gazing upon bloodstained hands and wondering whose blood it was, my own, or my son's, and how strange it was that, now, there was a difference. How that difference, that separating, would mark me for life, as one whose body had been broken, as one who had glimpsed death to give life. And mostly, left wondering why there was nothing I could seek from my own church community, why there was no ritual for this, no rich source of women's history, no liturgy, no balm of healing that I could access. I called my priest, and I suppose in a way I was churched. I didn't know what else to do.[40]

Reverend Watson told me that the value of the Churching of Women lay in the fact it was entirely focused on the woman and not the child. For her, the six-week medical check is 'the modern hangover of Churching' – both a checkpoint and a point that marks the return to 'normal life', although many women will find that that too focuses more on the child than on the mother.

Imagine a world in which the Church was the place that opened its doors once again to women who have found themselves bewildered after becoming mothers. In a world of declining Christian faith, yet one in which women have few outlets for marking the monumental moment of entering motherhood, the impact on women could be profound; it could be the Church's reparation for its collusion with the myth of perfect motherhood that leaves little room for women to grieve or seek healing for their broken bodies.

The in-between

In the birthing process itself, our broken bodies and subconscious minds may hold stories of sacrifice and death just beneath the surface. Here, we might identify not with Mary, but with her son, Jesus, and the atonement brought about by his painful death on a cross. Like the blood (signifying redemption) and the water (signifying life) that pour out of his side (John 19:34), we might feel the precarity of hovering between life and death, not necessarily because of a medical emergency, but because we find ourselves in an in-between space. Perhaps it is the smell and sight of blood; maybe it is the delirium and fatigue and, for some, the unspeakable pain. I am struck by the number of mothers – both religious and not – who have described this liminality. Lucy Jones writes in *Matrescence* of the sense of in-betweenness in which she found herself as she gave birth:

> In the first weeks of early motherhood, I had visualized the same scene repeatedly: an enormous, thick, purple velvet curtain hung from ceiling to floor in a cavernous temple, ripped from top to bottom. It took a while to remember it was an image from the Bible. The curtain of the temple is torn in two after Jesus dies. 'The earth shook and the rocks split,' writes Matthew, in his Gospel.[41]

In religious art, the lily has come to symbolise – among other things – this transition, the hovering between life and death. The lily represents both the beginning of life and the end of life: an Easter lily signifies Christ's death and resurrection, while a Madonna lily represents the announcement of Christ's birth. Historian Joanna Wolfarth describes the significance of the fact that images of Mary's Annunciation often include lilies. 'This was the moment that Mary's motherhood was set in motion,' she writes. 'A moment heavy with the promise of the birth of Christ. But of course, tied up in this is the story of death, and eventually, eternal life.' Wolfarth talks about her own experience of motherhood and the in-between space of life and death; the 'temporal shift' that took place when she became pregnant and started to count her life in weeks and months.[42]

As humans, we can fool ourselves into thinking we are unbound by time, that we will live for ever. We are living at a time in which death feels remote: death happens in hospital settings rather than in the home, as it did a century ago. We are living longer. Technological solutions are being developed, such as cryogenic freezing and virtual immortality, mind uploading and more ways to stave off what is – or at least has been until now – the inevitable. Yet being more cognisant of time – as I was during my own pregnancies – makes one more aware that it is limited. In those early weeks of my pregnancies, time slowed to a snail's pace. I was in a hurry to reach the twelve-week mark, so that I could breathe a little, the chances of miscarriage significantly reducing at that stage. Then I measured my weeks in trimesters, and myself against charts and development stages. Midwives knew little about me except that I was at a certain number of weeks' gestation, and consulted their computers so that they knew which checks to tick off or examinations to carry out. As the third trimester went on and on and my thirty-nine weeks of pregnancy turned into nearly forty-two, those final weeks dragged, just like the first had. My baby was outstaying his welcome in my womb and I was hoping to hurry things along so that I could meet him. As I stomped up and down Greenwich Park every morning, climbing up steep hills because I had heard that could help get the baby out, and as I ate spicy curries and drank pineapple juice and even went for acupuncture, my baby seemed to want to stay put. I was impatient, and desperate for time to speed up. In the early days after he eventually arrived, he and I were plunged into a timeless, liminal space once again. Day was the same as night: both consisted of feeding and burping and cleaning and bathing. Where the midwives once counted me in weeks, the health visitors turned their attention towards him: a two-day old baby, an eight-day old baby, a three-month-old. First, I counted his age in weeks, and then in months, remembering every date and milestone. Once he turned one, the months no longer mattered, and time seemed to speed up terrifyingly again. Pregnancy and those early days can make us more aware of time, but being a mother has also given me a unique sense of my own mortality, and of the pain of everyone else's – including my own children's. Again, Lucy Jones writes of this sense of the painful realisation: 'It hadn't crossed my mind, before giving birth, that by bringing a life into the world, I would also be bringing about a death.'[43]

Mary, like many other mothers, may have experienced the underlying whisper of finitude as she brought life into the world, but within a few weeks of giving birth to Jesus, her sense of his mortality would have become more acute, according to one account in the Gospels. In Luke's Gospel, she and Joseph take the baby Jesus to be consecrated to God at the temple in Jerusalem. Was he sleeping through the night? What had Mary expected him to be like, this Son of God, as a vulnerable baby? Did he feed well? Was he colicky, a crier? Did she stare at him in wonder as he slept in her arms, drinking in his scent and feeling his tiny heartbeat? Was she asking all the questions that we do when our babies are forty days old? Were these everyday thoughts of motherhood in her mind as she and her family went to the temple and were met by the elderly Simeon, who sang a song of praise to God about the birth of this precious child, but also indicated that there was pain ahead? 'This child is destined to cause the falling and rising of many in Israel,' Simeon said to Mary, 'and to be a sign that will be spoken against, so that the thoughts of many hearts will be revealed. And a sword will pierce your own soul too' (Luke 2:34–35). Was this the first time she would have sensed the sadness of the future death of her child, or was this sense always there, as it is for so many mothers?

Writing in *The New York Times*, existential philosopher Danielle LaSusa describes her relief at realising that death is a constant worry for many new mothers, and that her own thoughts were not unusually macabre. But she admits that, despite the realisation that natality and mortality go hand in hand – beginnings and endings – it is still painful. She writes:

> I am still gripped by the thought that this cute kid I have created, with pigtails and everything, will one day have to reckon with her own mortality. Even if she lives a long and happy life and then dies at 95 in a sun-soaked room, she still has to live with the knowledge that her death is coming, and the uncertainty of when it will arrive.[44]

The first time I gave birth, I had a very visceral sense of this liminality. Over three days, I laboured, slowly and painfully – the sharp thud of pressure crashing like waves that would crescendo and then subside. In my induced state, I could not sleep or eat; I was still being sick. When the pain became unbearable, I asked for an epidural. Relief; a pause; a ceasefire. A moment's rest. When the midwife told me I had fully dilated, I pushed for two hours and still no baby. In the pushing, I felt myself drifting in and out of consciousness as I held my breath and tried to evict my cannonball baby. 'Where am I?' I asked my husband. 'You're having a baby and you need to push.' I was jolted back into the land of the living. I could faintly hear my mum praying in tongues. She was right behind me, but her voice felt far away. Eventually, the cavalry was called in. Men and women in scrubs filled the delivery room. My husband will never forget the resuscitation bag. The doctor replaced the midwife and tried to get my baby out with a suction cap that slipped right off his full head of black hair. Finally, the forceps – the medieval instrument that I had prayed I would never see – yanked him out, and we were free. Free but still bound to each other. As someone placed him on me, my first feeling was shock. This was my baby? The one my heart already loved, but who seemed to have burst into the world as if we were part of a wildlife documentary, sticky and mewling. The presence of death left the room and what was left was this new life. He smelled of my blood. It was over and it had just begun. We hear much talk of near-death experiences. We have become so familiar with the idea that we recognise recurring patterns experienced by those who have gone through it: a bright light, floating above one's body, doorways, tunnels, choices to return or not; to go through the door, or come back to life. But it's funny that we don't talk about the profound nature of near-birth experiences with nearly as much regularity and openness, despite childbirth being a far more frequent occurrence than nearly dying.

Weird beyond words

On the first evening my two-year-old son returned from nursery after it had reopened following a few months of closure during the first lockdown of the Covid pandemic, I thought it possible to socially distance from him. I held his hand, slightly keeping him at a distance, I undressed him at the door of the house and put him straight into the bath and donned gloves to put his clothes straight into the washing machine. This distance between us lasted for only a few minutes until I realised it would be impossible to separate myself from him, nor would I want to. So I snuggled him as usual. He buried his face in the crook of my neck. I changed his nappy and cleaned his face decorated with that day's meals; and I thanked God we were all still here, despite a virus that was killing hundreds of thousands of people. Though he was no longer in my womb, he was still a part of me. Perhaps it would have been the same had I not given birth to him. Nevertheless, he was my son. He was me, and I was him; two and one.

Pregnancy offers us a way into thinking about ancient Christian ideas about the body. Philosophical ponderings about dualism and monism are felt in the 'both/and' of pregnancy. When my children grew in my womb, I felt both one with them and separate from them, our oneness and twoness expressing something of the ineffability of our connection with others in the body of Christ. This idea is summed up in the southern African term *ubuntu* – I am because you are; what it means for us to be children of God with bodies that are temples of the Holy Spirit. It also gives some new insight into the hard-to-grasp idea of the Trinitarian God.

One does not need a doctorate in theology to get a sense of this strange and unexplainable sense of connection and separateness. In a study of maternal identity change, Wendy Hollway interviewed a group of first-time mums in Tower Hamlets in east London. Hollway noticed similar language being used by the respondents to describe their pregnancies: the idea that it was 'weird' in some way, and hard to describe. One participant said, 'I can't explain, it's like weird knowing that you've got a life growing inside of you and you can feel the life every day.' For some, the weirdness begins when their pregnancy is confirmed, while for others moments like attending the first scan – often at around twelve weeks – are when they encounter a feeling that is 'weird beyond words'. For both of my pregnancies, we paid for early scans with private companies because I was impatient, but also perhaps because I could not really believe I was pregnant until I saw evidence of life – a life that had a body – the grainy black-and-white blobs making real that feeling of something I could not describe taking place inside me. And although the sonographer enabled us to listen to the baby's heartbeat – the gentle patter of life – I experienced a sense of displacement. It was as if my own heart was beating inside and out, part of me and separate from me. We were two and one, together and apart. Hollway describes the paradoxical feeling: 'My life was no longer possible to treat separately from the life of my baby, so the vulnerability of either was the vulnerability of both.'[45] For me, I felt a sense of loss when my baby's umbilical cord was cut. That undeniable interconnectedness – the oneness and twoness – I had felt for nine months provided a sense of comfort and control. My baby was inside me, and in the darkness of the womb, he was safe from the hazards of the outside. In the cacophony of feelings that accompany every birth, there can come a sense that something has shifted as your baby, your heart, now exists outside your body.

Mater Ecclesiae

This idea of the oneness and twoness of a mother and child during pregnancy and early motherhood can act as a way in to illustrate the relationship of Mary to the Church – here, read all Christians – as outlined in particular by the Catholic Church, and also to illustrate the idea of community and interdependence so central to Christian ideas of what it is to be humans made in God's image. Ambrose of Milan first used the term *Mater Ecclesiae* (Mother of the Church) in the fourth century, but it has been used much more frequently by more recent popes, including Pope John Paul II, who, in 1997, explained how the Blessed Virgin Mary was both mother of Christ and mother of the faithful, and how she also acted as a model for the whole of the Church.

The Church itself has also been described as 'Mother' – Mothering Sunday, for example, is named as such because it is traditionally the day we are to return to our 'mother church' – the one in which we were baptised and welcomed into the family of God as a child of the Church. It is strange, then, that though there are many metaphors of the body as a description of the unity of the family of God, none employ the example of pregnancy. It is perhaps of course more understandable when one considers the place of women in the wider context of first-century Palestine.

Body broken

The Eucharist began to take on new meaning after my own body was broken and my own blood spilled in the process of bringing forth new life. In conception, birth and recovery I experienced the spark of new life, the valley of the shadow of death and a slower-than-expected path to bodily resurrection.

Sometimes, I try to experience Communion through the eyes of those who do not believe in or belong to the Christian faith – this strange rite around which millions gather weekly to drink the blood and eat the body of their Saviour. In this sacred moment in which we consume the wine and the bread as symbols of our incarnate God, we partake in the understanding that Jesus was very much a body; and that that this body matters. When a priest holds up the cup and says, 'Take, drink, this is my blood' or holds up the bread, inviting us to 'take, eat, this is my body', we remember that Christ's horrific death through crucifixion symbolised his giving of his whole self for our sins. Writer Natalie Carnes puts it beautifully when writing about her own pregnancy:

I was Christ who, in my bone-sacrifice of calcium, lays down her life for her friends. I was only Christ in a shadowy way, of course. I did not give the church, the Eucharist, or atonement. I gave my body, blood, and bones, though not because I chose this sacrifice. Still, my gift was a faint echo, a sign, of Christ's gifts. Through pregnancy, my body became charitable, my life given for the sake of another. You were teaching me in my very bones the little way of love.[46]

Christ's death was not pretty. For me, one of the most profound representations of the world-changing moment is not the perfect, white, ripped body of Salvador Dalí's *Christ of St John of the Cross*, but the pock-marked, disease-ridden Christ of Grünewald's *Isenheim Altarpiece*. The manner of Christ's death means we cannot turn away from the reality that to be human is to bleed, to vomit, to leak bodily fluids and excretions. We are not ethereal beings, nor are we simply thinking minds; we are fully embodied.

I had never felt more embodied than I did during my pregnancy, while I was giving birth, and in those early weeks and months of my matrescence. Nor had I previously ever really resonated with the understanding of Christ's body broken for humankind or with the idea of sacrificing one's own body for the sake of another. That was until, as Jones puts it, 'a human animal grew inside my body'.[47] Wrapped up in popular understandings of perfect motherhood is the idea that we sacrifice ourselves, our bodies breaking and being given for our children.

When a woman becomes a mother, she may experience a profound sense of being decentred to make space for a child that is to become the main character in the story of the life in which she had mistakenly thought she was the star. For me, it felt that, from conception onwards, there was a gradual sense of my body being taken over. In a patriarchal world, where power is too often associated with masculinity, control and strongmen who put themselves first, this decentring provides a profound way to understand the nature of the self-giving and sacrificial love of God. It may seem paradoxical for a fully formed human to lay down their life for a child that is now-and-not-yet, and the same too for a God who lays down their life for that which God has created. But perhaps this paradox is the point. It makes little sense through the eyes of a society that wants us to put ourselves and our wants and happiness first.

Through the decentring of self that comes with pregnancy and motherhood, we can have a glimpse into the kenosis (the pouring out of self) that is described in Philippians 2, in which Jesus 'made himself nothing'. There is a profound beauty that can come from exploring the decentring that Christ demonstrated in his incarnation, death and resurrection. Nevertheless, the idea of decentring the mother for the sake of the baby is complicated and needs to be nuanced. We should not ignore the societal misogyny that calls for mothers to empty, diminish or make themselves void for the sake of their babies. Whether the decentring I personally felt came as a result of societal and Church influences or because of spiritual or physiological changes, I felt it. I no longer had power or control, but had to submit to a new – tiny – master.

The radical decentring I experienced during my pregnancies also provided me with lessons in humility. The sickness meant I could not be dignified, even if I tried. The most vivid lesson in humility for me during my first pregnancy came as I was on a train to London. As we drew near to Euston Station, I began to feel that horrific feeling – an overwhelming sense that I needed to vomit. I had been eating sweets throughout the journey to try and stave off the nausea; but this plan had failed. I rushed to the train toilet only to find it locked – out of order. As I had left not a minute to spare, this setback meant that I was sick all over myself, as the train rolled into the station. I tried to compose myself, not wanting to catch the eyes of other passengers. I stumbled off the train and sat with my head between my knees on a bench on the platform, as suited businessmen and-women walked past me with pity and disgust. I wondered how I would get home, smelling of sick; covered in it. Then a mobility driver – or perhaps a guardian angel – sidled up next to me and told me to get in. I will forever be grateful to him. This kind man delivered me to the entrance of the Tube so I could make my way home. It remains my most undignified moment – all sense of ego eradicated. This was far from the blooming pregnancy look I had been expecting.

One of course does not have to have given birth to experience the profoundly enfleshed nature of motherhood, or the required decentring. The physicality of motherhood is not confined to birth and delivery. While I still experience side effects of labour and pregnancy, I also occasionally see a doctor about the ailments I suffer from as a result of being a mother that have nothing to do with having given birth: the aches and pains of lugging around heavy children; the frequent transfer of diseases from the nursery to the child to me; the sheer exhaustion of caregiving. Irene Oh writes: 'For mothers, gestational or adoptive, the sheer physical labor of caring for a newborn or infant – frequent feedings and diaper changes; constant holding; and unpredictable, infrequent sleep for the caregiver – is formidable.'[48] The physicality of motherhood is also true for adoptive or foster mothers, non-birth mothers in same-sex-parent families, and those who have become mothers through surrogacy. One study describes the sense of alienation non-birth mothers can feel, saying: 'The concept of a mother in Western society is equated with the biological processes of pregnancy, birth, and lactation, which are assumed to produce a special maternal bond between mother and child.'[49] There are particular joys and challenges that come with being a birth mother; but motherhood does not begin with pregnancy, nor does it end in the labour ward. What follows in the subsequent years is a physical intensity unlike any other relationship. It comes with the territory of motherhood, whether one is a birth mother, or a non-birth mother. In caring for our children, we hold them close to us, skin to skin; we clean up their puke and change their nappies. We smell like them, milky-breathed and new-skinned.

Chapter 5

Hashtag Blessed

Perfect Motherhood for a Digital Age

'My Lady is beautiful, beautiful beyond compare; so
beautiful that when one has seen her once, one would wish
to die so as to see her again; so beautiful that when one
has seen her, one can no longer love anything earthly.'

—St Bernadette

In November 2022, as I was returning to work after six months of maternity leave and struggling with the constant, daily fails of being a frumpy working mother of two, reality TV star Heidi Montag posted a video on TikTok that went viral.[1] The former *Laguna Beach* star shared the video of herself sitting upright in a bed while a make-up artist applied foundation to her face. Next to the bed, her husband Spencer Pratt sat in front of his phone that was positioned on a tripod, posting his own video. In front of the bed was a photographer capturing the scene. But this was not just lights, camera, action on the set of a TV show. Heidi was in the labour ward about to give birth to her second child. This desire to be fully made-up while delivering a baby derives from a social media trend for visually documenting labour, and it is moving from the world of reality TV and celebrity to everyday mothers. At the start of 2023, videos linked to the hashtag #birthingmakeup on TikTok had already clocked up more than eighty-one million views.

These trends make clear to me what we all know: that women are judged on their appearance, and that for many women, to be beautiful is the primary way in which they can feel that they are of value. While these pervasive ideas about the way women look are well known, they take on new meaning, becoming even more sinister, when they take their place in the myth of perfect motherhood. We see more mothers in visual culture today because we see more images full stop, and rather than liberating women, the maternal body has become 'a symbol and the "management tool" for both the ideal fit body and "perfect" motherhood'.[2] Birthing make-up, maternity photo shoots and stories of how women exercised their postnatal bodies hard to 'snap back' to their pre-birth bodies are where the beauty myth joins hands with the myth of perfect motherhood to make us think that as good mothers, we must also be beautiful. Images of flawless-looking new mothers permeating social media feeds falsely suggest that giving birth is easy. Make-up and styling and lighting hide the realities of the chaos and brutality and blood and pain and bewilderment that can accompany so many women's birth stories. Perhaps they are a form of escape – they mask the darkness. Any woman who has given birth will know that behind the picture-perfect post-birth appearances of Catherine, Princess of Wales outside St Mary's Hospital in London lies the reality of imperfect motherhood. Perhaps society pressures women to make it look easy like this because we do not want people to know the realities of childbirth; the future of humanity literally depends on women not being scared of it. For those of us who find ourselves putting these perfect images forward into the ether, perhaps it is a way to try to convince ourselves that we are OK, despite our worlds having been irrevocably changed. Perhaps these perfect images are ways for us to take control, or to prove that we have what it takes to be perfect mothers.

This trend on social media to put forward a perfect image of oneself is encapsulated in a tongue-in-cheek way in the title of this chapter. 'Hashtag Blessed' (#blessed) refers to people telling picture-perfect stories about themselves – through images and posts that suggest they are living the life they have always wanted: a good job, a good car, a great partner, perfect children. Sometimes people will end their post with #blessed. For some this is done in a non-ironic way. While gratitude for what we have is good, and the secret to a long and happy life, too much public showing off clearly masks the reality that no one's life is perfect.

I think there may be a similar masking going on when we look beneath the surface of the increasingly popular 'tradwives' movement. 'Tradwife' – a portmanteau of 'traditional' and 'wife' – refers to a woman who is submissive to her husband and confines herself to, or prioritises, the domestic sphere. It is a trend that has been growing in popularity in more conservative circles, and there is a particular iteration of the movement that has become a social media phenomenon. While they vary to some extent in their political leanings (there are Conservative tradwives, alt-right tradwives, alt-lite tradwives), most of the tradwife influencers on Facebook, Instagram, TikTok and YouTube put forward ideals of homemaking and good old-fashioned child-rearing. There is also a sub-strand of *religious* tradwives (evangelical tradwives, alt-Catholic tradwives, Mormon tradwives, and even pagan tradwives) who take their anti-feminist, pro-natalist stances from their readings of their religious texts. Regardless of which faith they belong to, these religious tradwives share hints and tricks on mothering as a stay-at-home mum (#sahm), 'alongside homemaking and homesteading, and traditional notions of femininity'.

While the majority of the tradwife movement is white, there is a growing movement of Black tradwives – although they may refer to themselves as #blackhousewife. Many of them do not see themselves represented in the ideals of white motherhood presented on social media, but many are signing up to these ideas about biblical womanhood and traditional motherhood because they are tired. For some, 'traditional marriage is the key to Black women's liberation from being overworked, economic insecurity, and the stress of trying to survive in a world hostile to our survival and existence,' writes one commentator.[3] For them, marrying a man who provides for their material needs and leaves them to be responsible for the home is an attractive prospect, considering Black women's tortured history of working outside the home. As bell hooks writes in *Feminist Theory*:

> Historically, Black women have identified work in the context of family as humanizing labor, work that affirms their identity as women, as human beings showing love and care, the very gestures of humanity white supremacist ideology claimed black people

were incapable of expressing. In contrast to labor done in a caring environment inside the home, labour outside the home was most often seen as stressful, degrading, and dehumanizing.[4]

Despite the tradwife movement being very much of its time – a time when populism, women's reproductive rights, the strain of motherhood and a sense of foreboding about the times in which we are living have collided – it has a remarkably high concern with the past. Tradwives hark back to a perceived golden era of ideal womanhood, and motherhood – the 1950s. But mothers of the 1950s were, of course, living in a totally different culture. While things were more straightforward as regards where it was thought a woman's place *should* be, it did not follow that these women were happy within the comfort of defined domesticity.

In the years following the Second World War, many women had to return to a life of domesticity, despite having experienced freedom from the home during the conflict by taking on jobs for the war effort. For many housewives in the 1940s and 1950s, this return to a more confined life plunged them into a state of deep anxiety, and many suffered from depression. For some this may have been about the particular drudgery of home life and motherhood, but for others it may have been the result of being treated badly both by their husbands and by society as a whole, and of not feeling valued by either. By the 1960s, the Rolling Stones had released their hit 'Mother's Little Helper', in which they sang about the desperation of a suburban housewife who had become reliant on prescription drugs such as Valium to be able to cope.

The spotless mirror

Like stereotypes of a 1950s American housewife, today's tradwives – whether covertly or overtly – espouse an aesthetic of purity, whiteness and beauty, three 'ideals' that have long been intertwined. But perhaps the greatest of these is beauty. This has always been the case. Social media representations that put forward an unrealistic ideal of beautiful, perfect motherhood are today's version of Marian artwork and Christian iconography that represented the perfect woman as the most aesthetically pleasing – according to the beauty standards of the day. Just as Instagram tropes see women playing into motherhood ideals and aligning themselves with what it is to be 'good', so paintings of Mary of Nazareth have often been accompanied by a range of symbols to illustrate what we are supposed to think about her, and, in turn, what we are supposed to think about what it is to be a good mother.

Mary is often depicted in an enclosed garden – *hortus conclusus* in Latin. Medieval depictions of her often included the enclosed-garden theme in reference to verse 12 in Song of Solomon 4: 'Hortus conclusus soror mea sponsa, hortus conclusus, fons signatus' (a garden enclosed is my sister, my spouse; a garden enclosed, a fountain sealed up). Though these verses had nothing to do with Mary, the enclosed garden and the sealed-up fountain became symbols of her virginity and purity. This purity – which is conveyed in both visual perfection and an inward purity – is made manifest in another popular Marian trope: a 'spotless mirror'. Symbolising Mary reflecting the justice and righteousness of God, the spotless mirror derives from the apocryphal book of Wisdom 7:26 (NRSVA):

For she is a reflection of eternal light,
a spotless mirror of the working of God,
and an image of his goodness.

In her study of how women – including Venus, Medusa and Mary – have been depicted over the centuries, art historian Catherine McCormack writes: 'Images of Mary in Christian art have enforced her purity and chastity in very specific ways . . . The mirror also represents Mary's functions in Christian art as the ideal example of womanhood, which reflects back other women's inadequacies in comparison.'[5] Many mothers feel the pressure to play down their inadequacies and to highlight – and exaggerate – the ways in which they are doing well at mothering. But this in turn puts further pressure on other women, making all of us feel that we are just not living up to these idealised standards. There are very few people who are telling the truth about the shadow sides of motherhood, and social media only serves to exacerbate the false picture of mothering that is presented.

But, again, this positivity bias when it comes to the representation of motherhood is nothing new. In her 2005 study of what magazine advertising depicting motherhood between 1953 and 1998 tells us about the cultural ideas and ideologies about motherhood that were in the air during those decades, Karen Danna Lynch argues that 'it is not the real-life behavior of women as mothers that is revealed in these images, but the ideological construction of motherhood'.[6] These perfected images presented on social media platforms have had damaging effects on maternal well-being, especially among mothers who put a lot of pressure on themselves to parent perfectly. Becoming a parent has been shown to be one of the most stressful periods of a person's life, leaving new parents particularly vulnerable to experiencing poor mental health. The proliferation of images of motherhood on social media, as well as on parenting forums where parents seek advice or share parenting stories, can, instead of having a positive effect, leave people feeling that they are being judged for their parenting choices, or thinking that others seem to simply have it 'together'. Digital technologies make these unrealistic ideals more accessible, and leave mothers more vulnerable to comparison with others.

There is no greater scrutiny placed on a woman's body than during pregnancy and in the weeks and months that follow. In that time, the 'good mothers' are those who only put on weight in the right places when pregnant, and who shed the excess weight as soon as their baby comes out. There is little grace for women who do not 'snap back' quickly – at a time when many experience the fog of caring for a newborn, while battling the mental and physical challenges of doing so. It is unsurprising that we rarely see Mary depicted as pregnant at all, let alone as suffering from the ailments that plague new mothers. In Marian imagery there is not a stretch mark in sight, nor any dark circles of sleep deprivation. But portrayals of the ideal maternal body are not limited to pregnant women or those who have recently given birth. They include – or exclude – all mothers. A study released in 2024 by Moms First and the Geena Davis Institute on Gender in Media explored the ways in which fictional portrayals of mothers on television perpetuate unrealistic expectations for mothers. The study found that, in 2022, the majority of TV mums were white, young and thin, and that there were no examples of mothers with physical disabilities. It found that just 1.8 per cent of mothers on TV were fat. Mothers were also likely to be depicted as beautiful, with three times as many being presented as desirable to the viewer (or to other characters) as those who would be described as 'unattractive'. Nearly eight out of ten of the mothers appearing on TV were slim, as were six out of ten of the mums appearing with a child under the age of one. 'The necessary steps to achieving this level of physical beauty are not shown on screen,' the report said. 'TV moms rarely explain how they can afford beauty products, flattering clothes, and a gym membership or how they find the time to apply a full face of makeup, style their hair, iron their clothes, and exercise regularly. These unrealistic standards broadcast a message that attractiveness is effortless and affordable and thus should be attainable for the everyday mom.'[7]

Again, this is nothing new. The ideal of perfect motherhood that women have been pressured into conforming to for many centuries has simply found a new outlet in the vanity of social media. I confess that I myself am a prolific social media user. I flick from Facebook to X to Instagram, endlessly looping and refreshing new content. It is addictive. I like to think it also gives me a window into what is happening in the world, but also into *who* the world is telling us to be. Sometimes, I pretend to myself that it's my job that requires me to be a regular user of social media, and that forces me – against my will, of course – to put out content. I am a writer, a cultural commentator, a think-tank director, so I simply must be online and sharing viral GIFs and memes on WhatsApp chats with friends. I simply must follow and like Beyoncé's posts. And I simply must share content that paints a picture of everyday life with my children. I have fallen for the gimmicks that social media uses to entice me – the thrill of a new notification, a comment on my appearance or that of my children that makes me stand a little taller. The issue is, however, that I have never shared what I would consider a 'bad' photo of myself or my family online. I have occasionally swiped away clutter when taking a picture at home, lest someone learn my biggest secret:

that sometimes my house is a little messy because I live with small people. I have chosen not to share images that show me at an unflattering angle, or with a goofy or awkward face. I have on occasion asked my husband to take several pictures of me at a time, so that I can choose the one that I want to present to the world: good lighting, good hair, good posture. If none of the above are achieved, then those images will never see the light of day. What would happen if one of them did? I fear that people would judge me negatively, that they would think less of me as a person, and even worse, less of me as a mother. The unmaking of the myth of perfect motherhood will require all of us, me included, to intentionally choose to live more authentically – both offline and online. To choose to show the reality of motherhood – warts and all.

A 'remarkably perfect' Mary

When you imagine Mary, what do you think she looks like? I would imagine that you might not be able to describe her physical features in exact detail – save for the fact that she is probably white. If, like me, you have images of the Madonna ingrained in your mind, you might imagine her as serene, doting, passive, but you would also likely imagine her as beautiful. The fourth-century bishop St Epiphanius drew an image of what he thought Mary looked like. His Mary is described as not particularly tall of stature, but a little taller than average. Her skin colour is described by him as 'slightly bronzed', alluding to the Shulammite woman described as incredibly beautiful in the Song of Solomon. Describing Epiphanius's picture of Mary, 19th century French abbot Orsini writes of her 'light' hair and 'lively' eyes; her 'perfectly arched and black' eyebrows, her 'remarkably perfect' nose, rosy lips, oval face, long fingers. He adds:

> She was utterly full of Divine grace and loveliness; all the Fathers eagerly attest, with one accord, this admirable beauty of the Virgin. But it was not to this assemblage of natural perfections that Mary owed the power of her beauty; it emanated from a higher source ... The natural beauty of Mary was but the remote

reflection of her intellectual and imperishable beauties. She was the most beautiful of women, because she was the most chaste and most holy of the daughters of Eve.[8]

There are of course no descriptions of what Mary looked like in the Bible; so the above physical characteristics stem entirely from men's imaginations.

Mothers like me

What is different about social media messages as opposed to the constructions of motherhood that we have seen in art throughout history, as well as in advertising and the media industry, is that a lot of the content of these messages is driven by mothers themselves – albeit mothers who may have imbibed the messages that wider society has given them about what it is to be a good mother and a good woman. It is when there is dissonance with the experience of our peers as expressed on social media that we feel even more inadequate as women and as mothers. When Beyoncé posts iconic pregnancy photographs of herself on social media, we understand why. She is beautiful, yes, but she is also rich, with an army of people cleaning and cooking and dressing her and making her up, serving her every need. But when an old school friend posts her own images, looking similarly flawless, with well-dressed children and a spotless house and make-up, it might make us feel that it's just us who can't cope. A study of Canadian mothers' relationships to their postpartum bodies found that nearly all the women interviewed dismissed the 'get your body back after childbirth' messaging of commercial media as unrealistic, rejecting the images of thin celebrity mothers. However, the authors of the report said that these women frequently commented that social media sites and online forums for new mothers 'bothered them'. 'The appearance – online and in person – of women like themselves, who had babies but were thin, put pressure on women to get "in shape".' One mother, who said she had accepted her postpartum body, also said she was saddened by seeing other mothers 'all put together and I look like a mess'.[9] Writing in *The Guardian* in

2020 – the day before the Covid lockdown began in the UK – commentator Eva Wiseman describes her experience of being a new mother, getting sucked in by social media: 'Love makes every feeling bigger, even guilt and pain: unattainable ideals appear in the dark of a 5am feed like ghosts. Social media feeds your anxiety like fois gras farmers feed their geese.'[10] Perfect postpartum bodies are yet another way in which we are sold the lie that we can 'have it all': perfect families, perfect bodies – and wonder why everyone is succeeding but us. This all serves to keep women in their places of inadequacy in a world that values men.

We know a picture paints a thousand words, and hidden in social media photographs are symbols that attempt to tell the stories we want to put forward about who we are. Studies have shown that the pictures we post say far more about the message we are trying to portray than we would think. Families who lie outside the normative ideals might overemphasise the ways in which they conform. One study cites the example of a white mother posting a picture of herself and her two biracial sons sitting on the knee of her black husband, whose arms encircle the family, in a traditional and patriarchal pose: 'For this visibly mixed-race family, it could be argued, it becomes more important than for visibly normative families, to rely on these tropes to establish this normative "happy family" identity.' It goes on to analyse the positive comments that are left on the post – the most prevalent response being to describe the family as 'beautiful' – with the mother receiving validation from said comments.[11]

I am concerned too that this pressure to appear perfect as a mother leaves no room for the stark reality of maternal madness. There are countless stories of mothers whose mental health has suffered after they have given birth, sometimes with tragic consequences. These heartbreaking incidents can happen in the days after becoming a mother, or years afterwards. I'll never forget the heartbreaking story of Ariana Sutton, a thirty-six-year-old mother from Massachusetts who took her own life in 2023, just nine days after her twins were born. It was the second time that she had suffered from postnatal depression, having gone through it following the birth of her elder daughter five years earlier. Her husband, Tyler, spoke of how the first time around, she had begged him to not tell anyone else about her depression, describing the 'irrational sense of guilt and failure that stops people reaching out for help'.[12] Women's experiences of pregnancy and childbirth can be traumatic, leaving many scarred by post-traumatic stress disorder (PTSD) for years to come. On top of that there may be the daily stresses, strains or ennui that lead to depression in women. While there are psychological and medical, as well as contextual, realities that exacerbate these issues, I'm convinced that the veil of silence around the challenges of motherhood as magnified on social media surely cannot help. I recognise that I have had a hand in making other people feel inadequate about their parenting, by playing to the algorithm of the myth of perfect motherhood and being selective about what I post. If there is to be change, it will take all of us – me included – to tear through the veil of silence; to do something about it.

Barefaced motherhood

A decade ago, after writing my first book, *Am I Beautiful?*, I spent a few months leading women's breakfasts at churches around London. I called these gatherings Barefaced Breakfasts. I asked one thing of the women who were attending: that they turn up without any make-up on. For me, this was less about the make-up itself and more about wanting us to reject the dominant narrative that told us we had to look perfect at all times, even – and perhaps especially – in front of each other. It was also an attempt to invite women to peel off the masks that acted as a barrier to our telling the truth about how we were really doing; about the challenges and realities of what it is to be a woman today, including in the Church.

The first time I led one of these, I almost could not bring myself to do it. It took all my courage not only to leave the house without make-up, but to then stand in front of a room full of women and extol the virtues of being make-up-free. I felt naked and vulnerable. My discomfort stemmed from the fact that I had been used to doing all I could to hide my imperfections; to literally paint over them and create a face that was more beautiful than I felt I was.

It is strange to think how young I was when I was feeling that unbeautiful. I also realise that over the years since I wrote that first book, I and my body have experienced so much. The world might tell us that the wobbly bits and the stretch marks and the creaky joints are unbeautiful, but these are the brushstrokes that create the work of art that makes a mother. We are blessed not because of what we look like, nor because of the picture that we present to the world. We are blessed because we have experienced the joy and the vulnerability and the adventure that is bringing forth new life into the world.

Hashtag blessed

In Luke's Gospel account, we read of John the Baptist's mother Elizabeth declaring to Mary, 'Blessed are you among women' (Luke 1:42). Since the earliest days of Christianity, Mary has indeed been venerated as the most blessed, the most holy, the most spotless and worthy because she is the mother of God. Scroll through Instagram and you would be forgiven for thinking that many women today are attempting to knock Mary off the top spot, or at least to get closer to her on the podium, posting images of themselves giving flawless performances in the hope of winning points in the never-ending pageant of perfect motherhood. Some mothers use without irony the hashtag 'blessed' [#blessed] to humble-brag about how great their life is, or their family, or their mothering. Before I was a mum myself, I would notice endless images of often all-American families, smiling wide-eyed with perfect teeth and wearing matching outfits. The mothers in these images were always beautiful, and they were always white. Before I became a mother, I thought that's what motherhood would be like: shiny, spotless, sparkling white. A decade ago, there were very few people posting on Instagram about pregnancy sickness or mastitis or feeling deranged owing to sleep deprivation. Everything was happy-shiny; these families were #blessed. While aesthetics is one dimension in which many women succumb to the pressure to live up to a motherhood ideal, it goes beyond what we look like, leading us to tell inauthentic or incomplete stories about motherhood.

When it comes to the portrayal of Mary, what's clear to me is that we have dialled up the 'hashtag blessed' elements of her story, and dialled down the less-than-perfect realities that are plainly visible within the biblical narratives. But it is these vignettes in Mary's life that I find the most relatable. The scene in which I feel closest to Mary is the curious story told in Luke 2. Every year, Jesus' parents would go to Jerusalem for Passover, and after the festivities had finished, they would head home. On this particular occasion, following Passover, they had travelled for more than twenty-four hours, getting ever closer to home, when they realised their twelve-year-old son Jesus was nowhere to be seen. I've felt that that sense of panic; the overwhelming, crippling feeling in the pit of my stomach when I have lost sight of one of my children even for a few seconds while in a crowd. That devastating catastrophising: perhaps they have been stolen, maybe something has happened to them, maybe they're gone for-ever.

When Mary and Joseph realise Jesus is missing they quickly turn back to Jerusalem. They find him after three days. *Three days.* When they see him, the passage does not describe an emotional reunion. They find him in the temple courts, 'sitting among the teachers, listening to them and asking them questions' (Luke 2:46). I'm pretty sure that Mary's first thoughts would not have been to be impressed by his precocious behaviour. Perhaps the pride may have come later, as she pondered things in her heart. But her true maternal nature is expressed in the words: 'Son, why have you treated us like this? Your father and I have been anxiously searching for you' (Luke 2:48).

I am fascinated by the inclusion of this story in Luke's Gospel account – the only story we have in the canon of Jesus' childhood. Theologians – especially those Catholics who debate whether Mary was or was not sinless – have grappled with what this passage tells us. Some argue that Mary's anxiety as to Jesus' whereabouts was in itself sinful and so Mary was not perfect, while others try to find ways to describe her response as not sinful, or to separate the response from her sinless nature: for example, she did not sin, but Joseph may have.

Pope John Paul II sums up my motherhood journey perfectly when, in his Apostolic Letter on the Rosary, he describes Luke's Passover story as 'joy mixed with drama'.[13] This is the truth of parenting: it is neither wholly perfect and summed up in the hashtag 'blessed', nor is it wholly awful. Pope John Paul II describes here how Mary can help us into a deeper understanding of the 'realism of the mystery of the Incarnation' and to 'discover the secret of Christian joy'. Incarnation embraces the full reality of human life. To present a one-dimensional image of motherhood – as in the motherhood archetype of Mary and in the social media posts of mothers that have come two thousand years later – is not only false, it is unbeautiful. The beauty of the incarnation is that God steps into the joy and the laughter and the community, yes, but also into the chaos and the fear and the anxiety that accompany all aspects of life, including motherhood.

You can find this range of experiences on parenting networks such as Mummy's Gin Fund and Mumsnet, in which people share their fears and joys and anxieties with other parents. Often they are seeking advice, but I'll admit that I am one of those who lurk in these pages simply to make myself feel better about my own parenting fails, read advice, or check we are doing the right thing. I'm glad that such spaces exist online in a way that they have not previously, giving women a sense of solidarity with others; but the problem arises when they become spaces of competition, exacerbating the sense of inadequacy.

I am a sucker for a parenting hack, too, which is also part of the new trend in online parenting advice. I save videos posted by 'mumfluencers' about how to cook quick and healthy meals – apparently even for fussy eaters. For such advice on feeding my own such fussy eaters, I follow Kids Eat In Color, where one mum posts tricks and tips to help your children have a good relationship with food. I follow accounts like Five Minute Mum, with posts describing regular easy, fun games and activities for busy people to do with their young children. All of these women seem to have it together. They are the mothers I aspire to be, on top of everything else on my to-do list.

Motherhood and ageing

We rarely see images of the mother of God imagined in her later years. Ageing does not fit into our narrow ideal of perfect mother-hood. James Tissot's *La sainte Vierge âgée* ('The Holy Virgin in Old Age') – completed in around 1894 – is one of the few I have seen. It is a ghostly image, depicting a distraught grieving mother. This is not the youthful Mary we are familiar with, but draws out the pain of an older mother whose thirty-three-year-old son has just been murdered. Tissot imagines her praying as she looks down at the hole left where her son's cross had stood on Mount Calvary. Behind her are other women, whose faces are downcast after the trauma they have all just been through.

The most famous artworks imprinted on our collective imagi-nation are those picturing Mary as a graceful, beautiful young woman. But the Mary we meet later in the Gospel accounts is someone who has been a mother for thirty years. She may be a young mother to an adult child by today's standards, but she is no child. She has lived. Her motherhood would have grown as her child developed, each new phase of life bringing with it new requirements of her. Like every mother, Mary would have had to adapt from the oneness of those early intertwined months and years, when it is not clear where the baby begins and the mother ends. Like every mother, she would have had to learn to let go – bit by bit as the little one who once was helpless took his steps into the big wide world – tentatively at first, and then confidently. Like every mother, Mary would have pondered all these things in her heart and looked on as her heart inhabited another's body. Like every mother, she may have felt the timelessness of the early years – suspended in new maternity – and then watched as time sped up, and she felt herself tugging at it to slow down. When I first read the following words from Celeste Ng's *Little Fires Everywhere*, about the pain of separation as children grow, I felt devastated by the prospect of it. In the middle of the chaos of mothering my young children, I felt sadness at the thought of one day having to face them slipping away from me into adulthood. She writes:

Parents, she thought, learned to survive touching their children less and less . . . It was the way of things, Mia thought to herself, but how hard it was. The occasional embrace, a head leaned for just a moment on your shoulder, when what you really wanted more than anything was to press them to you and hold them so tight you fused together and could never be taken apart. It was like training yourself to live on the smell of an apple alone, when what you really wanted was to devour it, to sink your teeth into it and consume it, seeds, core, and all.'[14]

Mothering beyond the early years remains largely unexplored in public. I find there is a lot out there discussing pregnancy, birth and the early years. But I know very little of what it is to be a mother to a teenager, or about the particular experiences and feelings of women with adult children. A friend of mine, Alex, once told me that she found being a mother of adults in their twenties took up as much of her heart as it did when they were babies. 'It is just less of my practical time now, and I am less in control,' she said.

The overemphasis on young motherhood and the relative invisibility of older women is also present within churches, as demonstrated in the dominant image we have of the mother of God. A group of feminist theologians from the Asia–Pacific region noted:

The Church's tradition has excluded old women and widows from honor in what it has said about Mary. She is venerated as virgin and mother, as lady and queen. However, the young woman who sings of revolution *does* age. The woman who stands with other women, at the foot of the cross, and who is present with the community at Pentecost, is an older woman, a woman of wisdom and strength, who suffers, with God, the loss of her son – the consequence of commitment to live for change . . . It is time for us to claim and celebrate the presence of the Spirit in old women. We need them.[15]

The danger of a single motherhood story

In 2019, an estimated 600,000 young people attended World Youth Day in Panama – nicknamed the 'Catholic Woodstock'. During the series of events, young pilgrims from all over the world swapped flags and crosses and Catholic icons as a sign of cross-cultural unity. The highlight of the event was Pope Francis's public appearance in the 'Popemobile', and his celebration, early in the morning, of Mass, which thousands of young people had camped out overnight to attend, and in which he delivered a speech on young people and social media. 'The young woman of Nazareth was not part of the "social networks" of the time,' he said. 'She was not an "influencer", but without wanting or trying to, she became the most influential woman in history.' He then asked the young people: 'Are you willing to be an "influencer" like Mary?'[16]

If Mary were an influencer in today's world, which Mary would she present to the world? The Queen of Heaven, the perfect mother, the prophetic revolutionary activist, the grieving woman, or simply the mum? Perhaps the one-dimensional portrayal of what it means to be 'hashtag blessed' is the problem.

It is 7 March 2024, and I have found myself saying to my toddler in a frustrated voice, 'Please! You are not going to ruin this for me.' Yes, today is World Book Day; and, as it is for many parents – predominantly mothers, of course – in the UK, this is my big day. For the past few years, I have engaged in what is the height of competitive parenting: dressing each of my children up as a character from a well-known book. This year, my older son is dressed in a pristine white astronaut outfit complete with a NASA logo. He is Neil Armstrong, as featured on page 118 of one of his favourite non-fiction books, which tells the story of the moon landing. My toddler is dressed as Elmer the patchwork elephant in a second-hand outfit I bought from another mother online. The *pièce de résistance* of this outfit is of course the patchwork elephant head. But he will not wear it. I really do not care whether he continues to wear it after I drop him off at nursery; all I want is the photo of my costume-clad boys for 'the Gram' (Instagram). After a stream of attempts – outtakes – we get a few shots of my cherubs smiling, looking adorable in their outfits, and miraculously both looking at the camera at the same time.

After the school run, I sat on the train, uploaded the photos to my multiple social media accounts, and waited for the comments to come in. They did, of course, because people love cute kids in fancy dress. Friends liked and hearted the photos and my mission was accomplished: I got that warm sense of others' appreciation of my kids. But I also felt something else. I yet again felt part of a club of women seeking affirmation from the ether for our great parenting. We were the good mothers. Instagram told us so. The story social media portrayed that morning omitted a few things. I had told only part of it.

I did not describe how I felt the weight of the year-round burden of child admin: school creative projects, dress-up days, homework, uniform replacements, parents' evenings, school trip volunteering, assembly attending, spelling test preparing, multiple school and nursery app checking. I did not include how I felt as if I could not cope with one more day of attempting to hold all of this together while managing a full-time job, writing a book, volunteering, looking after a home, nurturing my marriage and trying to look after my physical and mental well-being. There was no snapshot of me a few seconds before the images I shared, shouting at my children as they ran around screeching or not eating their breakfast or not cooperating or not getting dressed. It told a single story. These single stories in which we collude in creating a perfect image of motherhood harm other women. They also tell a patriarchal society that already has unrealistically high expectations of women that such a simple story is possible. Christians talk about the invisible being made visible, but when it comes to social media such as Instagram, it is the visible things – the real, hard stuff of life – that I make invisible. Swept under the metaphorical carpet.

Things are changing, though. Just as some celebrity women are boldly sharing their stretch marks and wobbly bits on social media as a backlash against the beauty ideal, so some mumfluencers are deliberately sharing their warts-and-all stories to break the spell of perfect motherhood.

The mechanics of social media platforms such as TikTok and X and Instagram are designed to force us into binary, bite-sized stories.

They leave little room for nuance, encouraging us to squeeze ourselves into tropes of good motherhood. But I believe social media *can* be used as a way to demonstrate the range and complexity of the realities of motherhood. I feel this every time I see an honest post from another mother that shares the challenges of motherhood: the vacation mishaps, the messy homes, the children with food all over their faces. The tantrums in all their glory. It is possible for them to deconstruct the vision of perfect motherhood that has been passed down to us in the imagery of the Virgin Mother. But the thing to remember about social media images is that they are snapshots in time; they can be constructed to create a one-dimensional, single story of motherhood. When I do hear other mothers share realistically about their struggles, I feel a sense of connection to them because I recognise that this is someone who might understand my own imperfections. What if the Church could be known for playing a part in making space for mothers to come together and share their lows as well as their highs? It could go some way towards relieving the burden of striving for unattainable ideals.

Chapter 6

This Woman's Work

The Mental Load and the Myth of Having It All

'The wife, the employee, the mother and the housekeeper
all take it in shifts. You're more than *a* woman. You are
many women. You are every woman. They're all in
yoooooooooou. It's kind of cool. You get to live many lives.
Who doesn't want to do that? That is the ultimate dream of
mankind! The only niggle is, that they all happen at once.'

—*More Than a Woman*, Caitlin Moran[1]

'This is a generation of mothers that are burning out,
losing out, breaking down trying to simply exist. As a
family. With a career. It's not about "having it all", it's
just that we are doing it all. And it's too much.'

—Mother Pukka, Instagram, January 2024[2]

In May 2024, a US college commencement speech was the subject
of both praise and fierce criticism for suggesting that most women
are deep down much more interested in looking after their family
than in having successful careers. Delivered by Kansas City Chiefs
star Harrison Butker at Benedictine College, a Catholic liberal arts
school, the speech began by exhorting men to 'fight against' their
'cultural emasculation'[3] before telling the women graduating that he
guessed most of them were more excited about marriage and children than about making it in the workplace.

Butker, who was twenty-eight at the time, welled up as he spoke
of his wife's sacrifice, and did something that few men do publicly

– he acknowledged the invisible work of his supportive wife in contributing to his success. However, he also did what many men have done throughout history, making it clear that a woman's place is in the home, and presenting a binary choice between working inside the home and outside of it, and being unequivocal in which of those he thought was the right choice. The sisters of Mount St. Scholastica – the founding institution and sponsor of Benedictine College – were unsurprisingly not so impressed with the idea that a woman's highest calling is to be a wife and mother.

The debate over whether a woman's – and especially a mother's – place is in the home existed long before the sexual revolution and third-wave feminism. In 1915, suffragist and trade union activist Clementina Black, who worked mainly among communities living in poverty in London, undertook a study of married women's work and challenged the residual Victorian middle-class idea that the 'working for money of married women is to be deplored'. Black wrote:

> Wives who work not for their own or their children's bread, but rather for butter to it, are regarded as at least somewhat blameworthy. The underlying implication seems to be that a wife and mother who thus works must be withdrawing from the care of her home and her children time and attention of which they are really in need. Pictures rise before the mind of rooms unswept, beds unmade and dishes unwashed, of children hungry, ragged, unkempt and running wild.'[4]

In her visits to many homes of women who worked, she found numerous positives, and that neglect was not a given, exploding the myth that working mothers were *bad* mothers. What she did identify, however, was the strain on women both at work and at home. Black described as a 'horrible boast'[5] the claim by those who would tell her that they 'never missed but one week's wash with any of my babies', because she recognised in it the strain that women who worked put themselves under to live up to some ideal about what a mother 'should' be doing at work and at home. Women have for centuries faced the contradictory portrayals of mothering as a woman's ultimate work and yet at the same time as mundane and of little importance.

For most of my life, when I've heard the Annunciation story told, and how, on hearing the news that she was to give birth to God's son, Mary 'pondered all these things in her heart' (Luke 2:19), I have imagined her storing up great theological questions. I've imagined her contemplating, her head tilted to one side, as she considers great theological truths about the nature of divine love, Christology, soteriology and eschatology. This is such a profound happening that her mind is surely set on these big, lofty questions.

But what if Mary's ponderings were a little more grounded? These days, I also imagine Mary pondering in a way that it seems many mothers do. Storing up all the practical things that we have to do and hold in our heads, the things that keep our families going. Of course, women are some of the greatest theologians and do ponder eternal truths; but the reality of motherhood is that alongside these profound thoughts are the more incarnational. The things I ponder in my heart and head comprise a mental to-do list – an ever-streaming number of tasks and questions: what's for dinner? What's for breakfast? What are this week's spellings? When will I do the laundry-grocery-shopping-birthday-party-RSVPing-present-buying-gift-wrapping-bathroom-cleaning-playdate-organising-bike-fixing-karate-club-paying-school-performance-ticket-buying-bath-time-supervising-memory-making?

This is the hidden work of motherhood. The world does not pay attention to it because – like so much of supposed women's work – it is invisible. Many studies in recent years have attempted to make visible the hidden work that many women undertake. Broadly this falls into three categories: cognitive labour, emotional labour, and the mental load. Cognitive labour describes holding in mind all the practical domestic needs and activities such as knowing what groceries are needed, organising social activities, and planning. So much planning. Emotional labour relates to the responsibility for the family's emotional well-being: worrying about whether children are happy at school, or thriving in their friendship groups. The mental load is the place in which the cognitive and emotional labour intersect: 'preparing, organising and anticipating everything, emotional and practical, that needs to get done to make life flow'.[6]

Locked down

The pandemic made these things more visible, though, and for a time the western world could see how unrealistic the pressures we place on mothers are. While on one of my permitted daily walks in 2020, I called a friend and confessed to her how much I was struggling. 'I feel like I'm about to crack,' I said, in tears, as I paced around the park near where we lived. The world was experiencing a once-in-a-century trauma, and at home I felt as if I was drowning. When UK prime minister Boris Johnson told us to stay at home to stop the spread of Covid, I invited my sister to come and stay with us because I could not bear the thought of my extrovert sibling being alone for weeks on end without human company. I also felt responsible – for everything. I have always felt this way, but there is something about the myth of perfect motherhood that exacerbates this sense of not being able to let go, of needing to keep all the plates spinning, lest the world fall apart. I had thought that the narrative in my head was one that most parents have: the constant to-do lists circling round my brain, items being ticked off at a curiously slower rate than they were being added. As well as the actual physical tasks of mothering, there is the cognitive burden – thinking about everyone and everything all at once. Motherwork – described by Andrea O'Reilly as 'doing, caring, nurturing, sacrificing, subsuming oneself in order to let another thrive'[7] – is not just in the acts themselves, it is also in the thinking about the acts and feeling that it is part of your job description as a mother to do so. I once confessed to my husband that despite working more than full time and striving for equality in our relationship, I couldn't shake the belief that if the house was untidy or if the food wasn't cooked or if the children looked dishevelled, then somehow I was failing in my responsibility. I asked him whether he ever felt the same – that the domestic duties were *his responsibility*. He said 'never' – and also stated how ridiculous it was that I should ever think of them as my own either. Academics have found, however, that people believe that women do more housework, and also that women *should* do more housework, than men. Domesticity is synonymous with femininity. I experienced this most starkly in the examples of good Christian mothers in churches I was raised in, where expectations about the maternal ideal can be vividly played out. We are socialised to judge women more harshly than men for having messy homes, holding women to higher standards of cleanliness. It has been argued that women therefore might engage in more housework not because they want to, nor because they are better at it, but because they know they will be judged more harshly for not doing it. Meanwhile, men may avoid doing too much housework for fear of being seen as less masculine.[8]

In the months after lockdown, when bubbles and social distancing became but a memory – like recalling a weird dream – I noted how many books about the challenges of motherhood were released. So many seemed to be finding they needed a release from the pressures that the pandemic had placed on them, which had exacerbated the strain of the juggle many women routinely experience as they navigate their lives between work and home. Data published in the *British Medical Journal* showed that women were spending a disproportionate amount of time on unpaid care work – around a billion hours a day – comprising caring for children, older relatives, those who are ill, or those who are disabled. While the pandemic increased care and domestic work for both men and women, studies have shown the intensity of this work was much greater for women, with projected detrimental impacts on women's mental health.[9] As Triantafyllia Kadoglou and Katerina Sarri write: 'A society which assigns the bulk of responsibility for child rearing to women will result in a female population which feels constantly guilt ridden and often frantic.'[10]

The dominant portrayal of Mary seems to provide little that will help working mothers navigate their journey of motherhood and work. As Trudelle Thomas writes: 'Often Mary is regarded from a needy child's point of view, not the hardworking mother's.'[11] The Church, in my experience, has not been helpful in relieving this burden on women, either. I have heard countless stories of another Mary in the Gospels (Luke 10:38–42) – and her sister Martha, who, while Mary sits at Jesus' feet listening to him speak, busies herself with the household chores that so often fall to women. I've always heard, in the retelling of this story from the church pulpit, an admonishment to be more like Mary than Martha, and sit at Jesus' feet. The

Church criticises us for being preoccupied with so-called women's work, yet doesn't offer a helping hand, or come to our aid with a dustpan and brush. Instead, we are left with the impossible task of doing it all.

A good mother doesn't work outside the home

One afternoon, I sat in a toilet cubicle in central London crying my eyes out as I looked at pictures of my baby on my phone. It was my first day back at work. I had chosen to leave the new job I had started while a few weeks pregnant, opting instead to work in a role that was more manageable, at an organisation in a location that was more amenable to nursery pick-up times. I had been a mother for nine months. Nine months in which I learnt that maternity leave was not the holiday that I had expected it to be. I had been lined up to write a book while I was off, thinking that I might have time to write while the baby slept. It took me one week to realise how laughable a notion this had been. I had no time to think, no time to drink a glass of water, or a cup of hot coffee, let alone write. Every waking moment – and there were more of them in a day than I had realised were possible – was taken up by the baby. When he slept, I ran around like a woman possessed, trying to fit in everything else before he woke up. Checking emails, answering friends, doing the laundry, washing up, eating, showering, and maybe even going to the toilet alone. Those nine months were some of the darkest yet also some of the most joy-filled of my life. They were also relentless. I longed to go back to work. It was at work that I felt my real self: a thinking, doing, problem-solving creative whose brain sparked at talking about ideas with adults, and meeting new people. We had agreed that I would take nine months of maternity leave and then Mark would swap in for two months of parental leave. Though leaving my baby with his dad rather than with a childminder or in a nursery when I returned to work helped the separation anxiety, the ache was overwhelming. As I sat on the train, coffee in hand, wearing a new – and clean – dress, I exhaled. I felt free. Yet at the same time, I felt incomplete – that niggling feeling that I had forgotten something. As I was shown my desk and the rest of the building, I was excited. I took my new team to lunch and asked about their roles and their lives and their passions. It was strange to be in conversation with adults without talking about my son. Here they were seeing me like an autonomous individual: the new boss. No baby at my hip. No buggy, no wet wipes. I think I must have looked confident and present; but I was distracted by thoughts of him. *What was he doing right now? Was he napping at the right time? Was he eating well? Was he wondering where his mummy was?* Here I was in the place I had been longing to be, but this work had torn me away from the object of my obsession. And so the first opportunity I got to steal away, I let the tears come. Alone in the cubicle, as I looked at his face, I let the grief of separation wash over me. The grief was accompanied by a profound sense of guilt.

I was a feminist who had been raised by a mother who worked and achieved and broke glass ceilings. But in that moment, I felt a flicker of doubt. Maybe mothers *should* stay at home. Maybe we were not designed for this – to work, when our babies needed us. It's no surprise I felt like this. Despite years of women's liberation, we have been presented with images and archetypes of the maternal ideal – the Madonna who puts aside her own wants and ambitions for the sake of the family. Perhaps I *was* a bad mother.

In Germany, I might be referred to as a *Rabenmutter*. Few languages make explicit the judgement of women who fail to live up to a perceived standard of motherhood. But the Germans have a way of giving voice to the things we feel or experience that have no equivalent word in English. *Weltschmerz* describes a sense of world-weariness, an awareness of all the tragedy that exists in the world; *Verschlimmbessern* describes making something worse when you had intended to make it better; and *Rabenmutter* is the derogatory word used for a bad mother.

The word literally translates as 'raven mother' and refers to the incorrect belief that raven chicks leave the nest before they can fly because of neglect from their mothers. In Germany today, a mother who works is often described as a 'Rabenmutter', alongside mothers who spend extended periods away from their children, including giving them up for adoption. The opposite of a raven mother is a 'lucky mother' – again a derogatory term, this time meaning an overprotective mother. Women cannot win. The fact that the term *Rabenmutter* exists in German goes some way to explaining the attitude towards working mothers made manifest in Germany's socio-economic policies. German women are much more likely to end their career and stay at home to look after their children than women in many other parts of Europe, or to not have children at all to save themselves being labelled a *Rabenmutter*. The thing is that the term is used as a way to denigrate all women – whether mothers or not. Former German Chancellor Angela Merkel, at the time one of the most powerful women in the world, was called a *Rabenmutter*, despite not having any children. The same term was used to describe German Ursula von der Leyen, president of the European Commission and a mother of seven. That both Merkel and von der Leyen could be labelled raven mothers tells you all you need to know about the impossible standards against which all women are measured. This negative view of working mothers, and the lack of familial, societal and state support parents have in raising their children, presents existential questions for the German nation. The birth rate has declined significantly since the 1950s, seemingly as women choose to forgo having children so that they can continue their careers. 'The question is not whether women will work,' von der Leyen once said in an interview. 'They will work. The question is whether they will have kids.'[12]

A woman's place

There are few places in which the pressure to conform to the 'good mother' trope is more keenly felt than in the Church. Despite much progress being made in recent decades on women's place in the Church of England, including in the ordination of women, questions about the practicalities of women in leadership still betray a discomfort with the idea of working women. A 2024 audit into maternity provision within Anglican dioceses in the UK found a great disparity in both treatment and pay for women clergy who were pregnant or who had children, with poor maternity provision in some dioceses, and even instances of families being made 'effectively homeless by the church'.[13] The message that this sends women clergy is this: you do not belong here, because a woman's place is in the home. Rev. Dr Isabelle Hamley, principal of Ridley Hall, a theological college in Cambridge, said: 'The default understanding in the Church still seems to be anchored in social mores from long before the ordination of women, when women cared for children while men went out to work.' She also added that it was 'disturbing' to see the ways in which the Church was less caring, and less supportive of families, than secular workplaces, in many instances.

Saint Birgitta, the supermum

The pressure placed on Christian women to confine themselves to the home rather than go to work can be traced back to historical ideas that suggested mothers are responsible for bringing up their children in the faith, for moulding them into godly adults. The mother is ultimately responsible for her children's souls, as we see in the story of Birgitta of Sweden, a prominent figure within Christian mysticism in the fourteenth century, and – reluctantly – a mother of eight children. Part of a noble family, Birgitta was in effect forced at the age of thirteen to marry, despite her early commitment to virginity and singleness in order to devote herself to God. In fact, she had been so opposed that 'she would more willingly have died than married'.[14] When she did marry Ulf Gudmarsson, she persuaded him to wait two years before consummating the marriage, and prayed that each time they had sex God would 'give them a child who would serve him continually and never offend him'.[15] They went on to have four sons and four daughters, 'only' two of whom died before reaching adulthood. If anyone was a supermum, it was Birgitta. For nearly thirty years – before her husband died – she was a devoted wife and mother, and also managed a large estate. Clarissa Atkinson writes that Birgitta also 'carefully supervised the religious education of her children, tended the poor and sick, and observed strict ascetic practices as far as these were compatible with married life'.[16] Birgitta is reported to have had a strong identification with the Virgin Mary, of whom she regularly had visions.

The life of Saint Birgitta demonstrates the belief that a good Christian mother tends to the souls of her children. For Saint Birgitta, there was nothing more important than her and her children's relationship with God, Jesus Christ and his mother Mary. Every day, she would rise at dawn – just like the Proverbs 31 supermum who 'gets up while it is still night' (Proverbs 31:15) – and pray for the souls of her children. She would take her daughters to visit the sick. She would weep when her son forgot a saint's day. Birgitta's motherhood was affirmed in a visitation from Mary, who praised her efforts: 'You pray God that your children will please God. Truly this is a good prayer. For if she who is a mother pleases my son, and loves him above all other things, and prays for herself and her children, I will help her prayer to be effective.'[17]

Since Saint Birgitta lived far longer than most women in the fourteenth century, she witnessed the deaths of a number of her children. With each death, she had to wrestle with the guilt of whether she had done enough in their formative years to save their soul. Her son Karl was described as the black sheep of the family. 'Even on his best behaviour, Karl caused his mother embarrassment,' writes Atkinson. Towards the end of his life, he started a scandalous affair with Joanna, the widowed queen of Naples. It was while this affair was going on that Karl – who was accompanying his mother, Birgitta, from Rome to a pilgrimage in the Holy Land – died, likely of tuberculosis. On the outside, she accepted his death stoically – as she had done with those of her other children – not letting on that she loved them more than she loved God. But on the inside, Birgitta was deeply troubled. In a vision, she saw Mary alongside Karl in his death, protecting him from evil fiends and the fury of hell. 'It took two mothers to keep this sinner out of the Devil's clutches,' Atkinson writes, adding: 'The judgment of Karl, with its dramatic presentation of maternal power, makes a strong, explicit statement about a mother's responsibility for her child's salvation. Even though Birgitta was constantly reassured by Mary and by Christ that she was a good mother, she suffered from horrifying visions of the uses of maternal power by bad mothers.'[18]

This idea that it is God's will for people to have many children, whose salvation can be assured through a mother's prayer and commitment, is not just a thing of the past, but has found a place today in Quiverfull, a Christian movement. Found predominantly in the Anglo-American Global North, Quiverfull is a conservative Christian theology that arose as a backlash against advancements in birth control during the twentieth century. The Quiverfull movement, in which adherent couples do not use birth control or any form of family planning, takes its name from Psalm 127:3–5:

> Children are a heritage from the Lord, offspring a reward from him.
> Like arrows in the hands of a warrior are children born in one's youth.
> Blessed is the man whose quiver is full of them.

Examples of Quiverfull families include Jim Bob and Michelle Duggar – the father and mother known for their reality TV show *19 Kids and Counting*. One of the main tenets of the Quiverfull movement is the return to so-called traditional gender roles, where the father is the head of the household, and the mother submits to his authority and is responsible for the domestic elements of family life, including the moulding of Christian minds and the shaping of a Christian nation. For some people, the more children a woman can have the better; because more children equals more souls saved; and more souls saved appeases a Holy God.

Nancy Campbell is one of the most influential voices in the Quiverfull movement thanks to her Above Rubies ministry and accompanying magazine with a circulation of 160,000. Above Rubies takes its name from Proverbs 31:10, where the virtuous wife extolled in the passage is described in some versions of the Bible as having a value 'far above rubies'. For Campbell, 'mothers determine the destiny of the nation'. 'We're in a battle for the kingdom of God . . . And our children are all part of that battle.'[19] For Quiverfull families, the strategy of producing offspring is not just for the sake of the new lives that are to come, it is in order to have children who can influence national political life. Their souls having been shaped by the sacrifice of good Christian mothers, it is often hoped that these children will go on to vote for Christian policies and create a nation under God, where the alternative – according to them – is being outbred by high rates of birth among Muslim immigrants, while they view feminism as hindering God's commandment to go forth and multiply because birth control and abortion prevent the births of good Christian (white) children.

This idea that mothers drive their children's spiritual and moral beliefs is found not just on the fringes, but also within the mainstream Church. A study by US Christian research organisation Barna found that mothers – more than fathers – are responsible for their children's faith formation.[20] Mothers can of course shape their children in both positive and negative ways. Despite the ways in which Mary has been portrayed over the centuries as subservient and passive, in keeping with the dominant historical view of a woman's place, former Archbishop of Canterbury Dr Rowan Williams suggests it would have been Mary who had much to do with the shaping of who Jesus was. A group of feminist theologians from the Asia–Pacific put it like this:

> She who responds, 'Thy will be done,' is the mother who teaches her son the same response. These are also his words in the garden of Gethsemane. We learn from this that Mary's servanthood is the same as the servanthood of Jesus … With the singer of the Magnificat as his mother, it should not surprise us that Jesus's first words in Luke's account of his public ministry are also a mandate for radical change.'[21]

Margaret Hebblethwaite suggests the dominant Christian perception nowadays of Mary as an uneducated, illiterate peasant girl from a backwater town (John 1:46: 'Can anything good come from Nazareth?') may be a myth. She deduces that, yes, Mary was poor, but that was because she was a refugee. Nazareth is not where she was originally from; it was her adopted home, as Matthew implies, his Gospel account giving a different explanation from Luke's as to why Jesus grew up in Nazareth.[22] For Jesus to have known so much about Scripture by the age of twelve – as we see when he is found in the temple in Luke – he would have to have been shaped by his parents. While some commentators suggest it was Joseph who taught him, it is – according to Hebblethwaite – more likely to have been

Mary, who the Gospels present as the more involved parent, the one who reproaches Jesus when they find him in the temple, and the one who was still around when he was a young man. Mary would have been more exposed to theological education if she grew up around Jerusalem, which was surrounded by scriptural scholars and learned men, rather than in Nazareth, which was a small, provincial place, as Jewish writer Schalom Ben-Chorin suggests.[23] For Hebblethwaite, this idea of Mary as Jesus' first teacher makes logical sense. 'It would also deepen our understanding of Mary's role,' she writes. 'In place of the stereotype of a simple, submissive woman, she emerges as an educator.'[24] She adds that this is 'something already instinctively glimpsed' in paintings that show Mary teaching Jesus to read, such as sixteenth-century painter Ambrosius Benson's *The Madonna and Child* at Campion Hall, Oxford. In fact, from the Middle Ages onwards there emerged a strong – though lesser-known – tradition of imagery of the Virgin Mary reading from a book in the Annunciation scene – although of course books as we know them would not have existed in first-century Palestine. Such imagery was packed with symbolism. In some examples, Mary's solitary reading symbolised her piety, contemplation and devotion. In others, a scholarly Mary was simply an inevitable accompaniment to her perfection. Writes Laura Saetveit Miles: 'Part of Mary's exemplary status as virgin includes her studiousness, her bookishness as a well-read virgin. Her physical purity both justifies and enables an intellectual purity. With body and mind morally aligned, both distanced from the worldly downfalls of her sex, Mary gains access to the written word of scripture.'[25]

In some of the artworks, the book represented the incarnation – the Word made flesh. 'Mary is the student of the Word, the one who absorbs and attends to the Word so utterly that she is able to embody it as no other before or after her has done,' writes Nicola Slee. 'So she becomes a template and a role model of all assiduous learners and students of the Word.'[26] This insight feels so familiar to me as one who has given birth to two children. When it comes to knowledge about my children, I am an A-star student. I know every curl on their head; I study their faces as they sleep. I take notes on their likes and dislikes, their loves and their hates, their sleep times, their feeding schedules. There is no one so devoted to knowledge about them as me. Of course Mary would have been the same with Jesus, the subject of her maternal thesis. But, like any mother, not only was she shaped by her knowledge of him, but she too shaped him.

Mothers have long been held responsible for their children's formation – both intellectual and spiritual. The cognitive load of motherhood includes this responsibility, which is both a privilege and a burden. It is not just about the homework and spelling tests and holiday projects, it is also about the shaping of children's values, ethics and beliefs. It is a wonder to watch children grow into curious beings who are fascinated by the world and ask so many questions. Once my elder son could ask questions, he did not stop. I felt the weight of his intellectual and spiritual formation. I knew that not only would he be shaped by our answers to his questions about the world, about other people, about God, but he would be shaped by what he saw us doing, how he saw his parents living, what we valued, what we feared, what we thought about what it is to be human.

The myth of perfect motherhood attempts to suggest that when a woman has children, she must put to bed any previous ambition outside the home, as we saw in the example of Butker's commencement speech and advice to 'the women'. It also suggests that motherhood should put an end to any intellectual pursuits full stop. This idea is strong within the evangelical tradition, although Nadya Williams, an American evangelical writer and thinker who gave up a career in academia to become a full-time home-schooling mother, thinks differently. She argues that motherhood itself requires 'a robust life of the mind'. 'Too many Americans today find traditional women's activities, like motherhood and homemaking, to be intellectually worthless.'[27] She recognises, though, that the sheer practicalities of motherhood – such as having to breastfeed for 1,800 hours – make the pursuit of cerebral knowledge more difficult, and that women, just like the greatest male thinkers in history, need supportive networks and frameworks to enable them to have space to think. Williams laments the women in history, such as the English novelist and playwright Dorothy L. Sayers, who have felt they had to choose between their mind and their motherhood, forgoing one or the other because of the myths that place limits on what women can and cannot do. In

1924, Sayers had a son out of wedlock. Her sense of shame at this, the potential effect of that shame on her literary career, and the seeming impossibility of career success while bringing up a child alone led Sayers to ask her cousin Ivy to raise him. When Sayers died, people were surprised to learn she had been a mother.

Spinning plates

Ideas about what a perfect mother is leave women feeling that they can never measure up. Through the centuries – and often because of the growth and influence of the Church – women have been trying and failing to live up to whatever impossible standards are set for them in their day.

But it seems that women today are under particular burdens, ironically brought about by the gains we have made in equality in society and the workplace. There are particular pressures women face in the twenty-first century that our foremothers could simply not have imagined. Alongside the feminist gains there has arisen an almost nostalgic desire to return to the perceived golden age of mothering in Anglo-American societies: the 1950s. Many women today are buckling under the weight of trying to be both a working professional and a mother who fulfils all the duties of a 1950s housewife, complete with a pristine, spotless home, a perfect body, a great relationship and well-behaved children. It can all get a little exhausting.

According to a 2023 report entitled 'Bringing It All Back Home', mothers in 2015 were spending 68 per cent more time each day on childcare than mothers in 1961.[28] What is particularly striking about this report is that it shows that in the twenty-first century, it is professional women who are likely to be educated to degree level who spend the most time on childcare, despite having the longest working hours since the 1980s. There are complicated and entangled reasons for this, according to the author, Dr Giacomo Vagni. Since the eighteenth century, western societies have slowly transformed the ways in which children are viewed. There began to be a shift from the 'children are to be seen and not heard' approach to parenting that was prevalent when families had large numbers of children, some of whom might not grow up into adulthood, with middle classes starting to turn their efforts towards investing in and cultivating just a few children. These shifting attitudes were also inherently class-based, just as they are today.

In the early part of the twenty-first century, the concept of motherhood in Anglo-American cultures includes the ideology of 'intensive mothering', where mothers are the primary caregivers tasked with creating emotional and physical well-being in their children. This approach to motherhood has been described as 'child-centered, expert-guided, emotionally absorbing, labor-intensive, and financially expensive'.[29] A middle-class parent who spends time they do not actually have on childcare harbours the subconscious belief that nurturing and paying more attention to your children while they are young will lead to better outcomes when they are older: they will get to top universities that lead to top jobs that lead to family security. Of course, working-class mothers would want that future security for their offspring too, but for them, the unpredictability and precarity of their work, with non-traditional working hours and shift patterns in unskilled and low-paid jobs, make preparing their children for such a future a luxury beyond their reach. Vagni added that the physical demands of working-class jobs might also leave mothers simply exhausted after a hard day's work, and just not able to give as much time to childcare as white-collar mothers.

This pressure to mother intensively begins even before the child is born. I remember when, during our antenatal classes, one of the other couples mentioned the importance of playing classical music while the baby is in the womb. Despite no definitive proof, the so-called Mozart effect has been promoted to parents to enhance the baby's brain development and boost their IQ.[30] I returned home that day and – maybe for the first time in my life – put on some Schubert on purpose. In the early months after my son was born, we attended Bach to Baby concerts. Yes, classical concerts for parents and little ones. Some studies have suggested that listening to classical music might relax the mother and help reduce perinatal anxiety,[31] even if it does not have much effect on the baby. But perhaps what might be more relaxing is for mothers to be freed from the myths of the Mozart effect and perfect motherhood.

To some extent, the trend in intensive mothering – which experts would now consider the norm in western countries – particularly relates to *white* middle-class mothers. Some studies have found that mothers from minority ethnic communities like my own face conflicting cultural ideals. One, for example, showed that for Black women, the health and happiness of the mother are a priority rather than taking it as given that the child's needs must always come first. In Black and Latin American communities, there is much more of a sense of the care burden being shared among the wider kin or community. This does not mean that those ideals of intensive mothering are absent in these communities, just that there are other competing cultural norms to bear in mind.[32]

Motherhood is hard enough without having to also deal with the realities of daily life. For many middle-class women, the day-to-day practical and mundane tasks of mothering feel so challenging because they are so different from the space we have occupied for much of our lives up until that point. They feel alien because our education and our work lives have made us feel important in a completely different way – of value because we use our brains.

I am aware, however, that I feel this way because of the privilege that I have. Although I am a Black mother, I am a middle-class, Oxbridge-educated one. For many mothers living in poverty, including those from minority ethnic communities, coping with domestic life within their own family setting is far less stressful than facing the disrespect, racism and hostility they meet with outside the comfort of their home.

While concerns about a child's future are a natural expression of the love we might feel for our family and the instinct we have to protect them both now and in the future, the expectation that we will be able to control what happens in years to come because of how we mother our children now is yet another burden placed on women: perfect motherhood must of course create perfect futures for our children.

In a 2018 study on parental burnout, it was found to be this concern with their children's future that led women to crack under the weight of it all, with mothers stating that responsibility for a child's future could feel overwhelming. One participant in the study – Bénédicte – said:

What I experience, is fear actually. The fear of who my child is going to be, the fear that my child believes he is not loved enough, the fear that . . . I have this on my mind all the time . . . to know that what I do now is what will contribute to make my children happy or unhappy in the future. My only goal is to make them happy later. That's my problem: the fact that my goal is not to make them happy now, but to make them happy later.[33]

I want to have it all. At work, I want to be a stellar leader. I want to be clever and wise and organised. I never want to drop a ball. The problem is that this is what I want for my home life too. To be a perfect mother. I never want to drop a ball at home. What I want is impossible; and the sooner I realise that, the sooner I can let go of the unrealistic expectations I have placed on myself both at home and at work, not to mention at church.

The myth of perfect motherhood tells us that perfect parenting actions lead to perfect children and adults. But this is not true. We need to give ourselves some grace. Child development psychologist Alison Gopnik suggests that we should see our role in raising children as more like a gardener creating 'a protected and nurturing space for plants to flourish'[34] than a carpenter who needs to do certain things to create a precise, perfect product. 'It takes some work,' writes Jonathan Haidt, author of *The Anxious Generation*, 'but you don't have to be a perfectionist.'[35]

The unnecessary supermum

I want to let you into a secret. There is no greater compliment you can give me than telling me I am a superwoman. Well, there is one: telling me I'm a supermum. When someone tells me what I want to do simply can't be done, that is my motivator to get it done. I rage at the limits women place on ourselves, and at the ceilings society – as well as the Church – places above us. Women already face so many barriers to forging careers and achieving their ambitions before they become mothers. When I became a mother I wanted to shatter the glass ceilings placed above mothers' heads, too. I also wanted to show others that life does not have to stop when you become a mum. I was determined not to let the fact that I had had children become my overriding identity. But this stubborn determination led me to do some things that placed an undue burden on me. Bringing babies to public-speaking engagements, board meetings and team away days. My only reason for doing such things was to prove to myself – and to others – that I could do it. But what I was left with each time was an overwhelming sense that I could not in fact do it all.

I have thought this several times in the course of writing this book. I have attempted to prise my eyes open every evening to stay up and write after the children have gone to bed, and I have woken every day at 5 a.m. to write before they wake up, and I have taken my laptop with me everywhere to grab precious minutes away from my day job, or other events, where I could to write. I found a kindred spirit in Toni Morrison, in the description of her juggling writing around her two children. She wrote at night, or at 4 a.m., working 'with and around them, but never in those early years without them', writes Jennifer Banks. 'She would write in the middle of the day, too, with her children all around her . . . She once described writing around some vomit her son had left on the page. She simply needed to get that sentence down before she forgot it. The wiping up could wait, but the sentence could not.'[36]

A simple reading of Mary's story might suggest Jesus' mother knew little of the juggling act that modern women have to perform. That roles were simpler then: if you were a mother, then all you did was *mother*. Such a reading would in the first instance fail to recognise the immensity of mothering, let alone of doing anything else as well. But the reality was that, as well as being a mother, Mary was a leader in the earliest days of the Christian faith, too. Though you might be forgiven for thinking she was purely a passive vessel who bore the son of God, Mary was known to be a strong and courageous leader at her son's side during his ministry, and after his death and resurrection. Ally Kateusz uncovers the hidden leadership of Mary in her book *Mary and Early Christian Women*. Kateusz critiques the ways in which the role of Jesus' women followers in the movement has been downplayed, reducing them to one-dimensional caricatures with little nuance. 'A woman, after all, can be both a mother

and a leader,' Kateusz writes, 'and vestiges of the strong role that
Jesus' mother played are in the canonical gospels themselves.'[37]

The myth that surrounds the mother of God – that she is submissive,
small and powerless – must be unmade and reconstructed to convey the
truth – that she was a powerful, mighty woman, reflecting the image of
God, just like every mother today. No matter what she does.

Recent years have seen a significant rise in the number of people in
western countries experiencing parental burnout – a condition due
to chronic parenting stress.[38] Unlike its sister syndrome, postnatal
depression (PND), which happens in the weeks and months after
giving birth, parental burnout seems to be sparked by months and
months of pressure building up. The 2018 parental-burnout study
mentioned above found that one of the drivers of parental burnout
was a great sense of duty among the mothers, self-pressure, an obsession with not wanting to ruin their children's futures, and perfec-
tionism. One participant, Violette, said:

> We are driven by a kind of archetype of a perfect behaviour which
> leads us to set goals that are hard to achieve. When we do not
> achieve our goals, we get a sense of failure. Maybe such goals are
> unrealistic . . . I think that's why I got exhausted. If I had been
> able to let go instead of wanting everything to be perfect, maybe
> I would not have gone crazy.[39]

For the study participant Bénédicte, it was not the desire to achieve
goals that contributed to her burnout, it was the constant sense of
doubt about whether she could in fact be a good mother. 'I did not
even believe that I could do better,' she said. 'I used to always question my very ability to get things right. I used to be always in doubt
about myself, and therefore I would continue to seek to do more and
better . . . all the time.'

What I have noticed in my conversations with others, and from
my own experience, is that it feels as if part of being a good mother
is being convinced that you are a bad one; and not only that, but that
everyone else but you is a good mother. The perfect-mother trope
that hovers in the air around us seems to tell us that, whatever a

perfect mother is, it is certainly not us. Being a working mother is not ideal; being a stay-at-home mum is not ideal; trying to have it all is not ideal.

I am a sucker for New Year's resolutions. Even though I know I will likely fail a few months down the line, each January begins with a new productivity technique or habit tracker, a new system of life hacks to make everything more manageable. A commitment to be a better friend, to be more well-read, to be fitter, healthier, slimmer. This particular year, wrapped up in my new schemes was a commitment to being a better mother. I wanted to be one of those women who has dinner on the table for everyone at 6.30 p.m., despite having worked all day. So I enlisted the help of a weekly meal box to cut out the mental load of planning and shopping for ingredients. The thing was, I still had to cook the meals. So I would rush to the kitchen and try and rustle up dinner, while my children – also frazzled from long days – would not leave me alone. My big boy wanted help building things and demanded that that help came right that minute. Meanwhile, the toddler wrapped his arms around my ankles, wanting to be picked up, while I desperately tried to cook. *Mama, mama, mama, mama!* His cries became louder and more urgent the more I tried to ignore him. Again, the mismatch between the scene of domestic bliss in my head, which I wanted to recreate, and the reality of the chaos and noise and mess that I stood in was unbelievably frustrating. My husband was stressed and I was stressed and the children were stressed, and I screamed, 'I want to run away!' The desire to escape was overwhelming. I thought of walking out of the door, getting into my car and silently screaming into my steering wheel. I wonder why – despite the huge frustration I was experiencing – I felt the scream would have to be silent. Even in the fantasy of escape and abandonment, perhaps I still feared the judgement of onlookers hearing a mother who had come to the end of herself.

When I first read *Motherhood and God* by Margaret Hebblethwaite, the opening pages presented a warm and storybook picture of what becoming a mother is like, and what it can teach us about God. I began to feel pangs of inadequacy as I read about the author's first birth and how it gave her new and valuable insight into the nature of God. Of course, there are times – many times – when I have felt this overwhelming sense of love for my children, too. But I began to fall in love with Hebblethwaite's honest account of motherhood when she wrote about her experience of becoming a mother the second time round: the sense of claustrophobia and creeping insanity that any mother who has had to look after two children – or even more – alone has experienced. There is a feeling of being outnumbered, unable to exert control. There is much noise, much cajoling, much soothing, tears, trips and falls. It is hard to describe it to someone who has not experienced it, and we risk inviting people to question why we have had children at all, if it's so bad. If having one child afforded me the occasional moment of feeling that I was doing well at mothering, the arrival of my second child shattered the illusion of my occasional perfection. There were no longer such moments. Hebblethwaite writes of her own experience, becoming a mother of two and being alone, as her husband, who reported on the goings-on within the Vatican, had had to travel there following the death of Pope John Paul I in 1978. 'Once I had a child I was delighted in and was proud of,' she writes. 'Now, instead of two such children, every-thing had gone sour . . . Feelings of failure and guilt merged with those of disappointment and disillusion. I grew to hate children.'[40] In Hebblethwaite's account, I found resonance in the attempt to be a good mother – or at least a composed one – in the face of having children who seem determined to not let you win that accolade. Being a mother is more difficult than many of us had been led to believe. Letting go of the myth of perfect motherhood is vital to our survival. Rather than engage in the futile pursuit of perfection that causes untold levels of stress, sometimes we just have to call for help.

The icing on the cake

From my earliest memories, good motherhood and good baking had been intertwined. A good mother surely never bought her children birthday cakes from the supermarket, never outsourced the stress and strain that were part and parcel of the sacrifice of being a good mum.

When I was a child, my mum enrolled me and my sisters in sugarcraft lessons. We would arrive on Saturday mornings, clutching our sugarcraft boxes, complete with our essential tools: rolling pins, shape cutters, smoothers. As my first anniversary of being a mum approached, I dug out these instructions from the recesses of my mind. I revived the skills that had remained dormant, waiting for that point at which I myself would be a mother and, like my mother and grandmother before me, could bake to show my love.

So my first foray into this particular demonstration of mother-love was to create a huge blue cake topped with figures from my son's favourite TV show – the BBC's *In The Night Garden*. Over the course of a week, I crafted a Makka Pakka, an Upsy Daisy and an Igglepiggle out of fondant icing. I looked at my creations and saw that they were good.

These cakes showed that I was the kind of mother who slaved away in the kitchen for hours to give my little one these perfect gifts. My pride grew even further when friends and strangers complimented me on my cake skills – in real life at parties, and online as I unashamedly shared pictures on social media of my creations. People called me a supermum; other mums said how I was putting them to shame for their shop-bought celebration cakes. I felt like a Mother Superior.

But maybe motherly liberation looks like this: maybe sometimes, it's better *not* to make the cake.

In the autumn of 2023, I faced one of the busiest work periods of my life. The days preceding my elder son's sixth birthday were among the most packed. I had a trip to Washington, DC to speak at a conference, leaving my husband solo parenting while working full time. In the months leading up to the trip, I had been racked with guilt, knowing that crossing an ocean and leaving their family for several days and nights was just not something that good mothers would do. As the trip drew closer, I juggled work with party-planning for my son's birthday – sending invitations, booking a venue, ordering party-bag fillers. I still intended to do my usual ritual of baking a cake, despite having just twenty-four hours back at home before my son's big day. But when I looked at the number of hours I would have available to bake the cake, pick up the children from school and nursery, and eat and sleep, the maths just were not adding up. I was going to have to forfeit sleep to make this cake happen. But at 4 a.m. a few days after my arrival in Washington, DC, jet-lagged and anxious, I heard a still, small voice: *sometimes you don't have to make the cake.*

And with that thought, I decided on a plan of compromise. From my hotel room, I searched online for a cake-maker four thousand miles away back home, who could – with a two-day turnaround time – bake and cover a cake, so that all I had to do was pick it up and decorate it. We were going for a climbing-wall cake that year, to accompany my son's climbing-themed party. A few hours after landing back at Heathrow, I picked up the covered cake from the local baker's house, before spending a couple of hours putting the finishing touches to it myself. It wasn't my best work, but the world did not end. No one reported me to the Good Mother police. All that had happened was that I had loosened myself from the grip of wanting to appear a perfect mother. I get a buzz when people call me Supermum, or say, 'I just don't know how you do it all.' If I'm honest, there was a part of me that wanted people to say, 'Wow, you spoke at a conference in the US capital and then got back and looked after your kids and even stayed up all night, jet-lagged, to create a cake masterpiece? You are the best mother there ever was.' Aside from the Madonna, of course. Perhaps I felt this praise from others might assuage my mum-guilt for going away in the first place. But perhaps I too would be falling into the trap of pretending the juggle is easy, and of giving a false impression to those yet to have children, perpetuating the circle of expectation-versus-wide-eyed-reality that causes so much pain to new mothers. What I learnt from this was that sometimes, we have to let go of the myth of perfection, and call for back-up.

It takes a church

There is an opportunity here for the Church to be the back-up; to be what it's called to be. The Church can help to shatter the myth of perfect motherhood that harms women. A Barna study of Christian mothers in the post-pandemic USA found that both working and non-working mothers are roughly two times more likely than working women without children to say they feel nervous, anxious or on edge nearly every day. Commenting on these findings, Dr Heather Thompson Day wrote:

> I expect there are great spiritual, emotional, social *and* tangible needs churches might help women address . . . Support groups and spaces where women can be honest with others and themselves, whether online or in-person, have never been more valuable. Just as churches celebrate the mothers in their pews on Mother's Day, leaders should take time to ensure the programs their churches offer remember, support and empower mothers – not just once or twice a year, but year-round.[41]

If mothers are indeed responsible for their children's salvation, then the future of the Church depends on supporting them in any way we can.

We were never meant to hold it all together. Not by ourselves. We were meant to do mothering within the tender arms of community. In the days following the births of each of my children, we were held together by our church community. Each afternoon for two weeks, a different member of the church would visit us at home. These fellow church members were of course nearly all women, and we would sit and have a cup of tea together. They would ask the usual questions: about the birth and how the baby was sleeping. They would hold the tiny baby bundles and stroke their heads. They would sit down and simply provide a comfort, a presence and a listening ear. Sometimes there was silence heavy enough to hold the weight of the mental load – to provide space for the unburdening, in the prayers that passed between us, words unsaid.

They say it takes a village to raise a child. Anglo-American society could learn from other cultures around the world whose postpartum rituals and customs rely on family and community to nurture the newborn and prioritise the mother's well-being. In much of Latin America, *la cuarentena* involves forty days of rest with her family for the mother. In Japan, *Satogaeri bunben* sees the new mother move back to her family home to recuperate. And in my own ethnic group – the Igbo of south-eastern Nigeria – mothers benefit from the practice of *Ọmụgwọ*, which sees their own mother or another close relative move in for a few weeks to assist them in looking after their newborn and making sure they get plenty of rest.

Sometimes the village is a church. As more and more people live away from their families, the role of the local church in supporting parents has never been more needed. Aside from the meal trains in those hazy post-birth days, my church family have babysat my children and have taken them away for a precious few hours so Mark and I could sit somewhere and have a meal in peace. Up and down the UK are church halls that welcome bleary-eyed mothers and their toddlers in for play sessions, giving them space to exhale with a warm cup of tea and a biscuit, and a chance to speak honestly, if they would like, with other mothers like them. When my friend Claire, a solo mother of two, had her second child, the women of our church rallied around. A number of us, including her birthing partner, joined a rota to provide round-the-clock support for her, after a difficult and traumatic birth. It was in the darkness, as I held Claire's one-day-old daughter while staying overnight so Claire could try and sleep, that I knew this was what it meant to be the village. I recall those early days in which the women from our church and from Claire's local community would arrive, quietly handing over the baton of loving care as we slipped in and out of her house, filled with the hush of newborn stillness. 'I felt a really overwhelming sense of love. It was so powerful, so amazing,' Claire tells me. 'Because this was my second child, a lot of the women involved were also those who had had children. Whether they had given birth or adopted, it was women who knew what it was to raise little ones; and so there was a gravitas to the care because of the expertise shared. The quiet sense of loving care. That felt like motherhood. It felt like this was mothering together; that this was family love.'

PART FOUR

Death

Chapter 7

The Black Madonna

'The white fathers told us: I think, therefore I am. The
Black mother within each of us – the poet – whispers
in our dreams: I feel, therefore I can be free.'

—Audre Lorde[1]

As we pull into the station at Orléans, I feel an unsettling sense of
trepidation. I am here to meet Notre Dame des Miracles, *la Vierge
noire* – or the Black Madonna – who is believed to have protected
the ancient French town from much calamity over the centuries. I
have come with a producer to do some recording for our BBC radio
documentary on these mysterious Black Madonnas. Legend has it
that this particular statue's greatest miracle was helping Joan of Arc
defeat the English occupiers. In 1428, during the Hundred Years'
War between France and England, the English laid siege to Orléans.
The people of the north-central French town had long prayed for
Our Lady to grant them victory, and in 1429, Joan of Arc broke
through the lines of the English troops. For a week afterwards, she
stayed in a house with a private passageway to the chapel of the
Madonna – Notre Dame des Miracles – to pray at her feet. In the
battle that followed that week, Joan was victorious, and the English
were defeated.

As I step into the chapel, my eyes are immediately drawn to the
dark figure, bathed in light and raised up – standing at the highest
point in this stunning church building. Our Lady of Miracles takes
my breath away. Her dark body is dressed in a stunning white cloak,
sparkling under the lights that illuminate her, and nothing else. Her
baby – the Christ child – is dark, too. He is tiny in comparison with

his mother, but also wearing the same material, in the form of a christening cloak. Standing in this chapel, one cannot be mistaken about who is in charge here; who it is that has brought deliverance and miracles, and answered desperate prayers for centuries. Before we entered the chapel in which this Black Madonna holds court, we were stopped in our tracks by the beautifully coloured mosaics above the grand archways. They feature Joan of Arc in prayer to the Virgin. As we approach her, we see many more arches, with smaller mosaics – each dedicated to a different litany of Mary. The whole church is covered in panels engraved with people's messages of gratitude to the Black Madonna – *merci* for keeping us safe, *merci* for helping me to have a baby, *merci pour toujours*; it was a wallpaper of answered prayer.

We are in the chapel for less than an hour, and I am struck by the stillness of it; the quiet. This is not a busy tourist church, but a place of reverence – an oasis in a town of people going about their business on a Tuesday morning. But every few minutes, the door creaks open and another person steps into the chapel. They wend their way through the pews and make a beeline for the Madonna. On our way from the train station to the chapel – as we walked through ancient cobbled streets – I had not noticed anyone who wasn't white. Yet in this space, we watch as it is Black women who come to pray before Our Lady. I observe from a distance as some of them stand at her feet, hands clasped, reciting prayers. Some kneel in front of her. One woman takes off her sandals on this holy ground. One woman prostrates herself, her face pressed to the floor. It is extraordinary. Father Benoit, the priest at the church, tells us that Black women are drawn here rather than to any of the other four big churches in Orléans, including the magnificent cathedral, because of Notre Dame de Miracles. Perhaps they are in need of a miracle themselves and they know that for centuries others have given her thanks for theirs. Maybe they feel drawn to her because the Blessed Virgin is a woman who understands what it is to be a woman in a broken world. But perhaps more than that it is the Black Madonna's blackness, along with her womanhood, that makes them feel safe in her presence.

No one quite knows what a Black Madonna is. The term is given to all images, statues and paintings in which Mary and Jesus are depicted with dark skin. Many of them are thought to be associated with verse 5 in Song of Solomon 1: 'Dark am I, yet lovely'.[2] There are disputes among academics about whether they are actually Black – as in deliberately designed to depict a woman of colour – or whether this blackness is symbolic of some other idea that has nothing to do with race; or indeed whether the blackness of the images and sculptures has any significance at all. Leonard W. Moss and Stephen C. Cappannari, in a 1953 paper entitled 'The Black Madonna: An Example of Culture Borrowing', said Black Madonnas broadly fall into three categories: first, those that reflect the colour of the indigenous populations of the worshippers; second, those that are simply images that have aged and become darker over time; and third, those about which there is no explanation.[3]

The speculation and disputes over their origins and meanings only add to their mystique. Whatever they are, there are thought to be at least 450 of them in the world, with the majority found in Europe, and others in various places around the world, including in South America.

The meaning of their 'blackness' varies depending on where in the world they are found, and how they are perceived in the minds of the beholder. Wherever they are found the world over, Black Madonnas are 'focal points for pilgrimages, are regarded as miracle workers, and are among the most highly venerated of all Christian religious symbols, indicating that the blackness of these miraculous Madonnas still evokes profound and meaningful images and associations for devotees'.[4]

Whoever she is, it is clear that the Black Madonna draws people towards her. She has long been a popular figure in feminist and goddess spiritualities, and increasingly so as the decades-long rise in new religious movements has accompanied a decline in traditional religious affiliation, with more people describing themselves as non-religious. Within this category are those who might be termed 'spiritual but not religious'. Melanie Landman notes how the Black Madonna is seen as much more alternative than the traditional white imagery of Mary, with articles on her being found 'alongside article[s] on subject matters such as ESP, the Loch Ness Monster and Tarot cards' which 'position the black Madonna outside of mainstream Christianity'.[5] Much of what is said about the appeal of Black

Madonnas could also be said of the appeal of the Virgin Mary to her devotees: she is a representation of feminine divinity, a maternal figure who sings of liberation and gives voice to the voiceless, and who, in the Catholic tradition, acts as a mediator between humanity and God. Each of these roles fills a hole in the dominant perceived characterisation of who God is. But the Black Madonna also provides an alternative image to the dominant portrayal of perfect motherhood, which suggests that perfect motherhood is white. Women of colour are especially drawn to the Black Madonna because of this.

In *la Vierge noire*, Black women see themselves. But perhaps this is not just because of their literal blackness, it is also because of the fantastical stories that surround these Black Madonnas. *La Negre*, the Black Madonna of Montpellier, is believed to have saved the city from drought and plague. *Notre-Dame de Rocamadour* is thought to be able to resuscitate babies, promote fertility, free captives, and keep sailors from disaster. Wherever they are found, these Black Madonnas are thought to be in solidarity with those who are oppressed. Some of the greatest Black female activists have found themselves at the Black Madonna's feet. The late bell hooks spoke about the freedom she found in the Black Madonna, saying: 'Unfortunately, African Americans have not been interested in reclaiming representations of Black Madonnas . . . And this is a sensitive point, because most constructions of Black femaleness are tied to representations that are hateful and ugly, so the idea of an icon that can stand in resistance becomes further and further away.'[6]

When a Black woman in the West becomes a mother, she brings into her experience all the negative perceptions about her Black womanhood that she has heard all her life. The stereotypical beautiful woman in western art and culture has long been white. There are of course exceptions – global superstars such as Beyoncé and Halle Berry have been described as the most beautiful women in the world – but more often than not it is only light-skinned Black women who have broken through the veiled racism of beauty standards. Black Madonnas are 'unapologetically Black', as Dr Christena Cleveland describes them.[7]

Our nice white lady

It's not clear at what point Mary became white. There is a lot of discussion about the depictions of God and Jesus as white European males that have long existed in art history. But there is little about everyone else in the Bible, hardly any of whom were Europeans, including Mary. Just like Jesus, Mary was a Jewish woman from the Middle East – from Roman-occupied Palestine. It is unlikely she would have borne any resemblance to the porcelain-skinned Madonnas we see adorning churches and galleries across the globe.

There has been a centuries-long divide between the experiences of white women and those of women of colour. When it could still be said that Black women are the most disrespected, the most unprotected and the most neglected group, as civil rights leader Malcolm X once argued,[8] it is understandable that Black women might long for a sense of divine solidarity. While Mary's womanhood and motherhood resonate to an extent with Black women, it might be difficult for a woman of colour to feel truly safe with a representation of white womanhood that for centuries has been prized as the ideal. Not only that, the roles that white women played in the subjugation of Black men and women – whether during the Transatlantic slave trade or during colonialism more widely – might understandably put up a barrier between Black women and the mother of God – if, that is, she is represented as a white woman.

A while back, I took part in an event exploring women, slavery and the Church of England. My fellow speakers included American historian Stephanie E. Jones-Rogers, who shared stark and heartbreaking facts about the role of white women in chattel slavery. For the most part, I had assumed up until then that men were the chief orchestrators of this barbaric trade. Clearly succumbing to my conditioning about white womanhood, my assumption was that the women within slave-holding families were on the whole reluctant bystanders, themselves oppressed because of their lower status in comparison with their husbands and male relatives. But when I heard what Professor Jones-Rogers has uncovered through her painstaking exploration of first-hand slave narratives, I was shocked. What she reveals is that, rather than being shielded from the slave trade, wives and mothers often played an active part in it, including some of the most brutal aspects. As she outlines in her book *They Were Her Property: White Women as Slave Owners in the American South*, white women benefited from the institution of slavery and also enabled it to thrive. They were actively involved in the purchase of enslaved people,[9] sometimes buying slaves for their young children. They were also actively involved in making decisions about what the enslaved people did, and how they were punished. As enslaved women and girls kept on getting pregnant, the white women turned a blind eye to the brutal sexual violence meted out by their husbands. For these women, enslaved people were simply property. More enslaved people born meant more property, and more money to buy nice things. As Africana studies professor Eric Kyere states: 'The birth of a baby born into slavery meant profits that potentially lasted generations, a product requiring little investment.'[10]

Just as slave-holding men perpetrated violence against enslaved people, so too did slave-holding women. Sometimes the horrific cruelty was carried out against enslaved children. Jones-Rogers tells the story of eight-year-old Henrietta King, who was accused of stealing sweets. As punishment, her mistress made her put her head under a rocking chair, and then rocked back and forth on it, while her young daughter whipped Henrietta's body. Her face was mutilated. Scarred for life. Unable ever again to eat solid food.[11] Here for me is where the myth of perfect white motherhood is shattered – in seeing past the veil of purity and piety to the dark heart of a slave-owning mother's soul.

It is understandable that Black women – who live with the generational trauma of slavery – might feel uncomfortable bowing at the feet of a nice white Mary who resembles a slave-holding mistress.

Unmaking Mary requires us to separate the mother of God from her falsely constructed whiteness, and what it might represent. Just as Christena Cleveland's 'whitemalegod' describes not just the fact of whiteness and maleness, but also what those things symbolise, so white womanhood and its place in the collective consciousness of much of the globe is problematic because of what it symbolises: power, an unquestioning goodness and purity, an eternal supremacy. The words of the Magnificat resonate with a Black Madonna who takes her place among the oppressed, rather than prioritising the retention of her own power, prestige, privilege and status. This is why she has drawn people from marginalised communities towards her, including, but not limited to, Black women. In this way, the Black Madonna's arms are open to anyone who finds themselves powerless and voiceless.

To me, it is a shame that it is because of how God has come to be represented – as omnipotent, as male, and as white – that some feel they need the Black Madonna, or even a Blessed Virgin Mary at all, to find a place of welcome and solidarity, as they feel unable to discover those things in God.

Our Lady of the misfits

The thing about Black Madonnas is that they do not conform. They are surprising, intriguing, because they do not fit with the dominant image that we have of Mary in our heads – the Mary that has been constructed out of white, patriarchal Christianity and culture. Black Madonnas' non-conformity makes them also a useful lens through which to look at ways of mothering that do not fit the archetype either: adoptive mothers, single mothers, older mothers, LGBTQ+ mothers. When I think about the variety of mothers that are in my life, there are few of them – I would say perhaps none of them – that fit into the maternal stereotype of the white Blessed Virgin. For every mother I know, there is an element of struggle. For some, the struggle is due to a lack of material wealth, or of a partner who can in some way share the burden. The struggle may be about health or fertility, or about mental health issues within the family. Or they may worry about the unsafe environments in which they are having to raise their children. It is among these broken fragments of the strug-gle of mothers that the Black Madonna opens her arms and welcomes in the tired, the sad, the oppressed, the subjugated. For me, the Black Madonna's power is in her literal blackness, but also in her associa-tion with the wretched mothers of the earth. Just as James Cone writes that Christ's salvation is 'a story about God's presence in Jesus's solidarity with the oppressed',[12] so the Black Madonna represents the divine preference for those whose lives are not picture-perfect.

In the sixteenth century, Our Lady of Guadalupe is believed to have 'visited the marginalized and oppressed native people of Mexico, as one who was compassionately aware of their vulnerability';[13] and as theologian Jeanette Rodriguez writes, she 'embraces [and reclaims] that which the world has rejected. Guadalupe . . . offers God's loving embrace, not just for Mexicans and Mexican-Americans alone, but for [all] rejected people of the Americas.'[14] The alabaster-skinned mother who has it all together has no need for salvation, and does not have the incarnational understanding of what it is to be oppressed. So the Black Mother represents not just literal blackness, but also metaphorical oppression. God's presence symbolised in the Black mother, then, is a strategic one. If the least of us is free, then all of us are free. Christena Cleveland puts it like this:

> Social science scholars agree that what's good for Black women is good for *all* people. The liberation of all Black women requires the dismantling of all systems of oppression – white supremacy, patriarchy, capitalism, Islamophobia, homophobia, transphobia, and more. These systems harm all of us. So, if Black women are thriving and free, it also means the oppressive systems have been eradicated and we are all thriving and free.[15]

The oppressed themselves have more insight into this profound truth than those with power. Viewed through a white, patriarchal lens, the Black Madonna makes little sense. How can power arise from the powerless? In 1552, Archbishop John Hamilton wrote about the Black Madonnas in Europe: 'These statues darkened into something not far from idolatry . . . when . . . one image of the Virgin (generally a black or ugly one) was regarded . . . as more powerful for the help of supplicants.'[16] For this sixteenth-century archbishop, there would be little understanding about why poor Black women in Orléans in 2024 would choose to prostrate themselves before an 'ugly' Black representation of the divine when there are grand statues of the 'whitemalegod' in nearby cathedrals.

When I stand in front of a Black Madonna, I connect with experiences that have been integral to Black motherhood: feelings of solidarity, care, safety and a fierce protectiveness. Black motherhood, however, is a concept within Black communities that is not confined to people who have given birth. The mothering of Black women extends to the mothering that is done by all women: friends, sisters, aunties, mothers, grandmothers. This idea is central to womanism – a feminist intellectual framework championed by Black feminists that places anti-racism at its heart. The term 'womanist' originates from Alice Walker's 1983 essay collection *In Search of Our Mothers' Gardens: Womanist Prose*. Delores Williams describes the nature and role of mothering within this framework: 'For the womanist, mothering and nurturing are vitally important. Walker's womanist reality begins with mothers relating to their children and is characterized by Black women (not necessarily bearers of children) nurturing great numbers of black people in the liberation struggle' (for example, the American abolitionist and social activist Harriet Tubman).[17]

Here for me is one of the most powerful things about the Black Madonna: her alignment with all people, all who are marginalised, whether they are mothers or not; and in this, she challenges the perfect and restrictive ideal of motherhood that is presented to us in the myth of Mary. The Reverend Rachel Mann, a Church of England priest, writes:

In a world with few female role models, Mary runs the risk of setting women up to fail: insofar as she has been used to convince women that their holiest identity is to be mothers, she also shows how far short actual women fall of 'ideal' motherhood. Certainly, for very many women who cannot bear children, including me, the way in which Mary the mother is held as an icon for women has felt oppressive. I feel as if Mary's humanity has often been eroded away. So many statues and paintings of her are sentimentalized. She is presented as a middle-class simpering White woman dressed in pristine blue robes.[18]

For the Reverend Canon Kate Wharton, who does not have children, Mary is not an oppressive figure, but someone to look up to as an example of obedience to God. In November 2017, Kate held a ceremony at Liverpool Cathedral in which – in front of a hundred of her friends – she made a vow to God to remain single for the rest of her life. In this brave act, like the symbolism of *la Vierge noire*, she chose not to conform to the societal ideals placed on women, and often exacerbated within church contexts. For her, singleness was not a barrier to caring for young children and families that were not her own. For the past nine years, Kate has volunteered with a Christian charity[19] to provide regular support for children from families in need. 'I love children, particularly little ones,' she tells me, 'and had always hoped to have my own – and indeed had always thought perhaps one day I would foster or adopt. This is a wonderful way to be involved with the lives of families and little ones. It's church being church.' She wants to encourage this sense of church being church among her congregation, and does so through speaking regularly about her volunteering, and also by bringing children and families she volunteers with to church services or events. Through the process of caring for young children, Kate has gained an insight into how challenging parenting is, and an appreciation of the importance of having a 'village' around you to help look after your children.

I asked Kate for her thoughts on this womanist understanding of motherhood as something that non-mothers can do too, but she was not so sure about this. 'I have an interesting relationship with the word "mother",' she said. She confessed to finding Mothers' Day challenging, because of how poorly it is handled both within the Church and outside it. 'Even when people attempt to be considerate of those who might wish to be mothers but aren't, or have lost their children, they still often say things like "but at least we all have a lovely mum" – and that just simply isn't true! I've often spoken in church of "mothering" qualities, and of how we can honour those who "mother" us in various ways. I think I prefer to see myself as an aunty, and it is my greatest joy to have that title and role to lots of people. I'm just a bit cautious about using the word "mothering" for myself, for all sorts of reasons.'

The Mammy myth

In April 2024, just over six months before the US presidential elections, and before replacing President Joe Biden as the Democratic nominee, Vice President Kamala Harris was interviewed on actress Drew Barrymore's daytime TV show. During the show, Harris revealed some insight into her experience of being a stepmother to her husband Doug Emhoff's two children, Cole and Ella. She admitted, however, that because she did not like the negative associations of the word 'stepmother' – thanks to Disney characterisations of evil women who attempt to ruin the lives of their husbands' children – Cole and Ella refer to her as 'Momala'. What followed was a strange response from Barrymore that drew much media attention and conversation about the characterisation of Black motherhood in American culture, especially among white women.

Against a background of economic uncertainty, climate anxiety, the Russian invasion of Ukraine, brutal conflict in Israel and Gaza and rising political unrest, Barrymore said: 'I keep thinking in my head that we all need a mom.' With a quivering voice and an earnest expression, she went on: 'I've been really thinking we really all need a tremendous hug in the world now, but in our country we need you to be "Momala" of the country.' The audience, which I can only assume was not packed with Black women, broke into applause. Harris looked visibly uncomfortable as Barrymore then took her hand, pleadingly, saying: 'We need a great protector.'[20]

Who knows what was going through the vice president's mind as she attempted to respond to the bizarre scene. But for many who understand the 500-year history of misogynoir[21] and strained relationships between white women and Black women, the scene felt all too familiar. Black motherhood is sometimes expected to hold the weight of the world, to be responsible not just for one's own physical children but for others' children too, as well as to be a comfort and support to all white people who need them. This is best characterised in the symbol of the 'Mammy' figure. We will all recognise her. She is often depicted as a curvy Black woman, usually middle-aged, wearing an apron and speaking with a southern drawl. She is employed by a white family. She is there for the children's every

physical and emotional need. She is there for the parents' every physical and emotional need. She is fiercely loyal and has no thoughts for
her own welfare. She is utterly devoted to the white family's service,
and there to make everyone else feel better. In those ways, she is not
unlike the traditional stereotype of the Victorian Angel in the House
– the selfless mother. But this Mammy is not the great protector of
her own family. She is a martyr who lays down her life for white
families. As Melissa Harris-Perry writes: 'Mammy was not a protector or defender of black children or communities. She represented a
maternal ideal, but not in caring for her own children.'[22]

Black mothers do not have to have given birth to be pigeonholed
into the Mammy stereotype, and as Carolyn M. West notes, 'professional status and education cannot protect Black women from the
Mammy image'.[23] The 'Momala' incident on Drew Barrymore's
show was reminiscent of a similar happening more than twenty-five
years before. In 1998, John Gray, author of *Men Are from Mars, Women
Are from Venus*, was a guest on Oprah Winfrey's hit show and took
relationship questions from the audience. West recalled what
happened next:

> In response to an audience member's distress, he instructed Ms.
> Winfrey, one of the world's most powerful women in the televi-
> sion industry, to give the woman a hug. He went on to say,
> 'Oprah's going to be your mommy . . . She's the mother of
> America. That's why she didn't have time for her own kids. She's
> taking care of all the other lost children'.[24]

Examples of this racist stereotype in films and literature include Aunt
Chloe in Harriet Beecher Stowe's *Uncle Tom's Cabin* (1852) and
Hattie McDaniel's character in *Gone with the Wind*, who is literally
named 'Mammy', the ever-present help to Scarlett O'Hara. In 1940,
McDaniel won an Academy Award for her performance, as best
supporting actress. But critics within the Black community felt
uncomfortable about the glorification of the depiction of Black
women's service to white women. In *Gone with the Wind*, there is no
mention of Mammy's own children, whether they are dead or alive.
I am struck by the irony that six years after receiving this accolade,

McDaniel sank into a deep depression after initially being excited about what turned out to be a false pregnancy. She would never be a mother to children of her own.

What is particularly fascinating to note about the Mammy figure is that she never actually existed. She is a figment of white imagination. According to researchers, you would have been very unlikely to find older, curvy, dark-skinned enslaved women as house slaves, who were much more likely to be light-skinned teenage girls. Enslaved people lived in such brutal conditions that they were very unlikely ever to reach middle age, nor could they have been fat; and white families clearly preferred to have light-skinned enslaved women in their homes rather than what they perceived as 'ugly' dark-skinned women. Psychologist Chanequa Walker-Barnes suggests that 'Mammy was a largely mythical figure with little basis in the lived experiences of black women'.[25] Sound familiar? Just like the myth of perfect motherhood we see in the depictions of Mary, the Mammy too is a falsehood that bears little resemblance to real Black womanhood or motherhood. The myth led artist Andy Warhol to include a pop-art image of a Mammy in his 1981 'Myths' series, alongside characters such as Mickey Mouse, Father Christmas and Superman. The series invited viewers to 'reconsider the ways in which these figures shape our collective imagination and cultural identity'.[26]

Myths serve a purpose. The Mammy myth was devised by those who were in favour of slavery as a way to combat arguments by abolitionists about the brutality of chattel slavery and the need for its end. Its aim was to airbrush the cruelty and inhumane conditions enslaved people existed in, and make out that they were much loved by their 'families', and well looked after. The Mammy became even more prominent in the southern states of America during the Reconstruction era. Her purpose was to sanitise the legacy of slavery and racial injustice. In 1923, the United Daughters of the Confederacy even attempted (ultimately unsuccessfully owing to widespread outrage and resistance) to have a statue of a Mammy erected on the National Mall in Washington, DC.

I wonder for whom the Black Mammy statue – if she had ever been erected – would have been a destination for pilgrimage.

Who would have prostrated themselves at her feet and seen in her a place of refuge, strength and liberation? Drew Barrymore might have visited her at times of existential crisis to make herself feel better about the world. But for many Black women, this Mammy would have been a reminder of their subjugation, unlike the powerful, inclusive freedom-fighter that so many see in the Black Madonna.

Hypervigilance and Black motherhood

To be a Black mother is to exist in a state of hypervigilance because you have given birth to children who exist in Black bodies. The bodies of Black girls have been sexualised, oppressed and subjugated for centuries. The bodies of Black boys have been brutalised, violated and beaten for centuries. Our vigilance is necessary. The Black Madonna draws Black women to her because she is the ultimate symbol of Black motherhood; and because Mary is the ultimate symbol of a grieving mother who knows what it is like to bring a son into the world, a son who bears the scars of the world's brutality on his own body. It is Mary's proximity to suffering that has helped many oppressed groups find safety in her arms and at her feet.

It was this nearness to pain as seen in Mary's presence at the foot of the cross that led to Pulitzer-Prize-winning author Toni Morrison's conversion to Catholicism at the age of twelve. She was drawn to Catholicism because of its similarity to the magical and folkloric traditions of African American spirituality. But she was also drawn to it because of Mary. It was the Catholic veneration of Mary, 'a mother who gave birth, saw her son suffer, could not protect him, and was destined to watch as he was nailed to the cross', that caused Morrison to leave the African Methodist Episcopal (AME) Church she was born into. For her, Jennifer Banks writes: 'Catholicism stayed close to the bleeding body, the gruesome crucifixion. A son's tortured body presides over Catholic worship, reminding believers that Jesus's bodily suffering opened up eternity for all of God's children.' She adds:

The Madonna – her grief, her body, her child – was . . . iconic . . .
Later she'd say that Black women 'have held, have been given . . .
the cross. They don't walk near it. They're often on it. And they've
borne that, I think, extremely well.'[27]

As I look up at the Black Madonna in that chapel in Orléans, I am
struck with a profound sense of irony. Outside the doors, Black
women – many of whom work for and serve white people – are the
'mule of the world', as writer Zora Neale Hurston describes them.
Yet here, the Black mother is the centre of it all, and in being so,
invites Black women into a place where they are seen as those made
in the image of God, and therefore absolutely worthy of dignity and
respect and value. I watch as her crown twinkles under the light.
This is the Queen of Heaven, not the 'mule of the world'. She is the
Mary of the Byzantine era – crowned and bejewelled – but this time,
she's Black.

Miracle-working motherhood

Around the sanctuary that houses *Notre-Dame de Bonne Délivrance*,
also known as the Black Madonna of Paris, in a suburb of the French
capital, is panelling made up of tiles inscribed with messages of
thanksgiving, just as in the church in Orléans. These ex-votos give
glory to *la Vierge noire* for the miracles they attribute to her kindness.
I'm struck by how many of these little – and big – miracles show
gratitude for new life. Dating back centuries, the messages adorning
the walls give thanks for conception and safe delivery. Some of the
tiles name the children, whose existence the parents attribute to the
love of this mysterious Black Madonna.

Finnish theologian Elina Vuola describes being taken to *La Negrita*
– another Black Madonna, affectionately described by locals as 'the
little Black one' – when she was trying to conceive while living in
Costa Rica. Vuola's neighbour, an elderly Catholic woman, guessed
that she was not yet a mother despite wanting to be, and invited her
to go with her to the basilica of the *Virgen de los Ángeles*, the patron-
ess of Costa Rica, who was known for her miracles. The neighbour

suggested that they take with them a metal ex-voto in the shape of a baby. Vuola writes: 'My neighbour was convinced that only the Virgin Mary could help me – she was the one who both understands women's sorrows and has the power to intervene.'[28] Just as the blessing in the Churching of Women found in the Book of Common Prayer recognises the heartache, pain and horror of giving birth, so devotees of the Black Madonna believe she recognises what it is to go through this life-altering and dangerous rite of passage. As a mother, and as a Black mother, she knows what it is like for her body to be violated. The perfect, serene archetype of motherhood represented in the white Virgin Mary feels so alien from the experience of many Black mothers. Fear and suspicion of medical institutions today are rooted in a legacy that has traditionally harmed Black women, rather than healed them.

J. Marion Sims – dubbed the 'father of gynaecology' – is one of the most well-known perpetrators of experimentation on Black women's bodies for medical advancement. During the 1840s, he performed brutal surgery on enslaved women without anaesthesia, without their consent and without any form of pain relief. Today there is a striking monument that stands in Montgomery, Alabama – not far from where Sims carried out his procedures – which pays homage to three of the many enslaved women – most of whom were unnamed – who found themselves violated by his medical practice. Created by Black artist and activist Michelle Browder, who was named *USA Today*'s Woman of the Year in 2022, the sculpture entitled *Mothers of Gynecology* includes large statues of Betsey, Anarcha and Lucy. The womb space of Anarcha – who stands at fifteen feet tall – is empty, save for a single red rose where her uterus would have been. Inside her sit cut glass, scissors, sharp, painful objects and medical utensils. Another of the statues wears a tiara made from a speculum – a terrifying instrument for any woman who has been examined using one.

Browder told the *Washington Post* that she had created the figures out of recycled metal objects because these enslaved women were discarded. 'Never again will anyone look down on these women,' she said.[29]

Right from the moment they conceive, Black mothers face

significant disparities compared with white women, which continue through their pregnancy and through the birthing process too. In both the UK and the USA, they are much more likely to die from pregnancy-related complications than white women. They are more likely to experience life-threatening conditions like pre-eclampsia, blood clots and postpartum haemorrhage, as well as pregnancy-related complications such as pre-term birth and low birth weight.[30] Black women are also more likely to face poor maternal health outcomes during pregnancy and birth.

The burden of issues Black mothers face is exacerbated by the stereotyping, unconscious bias and racism they experience within the healthcare system. Sandra Igwe, founder of The Motherhood Group, which explores Black maternal health, said many Black women feel 'unseen, unheard and misunderstood' by medical professionals. 'Black women also disproportionately experience stressors like the weight of systemic racism. All of this compounds the already overwhelming transition to motherhood.'[31]

I am still mentally recovering from my own horrific experience of giving birth the first time round. I felt violated, brutalised. That no one was listening to me. I felt that I didn't have a voice, as if I didn't exist. A study of birth trauma released in May 2024[32] showed that one of the things that make giving birth in the UK so difficult for all women – and especially Black women – was the feeling that their concerns were not being listened to. For many women, the labour ward is a profoundly unloving place; it's a place that does not live up to the sepia-tinged images of giving birth to our children we have come to believe are the norm. It's time we put an end to this culture. But we cannot change it without holding it up to the light. Sharing our stories of the reality compared with the expectation is a step in that direction.

A barrel of ashes

American author and researcher Christena Cleveland has devoted her life to exploring Black female spirituality through the history, identity and place of Black Madonnas in France. She now spends several months a year in Europe, wandering, reading, sitting, and discovering these mysterious figures and what they mean for Black women's sense of value and self. In a basement in a bougie hotel in Paris where she is about to lead a pilgrimage of mainly American Black women, we sit over a coffee and talk about what she has learnt, the stories she has heard about these statues and images, and how she has changed.

Cleveland's book *God Is a Black Woman* detailed her first encounters with Black Madonnas on a pilgrimage as she moved away from the world of white American evangelicalism, where she had been a prominent thinker and speaker. As was to be expected, some took offence at her suggestion that God was a Black woman, describing it as blasphemous. I ask why it is important for her, why it matters. 'God may not be a Black woman ontologically,' she says, 'but I like to believe it because I think it makes me a kinder, more hopeful, more courageous person.'

As we speak I confess I get confused by who exactly the Black Madonna is supposed to be in the minds of devotees. Is she supposed to represent God, a generic understanding of divine femininity, an ancient pagan goddess, or Mary? For Catholics she is the latter, but understood in a way that transcends the earthly existence of the woman from first-century Palestine. For Cleveland, perhaps she is all of the above. But the key is that the Black Madonna understands in a visceral sense what it is to be an oppressed woman, what it means to be a Black woman.

Cleveland tells me the myths, legends and fantastical stories that surround some of these Madonnas. Like that of the abbess who got pregnant during the Spanish Inquisition, and prayed to the Black Madonna for help. The Black Madonna then helped the abbess deliver her baby safely, and took the baby to a family who would love and look after it, before returning to sew the abbess back up so that when she was examined by those who sought to kill her because of her sin, they would find her to be a virgin. I have found various versions of this story, but what they speak of, according to Cleveland, is that the Black Madonna has to find ways to 'work around the system', and that she is someone who understands. 'This is someone who knows what it's like to be examined when you're pregnant,'

Cleveland tells me. We can infer from the biblical accounts that Jesus' mother would have been examined too, when she got pregnant out of wedlock, and insisted it was a miracle. In the *Protoevangelium Jacobi* – the Gospel of James – which presents a non-canonical infancy narrative of Jesus, the midwife Salome attempts to examine Mary because she does not believe that Jesus was miraculously conceived. In the story, Salome's hand withers because of her lack of faith. Many women who have experienced a sense of violation during the birthing process as their bodies are poked and prodded will find solidarity in both the abbess's story and Mary's. 'This [the Black Madonna] is someone who knows what it's like for your body to be policed. Mary, as Jesus's mother, knows what it's like to have a child who's a victim of state-sanctioned violence. For her, this is not a TED talk, or a theoretical idea. This is her life. The fact that the Black Madonna can say "I relate to the estranged mother, I relate to the estranged child. I get you" – that's to me what's so unique about her.'

Another story Cleveland tells me leaves me speechless. On a visit to France a few months before, she had made a special trip to Clermont-Ferrand in the Auvergne-Rhône-Alpes region of central France. She was there, along with her Airbnb host, to see the *Vierge noire* in the church of St Julien. This Black Madonna – a striking twelfth-century Romanesque figure – had been targeted, like many other Black Madonnas, during the French Revolution. But legend has it that the villagers protected her by placing her in a barrel of ashes. She was found in that barrel, surrounded by those ashes, many years later – but her Christ-child was missing. Her baby had been taken away. Those who discovered her assumed he had been burned up, so created a replacement Christ to sit on the lap of the striking Black Madonna.

I'm reminded here of words from Jennifer Banks in *Natality* about what it was to be an enslaved woman during the barbaric chattel trade. 'A slave is someone who has lost her mother,' she writes. 'A slave is a person whose child will likely be taken from her, transferred to a different lineage upon birth. That child's children will in turn be taken from her. They, too, will lose their mother and their children will likewise be stolen from them. Slave mothers can grieve the loss of their children, but they cannot protect them.'[33]

But sometimes redemptive miracles do happen. In 2021, the Christ-child of the Virgin in Majesty of Melliers was discovered in a private home – more than two hundred years after his mother had been unearthed from her barrel of ashes. Experts examined mother and son and confirmed that the Christ-child did indeed belong to the Black Madonna. When Christena arrived at the chapel to see the statue, it was not there, however. The Black Madonna was being prepared to be reunited with her son. Because they had been living in different climates for two centuries, they would need to go through a nine-month process of reacclimatisation so that they could come back together without doing damage to each other. They have now been reunited.[34]

'I think of the barrel of ashes and what that means,' Cleveland tells me, 'especially for Black moms who have dealt with so much death and despair. I have so many friends who have Black sons who every day are not sure whether he is going to come back. This is literally every Black mother's worst nightmare. I think of the barrel and how they were separated, but how they found their way back to each other. Also this process of who do we need to be – after white supremacy, colonialism and patriarchy have devastated the intergenerational relationships between Black people – what kind of work do we need to be doing to be reunited without harming each other? I feel like this Black Madonna reminds us that there's always hope. So many people ask me – do you really believe what Martin Luther King said about the arc of the universe bending towards justice? Most of the time, I don't know. The evidence doesn't suggest that. But then I hear stories like this and I think: maybe it does.'

Our Lady of Ferguson

In the summer of 2014, black teenager Michael Brown was shot and killed by police officer Darren Wilson in Ferguson, Missouri, in the USA. The white officer claimed that Michael and his friend Dorian Johnson, aged twenty-two, got into an altercation with him, which resulted in a chase. Following Brown's death, protests ignited in Ferguson. Believing that Brown had had his hands up in surrender, or had shouted, 'Don't shoot' as he faced the officer's gun, protesters – in solidarity with Brown – used the slogan 'Hands up, don't shoot'. Ferguson became synonymous with civil unrest sparked by the reality of racial injustice and the pain at yet another shooting of an unarmed Black person.

Sometime after the killing, the Reverend Mark Francisco Bozzuti-Jones, an Episcopal priest at Trinity Church in New York City, commissioned iconographer Mark Doox to create a new image. The result was a Byzantine-style acrylic collage depicting Mary as a Black Madonna with her hands up. Doox named her *Our Lady, Mother of Ferguson and All Those Killed by Gun Violence* – for short, *Our Lady of Ferguson.*

If you were to visit her at the Cathedral of St John the Divine in New York City, where she currently resides, you would see that where her womb should be, there is a black silhouette of the Christ-child. Both Mary and Jesus have their arms out in the now iconic 'Hands up, don't shoot' pose. Mother and child are in the crosshairs of a gun, and we view them as people at the mercy of another human being, whose intention might be to harm them. Here in these crosshairs, they hover between life and death.

In her book *Motherhood: A Confession*, Natalie Carnes writes of Our Lady of Ferguson: 'With this image, the iconographer inscribes the stories of all mourning black mothers into the story of Mary suffering violence against her own child.'[35] It is here in Mary's suffering that the saccharine myths of motherhood fall away, and all mothers whose souls are pierced by the shadow of tragedy and death find solidarity in this sister-mother.

Chapter 8

A Pierced Soul

Death, Loss and Mother-love

'Crucifixion was a deliberately degrading yet public
form of execution. It's hard to imagine a mother not
standing by her son at his moment of greatest need,
channelling his pain into every fibre of her own body.
Was it there perhaps that she became a believer?'

—*Women Remembered: Jesus' Female Disciples*,
Joan Taylor and Helen Bond[1]

'I hoped faith would be an epidural for pain. Turns out to be a
midwife who says, "Push. I'm here. Sometimes it hurts." Dammit.'

—Brené Brown[2]

When my elder son was in his first year of primary school, he asked
me a question I had been dreading: 'Mummy, can children die?' He
had turned five in the weeks following the death of Queen Elizabeth
II. At school they had received commemorative bookmarks, had
talked about what Her Majesty had done for the country, and were
given a day off school to watch the funeral. As parents, we weren't
sure how to deal with this. He was only just grasping the idea of
death and it already felt like a loss of innocence. Yet here we were
attempting – and failing – to get a young child to sit and watch this
solemn, historic moment unfold on our screens. *Is the Queen in that
box? Why doesn't she just wake up? When people die, why can't God just
make another one?* During that time, he became obsessed with death
– a normal rite of passage, but perhaps exacerbated by the death of a

monarch happening in his formative years. Having spoken to other mums, I knew their children too were asking lots of questions about mortality. At some point, my son seemed to reconcile himself to the idea that people live to 100 years old and then they die. We could see him mentally calculating how old we were and how old his grandparents were, and being satisfied that there was still plenty of time left. But then came the question, as he sat in the back of the car while I drove: 'Mummy, can children die?' I winced as he said it, as if something had broken. Perhaps I had wanted to shield him from the world's brokenness. I remembered the crippling fear I had as a child of my parents dying. To my child brain, that was the worst thing that could possibly happen. But now, as an adult and a mother myself, I know the order of things; the reality of generations living and moving on and leaving legacies and homes and memories and stories for those that come next. But a child dying distorts this order. It is an abomination. You start to see the world differently when you learn that such a thing is possible.

Mary has a glimpse into this in the earliest days of her motherhood, when she and Joseph take Jesus to the temple when he is forty days old, as Jewish law requires, and meet a man, Simeon, who gives them a prophecy that may haunt his mother for the rest of her life. We explored Simeon's words earlier in this book: 'This child is destined to cause the falling and rising of many in Israel, and to be a sign that will be spoken against, so that the thoughts of many hearts will be revealed. And a sword will pierce your own soul too' (Luke 2:34–35).

To be a mother is to live in fear of your child dying. Try as I might to push the thought away, it is the dark cloud that intrudes into some of my most joyous moments – birthday parties and first days at school and play dates. It is the unsaid terror I hear made manifest in anxieties about breastfeeding and temperature checks and comparisons about child development. It drives this primal need I have to protect. It is the panic that leads to many trips to A&E departments in the early days of your child's life, where zombied, sleep-deprived new mums gather and wait for hours just to be sure that their baby's ailment isn't really serious. The saccharine images painted of what perfect motherhood is do not forewarn us of this ever-present dread.

In the poignant essay 'Mothers as Makers of Death', written for the *Paris Review* in 2018, author Claudia Dey put words to how so many of us feel:

> No one had warned me that with a child comes death. Death slinks into your mind. It circles your growing body, and once your child has left it, death circles him too. It would be dangerous to turn your attentions away from your child – this is how the death presence makes you feel. The conversations I had with other new mothers stayed strictly within the bounds of the list: blankets, diapers, creams. Every conversation I had was the wrong conversation. No other mother congratulated me and then said: I'm overcome by the blackest of thoughts. You? This is why mothers don't sleep, I thought to myself. This is why mothers don't look away from their children. This is why, even with a broken heart, a mother will bring herself back to life.[3]

I like to think of myself as a pacifist, but in the face of my children being harmed, I have no doubt what I could be capable of – as God is described in the Old Testament: 'Like a bear robbed of her cubs, I will attack them and tear them asunder' (Hosea 13:8). To be a mother is, as far as possible, to anticipate danger. Mums of young children enter rooms and carry out risk assessments within seconds, swiping away potential hazards that might harm their little ones. Mums of teenagers forgo sleep to pick their children up in the early hours of the morning rather than risk them making their own way home from nights out. Lucy Jones describes motherhood as constant watching, saying that as a mother, you are 'first and foremost, a sentinel'.[4] Always alert, always keeping watch for what dangers might lie ahead. Acting as a guard against an ever-present enemy. The possibility of a child dying is a thought too terrible to contend with. It is the worst thing that could possibly happen.

But sometimes the worst does happen.

For mothers who have experienced this unspeakable loss, the horror is not just a lingering threat, punctuating their thought life. It is a reality; a nightmare that has become their story.

An unspeakable loss

I first met Alexandra a year after her baby Evelyn had died at eleven days old. She is married to an old school friend of mine, and though we had never met, we both felt a sense that we should be friends. Strange, I know, but this kind of thing tends to happen to me a lot. It's as if I hear God's voice most vividly in the call to befriend another person – a magnetic, spiritual draw to build a relationship. In this instance, perhaps Alexandra and I were drawn to each other because we recognised that we could provide each other with a space to talk about the pain of motherhood as Christian mothers. When I ask Alexandra questions about Evelyn, I feel that I'm mustering a courage that I usually do not have. Generally, I am resolutely ostrich-like, sticking my head in the sand rather than facing hard truths, but as we sit in Alexandra's kitchen or across a dinner table, I find myself able to stare this, the most tragic thing imaginable, in the face. Able to not avert my gaze from the deep sadness in my friend's eyes. Wrestling with it and hating that it happened, while knowing that for me, the fear of my child dying has not manifested. For Alexandra and for her husband, Jonathan, it is not some intangible idea to be afraid of or to deliberate theological truths about. It is an ever-present fact that lingers; that will be with them for the rest of their lives.

In 2021, a few days after Evelyn was born, she caught a virus but never displayed the typical markers that would have enabled the doctors to try to save her. 'The virus she caught was a cruel one,' Alexandra tells me. 'It gradually decimates the organs. Even if they had picked up on the virus after a week, it could have seriously impacted her ability to live a traditional full and healthy life. Sometimes I find that knowledge a comfort.'

In the aftermath of Evelyn's death, Alexandra noticed the ways in which people responded. 'People always say sorry. Perhaps that is a reflection on British culture, though. Some people say that they don't know how I am surviving and still living. Which isn't always helpful as it makes me question if I should be! I have a husband and sons who I love and adore. I want to survive Evelyn's death, to strive to be present when the grief has had the potential to consume me, for them. For myself. I didn't ask for Evelyn's death and so I don't want it to be the only thing that defines me and who I am. Being her mother is fundamental to who I am now, even though she is the unrepresented and invisible person in any picture or telling of a recent thing that happened at home. It is me who feels so uneasy with that, probably more than others. I fear she will be forgotten, that growing her, seeing my tummy expand and swell and then to deliver her and hold her in my arms for those precious few times, is something only I know of. I can't use the terms 'my children' or 'the boys', as in doing so, Evelyn is excluded and forgotten. Maybe that will change over time, or maybe that will never be something I can do.

'Some people can never bring it up. They don't feel that they can say anything of worth, can't offer any help. I remember when returning to work, for both Jonathan and me, we had colleagues that, when they saw either of us, would avert their eyes or suddenly change direction. I am sad to say that some of my friendships have suffered profoundly from their silence. And also thankful that others have blossomed and become so important owing to their desire to walk beside me and check in. To be intentional and present, even if they haven't been able to do it physically.'

Dr Kathryn Mannix, a former palliative care doctor who is on a mission to get the public to talk more openly about death, notes that there is no word in the English language for a parent whose child has died. 'The absence of words in English renders it literally unspeakable,' she says.[5] In English, we are of course familiar with the terms widow and widower to describe someone whose spouse has died, but what of this gaping hole in our language that leaves parents who have experienced such loss floundering? In China, which implemented a strict one-child policy between 1979 and 2016 to bring down the population rate, the term *shidu* refers to a parent whose only child has died. *Shidu* also encompasses those whose children have been disabled owing to an accident or other life-changing event, and who have not gone on to adopt another child. *Shidu* parents are reported to have more severe mental and physical health conditions, including PTSD, than those with living children. Although this bereavement is obviously tragic for both parents, in Chinese culture the loss of an only child brings about very particular pain for mothers, who play a bigger role in raising their children and spend more time with the children than fathers do.[6] Germans have the terms *Verwaiste Eltern* and *Verwaiste Mutter* or *Verwaiste Vater*, which translate literally as 'orphaned parents', 'orphaned mother' and 'orphaned father'. In a Ukrainian Lenten hymn sung in Catholic and Orthodox churches around the world, Mary at the foot of the cross uses the word 'orphan' to describe herself in the wake of her child's brutal death:

> What becomes of me now, a lonely orphan,
> I'm alone in this world, as a blade of grass I stand.[7]

In 2006 Karla Holloway, an emeritus professor at Duke Divinity School and author of *Passed On: African American Mourning Stories*, described in an NPR radio programme how not having a word to describe a mother like her, whose child had died, made the pain even worse. 'Despite the generations of parents whose fate it is to spend their years shadowed by the memories only of the child or children they have lost, there is no name for us,' she said. 'I feel further punished by this empty space of language.' Holloway called for someone to find a word that would describe this near-indescribable tragedy. For her, it was an urgent challenge: 'Our numbers grow daily. With drive-bys and carelessness, with genocides, and accidents, illnesses, and suicide, war, and, yes, murder, the ways in which our children die multiply.'[8]

Later, she would discover and use the Sanskrit word *vilomah*, which means 'against a natural order' and refers to a parent who has lost a child. 'The grey-haired should not bury those with black hair. As in our children should not precede us in death. If they do, we are vilomahed.'[9] What does such a terrible thing do for one's faith in God? 'I have had people shocked to find out I still believe and trust in God,' Alexandra says. 'Because of Evelyn dying, they assume I would walk away from my faith.'

A taboo within a taboo

In the summer of 2023, I chaired a panel on death and mortality at the Greenbelt Festival, the annual arts, faith and justice festival held in Northamptonshire. The panel included Kathryn Mannix, the former palliative care doctor, and radical undertaker Ru Callender.[10] We explored topics we're not supposed to talk about, although for many of us, they are the thoughts that haunt our daily lives – such as *how do you feel about your own mortality?* At the end of the conversation, as I walked off the stage, I was approached by a woman who asked me why we had not touched on the subject of baby loss. Her name was Laura Francis, and she was a principal clinical psychologist in maternal mental health. 'It's a taboo within a taboo,' she told me. I felt a deep sense of regret. She was right; we had failed to talk about the thing that is so much a part of women's experience. In recent years, I had sat with many friends who had gone through this loss and who were forced to mourn in silence; to continue to work or to look after their living children, when death had taken place inside their body. I recalled one particular dear friend with whom I had sat and wept after her loss.

Chi fell pregnant in October 2018, a couple of cycles after she and her husband, Chris, had started trying for a baby. 'All was well with the pregnancy, and it being my first one, I was in blissful ignorance,' she told me. The couple went to Thailand for a 'baby moon' when Chi was around 20 weeks pregnant. They wanted to relish the final weeks of being just the two of them, before welcoming their new arrival. The morning after they returned, Chi woke up early to go to the gym. When she got up, she felt a sudden gush of water, followed by some light bleeding. The bleeding got heavier, so she drove herself to the maternity hospital, where medical professionals confirmed her waters had broken but said that there was still some water around the baby, and still a heartbeat. 'They admitted me and put me on antibiotics to reduce the risk of infection, and it was a case of sitting and waiting. At that point I don't think I grasped the seriousness of the situation. My brother came to visit, and we went for a walk around the hospital grounds. In hindsight this was the worst thing to do as it encourages labour – despite the midwife on duty encouraging it.'

Later that night, Chi was in some discomfort, with pains around her lower back and sides. In the early hours, she felt like she needed to go to the toilet, and that's when her baby – they would call her Olive – was delivered, in breach, and not breathing, at twenty-two weeks. 'That's the day my heart broke, and it hasn't really ever mended; and I don't think it ever will,' she said. 'To have your perfectly formed baby come too soon, and to feel that as a mother, you were not able to protect her and keep her safe, is a guilt – rational or not – that I feel every day, and won't ever go away. When you lose a child before they are meant to be born [it] means that you have a lifetime of mourning the lost future with your child that you started to picture from the moment you got that first positive pregnancy test.'

Olive's death was defined as a late miscarriage, and tragically Chi then had an early miscarriage before falling pregnant with her daughter Alisa, who is now three years old, and is my goddaughter. Alisa's birth story is traumatic too – she was born ten weeks early during the pandemic, when Chi contracted Covid-19. Recalling the terrifying circumstances of Alisa's birth, I remember how helpless I felt while Chi lay in intensive care for days. I prayed and prayed and prayed that God would save both of their lives – I could not comprehend that such tragedy could happen, especially in the light of Olive's death. Such a thing was surely unimaginable. But I knew that tragedy had befallen so many women throughout history, who died attempting to bring life into the world.

When Alisa was two, Chi and Chris started trying again, but then experienced the pain of three back-to-back miscarriages – each taking place before eight weeks. 'We are now facing decisions that so many couples face every day: do you continue to try, or do you thank God for the blessing of already having a child, and call it a day?' Chi, who was raised a Catholic, said that though she rarely thought about Mary, she found that the pietà imagery resonated with what she had been through. 'A mother holding her dead child's body is against the laws of nature,' she says. 'I chose to see and hold Olive – and we also gave her a private funeral. Whilst I am glad I did hold her and spend time with her, it is a memory that is forever etched in my mind. It immediately brings me back to that hospital room where my world fell apart. The feelings of helplessness and unbelieving that the unbelievable has actually happened are both feelings I imagine Mary also felt when holding her dying son.'

In Chi's experience, the societal stigma about baby loss is still so great that people just do not know how to react; they do not have the words, they don't know how to behave: 'I found a lot of people just said nothing.'

It is into this vacuum of not knowing what to say in the face of this pain and loss that the pietà steps in, providing a figure of solidarity for those who have experienced such profound loss. Just as Christ's incarnation places God close to our suffering, so Mary, too, in knowing the most heart-stopping of losses – the death of a child – shares our pain. 'Unless you have lost a child, you do not know what it feels like,' says Chi. 'This is why there are specialist groups for parents in these situations. I've joined these groups and they have been an invaluable support network: there are strangers who know more intimate details about our loss and fertility journey than many of my friends. And that's OK.'

It is remarkable how little the Bible says about the specific heart-break of unresolved fertility issues. Yes, many of the matriarchs of the Christian faith struggle to conceive, sometimes for years, but their stories have happy endings. In Genesis 18, Sarah – the first woman in the Bible who struggles with her fertility – laughs when God says she will have a child in her old age; and three chapters later, she is pregnant (Genesis 21:2). Isaac prays and his wife, Rebekah, becomes pregnant (Genesis 25:21). We read of Hannah's deep distress at her barrenness, as opposed to the fertility of her husband Elkanah's other wife, Peninnah. But in the end, God was 'gracious' to Hannah, and she gave birth to three sons, including Samuel, and two daughters (1 Samuel 2:21). How must such stories affect those who never have children of their own, despite their prayers? Those for whom the idea of perfect, fertile motherhood leaves no space to recognise their pain?

Theologian Karen O'Donnell confesses: 'I hate Hannah.' Dr O'Donnell, who teaches at Cambridge University, experienced multiple miscarriages, and finds little comfort in the story in the first book of Samuel:

The story of Hannah has been wielded like a weapon to the distress and misery of many people who struggle to conceive . . . These stories cut deeply. Why? Because all of them end in pregnancy and the healthy birth of a son. Barrenness, infertility, reproductive struggle in the biblical narrative is never a permanent state. It is always a temporary position that God is shown to intervene in and remedy with the best possible solution. There is no model in the Bible for ongoing reproductive losses or infertility.[11]

O'Donnell notes, however, that her hatred for Hannah may be because of the patriarchal lens through which Hannah's story – along with all the other biblical stories of those who struggle with their fertility – has been told. The stories that matter are the ones in which pious women – perfect godly mothers – are #blessed because of their devotion to God, and reward their husbands with male heirs, who continue the family line. But Hannah's story, as with those of other women in the Bible who go through similar plights, might have been more bearable for those who experience infertility if their voices had been heard – their experiences of miscarriage, the way in which they mourned, 'how they comforted and were comforted by other women in their communities', as Dr O'Donnell writes.[12] Perhaps it is solidarity that can – in some small way – soothe a pierced soul. Just as Jesus' incarnation brought him closer to the suffering of humanity, so Mary's motherhood enabled her to empathise – to find solidarity – with the suffering of all mothers.

The theological construction of Mary has at times like this been a help to mothers rather than a hindrance. Despite the one-dimensional portrayals of motherhood that can be seen in sweet images of Mary in Christmas-card nativity scenes, there are also many examples of Christ's mother experiencing the pain of her own child's brutal death as he takes on the sins of the world in the most gruesome way imaginable.

While the Madonna lactans artworks depict Mary's maternal nurturing and care through the feeding of her infant child, in the poignant pietà imagery such as Michelangelo's *The Deposition* (circa 1547) and William-Adolphe Bouguereau's stunning *Pietà* painting (1876), the nursing child is replaced by the dead body of the crucified Christ – still cradled by his mother. Mary's sorrow became a key symbol in how she was represented. Her grief was believed to be characteristic of the grief of all mothers, and her tears became a powerful symbol for all maternal suffering. Marina Warner writes: 'Contemporary prudishness has tabooed the Virgin's milk, but her tears have still escaped the category of forbidden symbols, and are collected as one of the most efficacious and holy relics of Christendom. All over the Catholic world, statues and images of the Virgin weep.'[13]

The *Planctus Mariae,* the poetic laments of Mary that spread far and wide in Europe in the Middle Ages, demonstrated – as Clarissa Atkinson notes – 'a wide fascination with Mary's grief over Christ's brutal death and her own piteous state – widowed, orphaned, deprived of all "family" by the loss of her son'.[14] As the example below illustrates, these laments emphasised the universality of the maternal experience, and the suffering that mothers bear witness to, including those whose children die – whether through miscarriage or illness or brutality and violence:

> All women that ever be bore
> And have bore chylder, behold and se
> How my son lyes me before
> On my skyrte, take fro the rode tre.
> When ye danse your chylder on your kne,
> Ye clyppe and kyse with mery chere,
> Behold my sone and behold me:
> For thy son dyghed my dere son dere.[15]

Atkinson writes: 'In one Middle English poetic dialogue, Jesus instructs Mary to recognize in her own agony the pain of every mother, to have compassion for all mothers and, through them, for all of suffering humanity. Maternal anguish became the emotional center of Marian piety.'[16]

Mother is here

In the last moments of his life, George Floyd called out for his mother. 'Momma!' he cried, while police officer Derek Chauvin knelt on his neck for more than eight minutes. 'Momma! I'm through.' In these moments in which he was brutalised, killed slowly in broad daylight, this forty-six-year-old man reached for the place where he knew he could find comfort and acceptance: in the arms of his mother. His mother who had died two years before. She was gone; and now his life was being taken away from him too.

It has often been reported in hospices and care homes that in people's dying moments, they cry out for their mother. In the American Civil War, as in wars before and after, injured soldiers were heard crying out for those who gave them life. Female nurses reported often being called 'mother' or 'good mother' by the injured men. Mary Seacole, who was born in Jamaica and travelled to the UK in the 1820s, devoted herself to treating people with cholera before travelling to the frontline of the Crimean War when it broke out in 1853. There she supported injured and dying soldiers. Later, soldiers would give accounts of her holding them and saying, 'Mother is here . . .,' which inspired her affectionate nickname, 'Mother Seacole'. Of Seacole, who had converted to Catholicism sometime before joining the war effort, author and broadcaster Joanna Bogle said, 'I am rather moved by the thought of kindly Mother Seacole responding to the cry of a dying soldier, so that at least he felt loved and caressed . . . and perhaps somewhere in all that is the thought that surely Our Lady hears their cries.'[17]

The Reverend Lyle, a priest on the front line of the American Civil War, recalled injured and dying soldiers often saying: 'Mother! Home!' According to him, these cries for their mother ranked 'second only to the blessed name "Jesus!"'[18]

Author Lonnae O'Neal writes of the 'sacred call' of the sisterhood of Black mothers, who have experienced the grief of the death and brutalisation of their children in the face of white supremacy. Of George Floyd's final moments, O'Neal writes: 'To call out to his mother is to be known to his maker, the one who gave him to her.'[19] Author and midwife Diana Spalding gives voice to the way I feel when I hear of people calling out for the comfort of their mother in these tragic moments. Of George Floyd's death, she writes: 'Somewhere in the depths of his being, he believed that somehow, someway, his mother could help him in his last, horrifying moments. Because isn't that ultimately what everyone believes in their core? *My mother will always come* . . . When mothers around the world heard this, we let out a collective wail. Because deep down in the depths of *our* beings, all we ever want to be able to do is come when our babies call us. *I'm here, my love, I'm here.*'[20]

When I hear my baby's cry in the middle of the night, knowing that I am the best salve to whatever terror he is facing – whether the perceived threat posed by night terrors or the pangs of hunger, discomfort or illness – it is a precious feeling to pick my child up, stroke his head, kiss his cheek and let his heartbeat steady to the beat of my own. For me, these are signs of the essence of God breaking into our reality. Sociologist Peter Berger suggests that a mother's love for their child is one of the 'signals of transcendence' in societies that claim to be secular. For him, this transcendence is best illustrated in a mother's words to her child: 'everything is alright'. 'The parental role is not based on a loving lie,' he says. 'On the contrary, it is a witness to the ultimate truth of man's situation in reality. In that case, it is perfectly possible to analyze religion as a cosmic projection of the child's experience of the protective order of parental love. What is projected is, however, itself a reflection, an imitation, of ultimate reality.'[21] Beyond the constructed myth of perfect motherhood, then, is a beautiful revelation about the nature of divine love.

Solidarity not theodicy

Christian theologians have long wrestled with the reality of suffering and attempted to reconcile its existence with the idea of a loving God. But just as God mothers us, loving and protecting us, I believe the God who experienced what it is to suffer also weeps with us, holding our hands as we walk – or crawl, or limp – through the valley of the shadow of death. This God doesn't stand apart watching and directing or orchestrating our ups and downs. In the same way that motherhood calls us further into our embodiedness, the incarnation of God represents the divine getting right into the poop and the mess and the pain and the suffering.

As we've discussed already, one of the most vivid images of divine love in the face of profound loss is the pietà image of Mary. In the many depictions of this image that have come down to us through the centuries, we see the mother of God cradling a dying and broken son, who is in fact God. It is profound and illogical, yet the pietà image has brought comfort to so many who have walked through tragedy.

Mary did not feature much in my friend Alexandra's formative years of becoming a Christian, but the story of Jesus' mother resonates with her now in a way that only a mother who has lost a child can understand. Reflecting on the pietà imagery, Alexandra says: 'After Evelyn died and we asked the medical team to stop trying to resuscitate our beautiful and fragile little girl, I held her in my arms. She still had tubes in her and there was blood in various places, but my goodness I was not going to let that opportunity to hold her one last time slip by me. I am – was – Evelyn's Mama Bear, her Lioness, I would have done everything within my power to keep her safe when danger threatened. But I could not. So I took the precious opportunity to hold her one last time, to stroke her face, hold her tight and weep. I can only imagine how Mary felt, with the selfish and primal desire of any mother to keep her child physically on this earth, even if he was the son of God. To know the helplessness of what was happening. Whether it was because of not becoming a Christian until my twenties, or not really being exposed to Christian teaching as a mother, or not knowing that the word translates to "pity and compassion", I still thought more of Jesus in those pietà images and statues, rather than Mary. I have reflected on Mary and on how God must have felt about Jesus' death in a totally different way since Evelyn died. It has made the sorrow Mary and God must have felt more profound and it makes God's clear love for us brighter, for how could anyone willingly lose their child, no matter what their age, unless the gift was forgiveness of sins and reconnection?'

It is this Mary that has been kept from many for whom she would have provided a profound sense of comfort, rather than being viewed as a figure onto whom all the 'ideals' of perfect motherhood were projected. Nevertheless, many mothers have been able to see through the gloss and into the heart of the beauty – and the pain – of Mary's motherhood.

'I don't think I have given Mary enough credit or recognition for her role beyond the Nativity story,' says Alexandra. 'I remember connecting more with her when I had my first son, thinking about how it must have felt to give birth to Emmanuel, how scared and bewildered she must have felt and fearful about her position if Joseph didn't stand by her after Jesus was born. I found life as a new mum exhausting and felt like I knew so little, and that was with a support-ive husband who was as committed as I was to helping our child thrive.

'I think of Mary more now and feel it is her time to shine, to give the role that women played in the Bible and story of Christianity more focus and attention; that she is more than just a stained-glass window or a heavily pregnant lady on a donkey. Maybe I am show-ing a very warped view of the teaching I have been exposed to, but I question if the twenty-first-century Anglican church has given her enough. To live and to love as she did is astonishing.'

I have no answers here. None that will satisfy or make sense of the unimaginable pain of losing a child. It must be the most earth-shat-tering pain conceivable. What I do believe is that God doesn't sit back and watch. God doesn't even just send flowers and cards of condolence, nor 'thoughts and prayers', as many of us have become accustomed to doing when we witness another's tragedy, whether in real life or on social media. To send thoughts and prayers is to remain at a distance from the pain. To see it, but still be separate from it. To have the privilege of being a step removed. Loved ones don't send thoughts and prayers from far away; they step right in, howling with you and holding you as you lie broken. The God I believe in goes further still. God steps into the pain. There is no separation from it in Christ Jesus, whose incarnation means he steps into the fragility and brokenness of humanity, and knows what it is to suffer. Mark L. Yenson points out that women's familiarity with suffering may explain Jesus' female disciples choosing not to abandon him follow-ing his crucifixion. In Mark's Gospel, Mary Magdalene and Mary the mother of Jesus witness the body. Yenson writes: 'When the response of the male disciples is to turn away from suffering, the response of the women is courageous accompaniment, sustaining community where none would otherwise exist.'[22]

Bright sadness

In my earliest days of being a mother, I felt that my life had become one marked by vigilance. My eyes constantly darted around to anticipate danger, and I held my breath daily as I checked on my sons while they were sleeping – exhaling only when I saw they were still breathing. I wondered whether I could possibly withstand the loss of a child. Dare I say it, I wondered whether I would rather not have experienced this crazy sense of love, because it also meant living with the possibility of losing these precious gifts. Yet the love I feel is uncontainable; it bursts out of my chest and I am forever grateful that I get to experience it. The Christian life is one of paradox; it requires us to walk in tension: the sacred and the profane, the body and the spirit, the now and the not-yet. In the Eastern Orthodox tradition, the term 'bright sadness' perfectly describes this feeling of joy and grief being intertwined.

When a young Mary is visited by the angel Gabriel, who tells her she is to give birth to the Son of God, he greets her with the word 'hail', which is an instruction for her to rejoice because of this incredible news of her impending and miraculous motherhood: 'And the angel came in unto her, and said, Hail, thou that art highly favoured, the Lord is with thee: blessed art thou among women' (Luke 1:28, KJV). She is *instructed* to rejoice. Some of us might know the familiarity of a feeling of being so overjoyed at the news that we are going to have a baby, yet at the same time fearful of what is to come: not just the risks of pregnancy and childbirth, but the challenge of parenting and the anxiety of protecting our children. Mary's response to the angel's news is not to say, 'Yay me!' but to be 'greatly troubled' (Luke 1:29). It is a lot. This tension is familiar to so many mothers. Maybe here Mary's story might resonate in particular with mothers whose children have died. Mary goes from trembling with

fear to singing a song of praise to God to being told by the prophet
Simeon that something bad is going to happen to Jesus. What is a
mother to do with such tragic news? How can she go on loving and
living while knowing that something – though she does not know
what it is – is going to happen to her beloved child? In Mary's case,
the worst thing imaginable happens, and more than thirty-three
years later she is standing at the foot of the cross having witnessed her
son face the most horrific pain imaginable. Writer Tish Harrison
Warren shows how Mary's suffering can help other mothers who go
through such loss feel seen and held. 'As the Gospel stories continue
through the life, death and resurrection of Jesus,' she writes in *The
New York Times*, 'we find in Mary's story that joy and pain constantly
intertwine. Her heart is full of all kinds of unimaginable memories
treasured up and her soul waits to be pierced. Her life story witnesses
to the profound vulnerability of mothers in a world where deep love
does not give us the ability to protect our children from all violence
or pain.'[23]

My own soul was pierced the moment I found out I was having a
baby. It was pierced in anticipation of the perils that my child would
face simply by virtue of existing in a broken world. Pierced by the
knowledge that I could not protect them from every unkind word or
judgement or act of violence or rejection. That I could not protect
them from death. A mother's heart is pierced in anticipation of the
knowledge of their child's mortality – whether it is faced at eleven
days old or at 100 years old. To be a mother is to be alive to the sting
of human existence. I want to protect my children from understanding that there is pain in the world. I want to keep them away from
the tree of the knowledge of good and evil. I want to keep them safe
– in this life and in the life to come.

What comes next

Along with the problem of evil, theologians have long attempted to
reconcile the belief in an all-loving God with the reality of death, as
well as grapple with the question of what happens after we die.
There is a strong tradition within Christianity of the idea that after

death, some will be reconciled with God in heaven – that heaven might be a place elsewhere, or it might be the kingdom of God residing in a perfect version of this world. For many Christians, there has existed alongside the idea of heaven the concept of hell. For some, this hell might simply be an afterlife lived separately from an all-loving God whom people either rejected or acted against through sin and from whom they did not ask for forgiveness, or it can literally be 'hellish': cue fire and brimstone, and eternal conscious torment. Alongside these ideas have also existed universalist theologies, which state that in the end, all will be saved, because of God's love.

While there have been prominent male universalist thinkers in Christian history – some would include C.S. Lewis among them – it is fascinating that hidden in the pages of Church history are stories of women whose motherhood led them to denounce the idea of a God who sent people to hell. Historian Sarah Apetrei details a debate that raged within the Baptist movement prior to the English Revolution in the seventeenth century, in which the controversial universalist views of a group of women (Mrs Belcher, Mrs E, and Sister Katherine) in London led to their facing excommunication. A manuscript written sometime between 1677 and 1682 describes one James Warner being tasked with examining the beliefs of 'Mrs E' before she could be admitted as a new convert to a London Baptist congregation. Warner describes Mrs E's 'faith that her Infants deceased were saved'. She also believed that those who had never heard of Christ would not be damned, and that Christ died for all. But it was the conviction that her children would not be damned that drove her beliefs.[24] Other popular female theologians, influenced by the radical theology of the English Revolution, also became fierce proponents of this doctrine. Dr Apetrei explains that 'women's heightened sensitivity to questions about the fate of lost infants played a role'. For such women, the doctrine of reprobation – the Calvinist view that some sinners are not part of the chosen elect group and therefore destined for eternal damnation, 'was not just repugnant, but nonsensical to those who identified divine compassion with a mother's unconditional love'.

Alongside mothers' inability to comprehend an existence in which their children could face eternal damnation was the idea that hell contradicted the idea of the divine, maternal love of God. Mystical radical Richard Coppin, a preacher, was arrested several times for blasphemy during the 1650s for espousing the doctrine of universal salvation, based on his understanding of the maternal love of God. On page 57 of her book, Apetrei describes his reaching for the maternal imagery of Isaiah 49 as an example: ' "Can a woman forget her suckling child, that shee should not have compassion on the Sonne of her wombe? Yea, they may forget, yet will I not forget, saith God." '

Commenting on the Isaiah passage, Jewish studies scholar Dr Malka Z. Simkovich said the writer understood the idea of a child's dependence on its mother, and the fact that the two are forever bonded by unconditional love. For her, the passage suggests that God's love is even greater than that. 'Because God has promised to maintain this bond and protect the people, Israel can call upon God to help in times of crisis. As mother, God is accountable, compassionate, protective, powerful, and bound to her children through love.'[25] That women – and often mothers – were among the fiercest proponents of universalist theology is no surprise to me. In the seventeenth century, such a belief was not orthodox, so 'the fact that some women were willing to nail their hard universalist colours to the mast', writes Apetrei, 'is striking; it speaks of the power and resonance of the idea for them.'[26]

I have lived most of my life with a concept of God being, on the whole, a God who exhibits the qualities and characteristics we have come to associate with maleness. Along with that, I have been drawn to the cross, with its promise of salvation and redemption from the wretchedness that I feel and from the many times I fail to find the grace of a God who loves us and puts aside the scales of judgement and takes on our sin and pain through the incarnation; through God becoming human. I do not know what happens at the end of things, nor the manner in which God will make all things new (Revelation 21:5). But what I do know is that I am drawn to the idea of a compassionate and loving God who welcomes us in.

Maternity and hope

For some, becoming a mother makes them fear death not more, but less. The act of giving birth and the notion of being reborn in the life that is to come are coupled with the profound existential insights many mothers can learn precisely because they are mothers.

I am stunned by the ability of mothers whose children have died – sometimes in the most horrific of circumstances – to just keep going. I'm certain that if such a thing should happen to me, I would descend into a kind of hell and never again want to resurface, never again care about anything or anyone else. Nothing else would ever matter. Alexandra told me that she felt like this, for a time, after baby Evelyn died. 'For the first year and a half, I couldn't and didn't ask people how they were, I couldn't take on anything of anybody. I just needed to survive. To not drown. I think I damaged relationships while I was in that hole. But I can't apologise for it. I needed to take everything offered by people I knew; it was 100% a one-way street. So for the most part, the things I remember the most about the aftermath of Evelyn's death is all the flowers we received, our incredible church family who fed us for two months, bringing us hot meals every day without fail, and crying lots while walking our dog. Of brave friends coming to visit me to go on dog walks or to sit with a cup of tea and cry with me.'

I would never blame a mother for feeling unable to face the world after such a loss. Which is why I find so extraordinary the stories of mothers who are able to look up from their own grief and pain and find something in them stirred to make a difference in the world.

When her fourteen-year-old son Emmett's brutalised body was recovered following his murder in Mississippi in the summer of 1955, after he was thought to have whistled at a white woman at a grocery store, Mamie Till-Mobley at first 'wanted to go in a hole and hide my face from the world'.[27] But then she decided to act, displaying an open casket before her son's burial in Chicago so that the world could see the violence and cruelty of racism. 'Let the people see what they did to my boy,' she told the world's media.[28]

When trans teenager Brianna Ghey was stabbed to death in a park in Warrington in February 2023, her mother Esther Ghey said she had 'never felt such grief'. Yet she found it within her to reach out to Emma Sutton – the mother of Scarlett Jenkinson, who, alongside her fellow perpetrator, Eddie Ratcliffe, killed Brianna – and see how they could join together to make a difference in the lives of young people. One expert in restorative justice called the mothers' meeting the most 'extraordinarily unusual' meeting they had seen in thirty years. Prior to meeting, Esther Ghey had said she did not blame Ms Sutton for what her daughter had done, and when they met they agreed to campaign together on the dangers of mobile phones for children.

I do not understand how these mothers could do what they have done, looking out at the world, when a part of them has died. I do not understand, but perhaps there is understanding from one who stood at the foot of the cross and watched – with a crushed heart, a pierced soul – her son crucified. Perhaps in Mary's story, and in her son's gentle words ('Woman, behold your son' (John 19:26, NKJV)), we see the possibility of grief never forgotten, but turned into action. I imagine how Jesus must have felt the night he was betrayed, drops of blood dripping down his face, as he asked for the cup to be taken away from him. He was carrying not only his own anguish and the weight of the sin of the world, but also the knowledge that his own mother would see him suffer in such a terrible way. This pain is heartbreakingly communicated in a vernacular poem written by thirteenth-century Franciscan friar Jacopone da Todi. Part of a tradition of religious poetry designed to educate the laity known as *laude*, the poem *Donna de Paradiso (Lady of Paradise)* illustrates a meeting between Jesus and Mary – whom Jesus calls 'Mamma' – ahead of his crucifixion, and after he has already experienced violence and humiliation at the hands of the Roman authorities. In the poem, Christ says to Mary:

> *Mamma, ove sei venuta?* Mamma, why have you come?
> *Mortal mi dai feruta* You cause me a mortal wound
> *Il tuo pianger mi stuta* For your weeping pierces me
> *Che'l veggio si afferrato.* And seems to me the sharpest sword.[29]

Perhaps in his final moments, he wanted to provide her with both comfort and purpose to move forward. As Andrew Greeley writes:

'Mary, having lost everything that mattered to her at the foot of the cross, was then able to give herself to the whole of humankind: "Son, behold thy mother."'[30]

All our children

Mary of Nazareth knew what it was to live under the terror of occupation, and stare death in the face while carrying Life itself. It is April 2024, and women in Mary's homeland are facing a horror so unimaginable that it turns my stomach to read about it. I'm doing so from the safety of my home, where I have shelter and heating and clean water and those little grocery shopping bags that fold down into tiny bundles so they can fit in my handbag. Everything seems so trivial held up against the darkness and horror of the Israel–Gaza war. I have heard that Hamas did horrific things to babies and pregnant women during its barbaric attack on Israel on 7 October 2023. I have heard that the months-long retaliation has separated children – sometimes newborns – from their parents. I have heard of a woman who, facing the Israeli attacks on Rafah, woke her six-month-old baby in the night to play. As the bombardment loomed, she thought it might be their last night alive. If this was to be it, she at least wanted the chance to hug her daughter one last time.[31] I have heard that at the start of the conflict, there were around fifty thousand pregnant women in Gaza. But I have heard there were no doctors or midwives to help them deliver their babies. No pain medication or anaesthesia. No sterile instruments to cut the babies' umbilical cords. I have heard that C-sections have been performed on dead women. I have heard a baby was born recently, delivered from her mother's womb after she had died, along with her husband and their other young daughter. The baby – named Sabreen after her mother – was born an orphan, prematurely, and weighing just three pounds. I have heard she lived just a few days and is now buried in her father's grave.

Motherhood has made me furious. It has radicalised me. It has woken me up to the injustices that exist in this world. I knew they were there before, of course – like constant melancholic background music. But the moment my son was born, this soundtrack became a loud ringing in my ear. Something I could no longer pretend did not exist. Journalist and Lutheran pastor Reverend Angela Denker described the feeling that many mothers were experiencing when, during the Rafah bombardment just ahead of US Mother's Day in May 2024, she wrote these words:

> It is hard enough to protect our kids, how can we save the children of Gaza? Couldn't we keep scrolling, purchase our way out of suffering and death? The truth is that the devaluation of children's lives anywhere means the devaluation of children's lives everywhere. This Mother's Day: For those kids and for our kids, I don't want brunch. We need a cease-fire.[32]

When I became a mother, I was no longer living for me or for now, but for my children and their future. It was as if my eyes were opened to the need to conceive of not just today or the coming year, but the decades and centuries to come. From the moment I became pregnant, a determination was instilled in me to clear the way for the future, for that which was not yet. But it opened my eyes too to the plight of all mothers and the future of all children, everywhere. In the words of Toni Morrison:

> It is abundantly clear that in the political realm the future is already catastrophe. Political discourse enunciates the future it references as something we can leave to or assure 'our' children or – in a giant leap of faith – 'our' grandchildren. It is the pronoun, I suggest, that ought to trouble us. We are not being asked to rally for *the* children, but for *ours*. *Our* children stretches our concern for two or five generations. *The* children gestures towards time to come of greater, broader, brighter, possibilities – precisely what politics veils from view.[33]

Where there is birth, where there is new life, where there are new beginnings, there is hope. Natality is a radical act, when all around is death, brutality, destruction and hopelessness. Jennifer Banks writes of the 'complex and dissonant truth' of experiencing birth, even celebrating it, 'while living amid death and destruction'. She adds:

'We arrive with our natality into a mortal world, and that natality is what a human world depends on. The world needs beginners, people who are committed to its rebuilding. Our oases are where we prepare for that beginning, that birthing, that rebuilding.'[34]

In the Magnificat, Mary's manifesto, we hear the cry of a mother who is singing of a future that seems far away from the reality of her present day. It is a prophetic pointing towards a kingdom in which all will be made new, where the mighty are brought down from their thrones, where God's mercy reigns, and where the sting of death and destruction is no more. All over the world, Mary's rallying cry has stirred mothers to rise up and rebuild a better world for all children.

PART FIVE

Assumption

Chapter 9

Mothers Rise Up

The Magnificat and the Future for All our Children

All things rising, all things sizing
Mary sees, sympathising
With that world of good,
Nature's motherhood.

—'The May Magnificat', Gerard Manley Hopkins

The future for me is always my children.

—Toni Morrison[1]

I have never doubted the existence of God more than in my first few months of studying theology at university. I arrived unprepared for the challenge it would be to my faith. As with my motherhood journey, I had expected it to be more straightforward, perhaps challenging, but not earth-shattering. Again, as with motherhood, it was the expectation of ease and my discombobulation at the reality that caused me to wobble in my faith as I wrestled with Big Bang theory and quantum physics and the psychological tricks at play in the charismatic worship that had formed the soundtrack to much of my Christian youth. In my attempt to keep my faith and hold on to God, I would sometimes go to three different services on a Sunday: a charismatic evangelical service outside the centre of the city in the morning, then evensong in the college chapel early in the evening, before going on to a 'happy-clappy' evangelical church straight afterwards. I emerged from three years of university with my faith just about intact, but with a newfound appreciation for choral music. A few years later, when I began to attend a thousand-year-old Anglican church, I realised I now found comfort in the familiarity of the Apostles' Creed, the voices in unison reciting the Lord's Prayer. I found my soul stirring, too, to the words of the Magnificat, as I sat in vast cathedrals and heard the voice of God in the song of Mary. Though I found these moments extremely moving and felt the presence of God in the ethereal music, there was something disturbing about it that I couldn't quite put my finger on. Something uncomfortable, something out of place. I now know what it was. It was that the words did not quite match the settings in which we were singing them. The Magnificat speaks of the overturning of a world order, but here I was sitting in historic Anglican pews, surrounded by grandeur and stained glass. Here, the Church seemed more like 'the mighty' than the poor.

In 1521, Martin Luther wrote a commentary on the Magnificat. For a man who was not afraid of revolution, his interpretation of Mary's canticle was not so liberatory. Instead, writing for young Prince John Frederick, the future elector of Saxony, Luther aimed his handbook on the Magnificat at leaders, demonstrating the ways in which he thought it showed that it was God who gave people power, including political office, and that it was God who could take it away. While of course this is one potential take, Luther, as Catholic theologian Margaret Hebblethwaite told me, 'missed the whole point' and ignored the fact that it was 'a cry of political liberation'.[2]

The myth of Mary has obscured her reality; it's made her pretty rather than powerful and prophetic. Hebblethwaite found a similar obscuring of her reality during a visit to the Shrine of Our Lady of Walsingham, shortly before we met. 'There was a lot there on the Annunciation, the Assumption, the Coronation in heaven. But where was the Magnificat? I didn't see any images celebrating it. Why? Because it did not fit with the idea of their ideal woman. In the Magnificat, Mary is a prophet and she spouts a kind of prophecy or psalm like in the Old Testament, with articulacy and eloquence. *She* says the words. The song is long, and very strong, and is a proclamation of liberation. It's revolutionary; and that's not part of the traditional Marian spirituality. It's not that they've rejected it, it just hasn't come to the fore.'

What might it look like if we unmade the version of Mary that has subjugated women, and has had us trying and failing and trying and failing to live up to a perfect standard? What might it look like if we told a more honest story, if we heard a new song, about Mary? Ursula King writes that it is time for this to happen:

> Women need to create new images of Mary through new insights and interpretations of the life of Mary and her role in the liberation of human beings. Paintings, images, and interpretations of Mary still exist that reinforce her weakness as a woman, and as a consequence the weak state of women everywhere. These images lead women to accept unjust systems because of their lowly positions ... Women need to ... work together in creating new images that will liberate them to see Mary as a catalyst in the liberation of all women.[3]

These new images are indeed being created. Mary is finding herself at the heart of liberation movements around the world, where her song – the Magnificat – is recognised as a song of freedom, and of the casting down of oppressive regimes and structures. It is this Mary who has become an emblem, particularly within Latin American liberation theology, where she is seen as standing in solidarity with the oppressed, because she herself knew what it was to be poor. It is particularly in the following lines from the Magnificat that those living in poverty, or those who are marginalised, can find hope, and they are the reason Mary 'becomes the symbol of the struggle of the poor and marginalized':[4]

> He has brought down rulers from their thrones but has lifted up the humble.
> He has filled the hungry with good things but has sent the rich away empty. (Luke 1:52–53)

The Magnificat is not about maintaining the status quo, but is a mother's prophetic cry for a world that will be turned upside down. The Reverend Lucy Winkett, who was the first female priest to join St Paul's Cathedral, described how 'Mary turns us outwards ...

We're called as women and men to steady our gaze on the suffering of the world as she steadied her gaze on her son.'[5] Speaking at the Greenbelt Festival in 2006, she recalled how a Kenyan woman's cry for justice reminded her of Mary's Magnificat. Reflecting on Mary's 'extraordinary declaration of the *Basileia* – the kingdom of God', Reverend Winkett recalled the testimony of Wahu Kaara, a global social justice activist, as she stood on stage in front of 3,000 people at St Paul's in 2005 alongside the then secretary-general of the United Nations, Kofi Annan, and the then UK prime minister, Gordon Brown. 'While everyone else quoted statistics, and said that every four seconds, a child died from poverty, she said she knew the faces of those people.' These were her family, and her neighbours, and it was a scandal that they were still poor. 'We could all hear in her passion and courage the cadences of the Magnificat,' Reverend Winkett said. 'God has filled the hungry with good things and has sent the rich away empty.' Sometimes these new messages of liberation are forged in song, just as they are in Mary's Magnificat.

There's something about singing

Civil rights anthems such as 'We Shall Overcome' strengthened activists during the civil rights movement in the 1960s. The 1897 hymn '*Nkosi Sikelel' iAfrika*' became the song of the anti-apartheid movement and South Africa's national anthem. Historian Beth Allison Barr ends her book *The Making of Biblical Womanhood* reflecting on the power of the patriotic hymn 'Jerusalem' within the early-twentieth-century fight for women's equality. In 1917, a year before the first women in England were allowed to vote, the women of the Royal Albert Hall choir performed at a service held to mark the female contribution to the Great War effort, with some having driven ambulances, or been nurses or part of the land army. At the service, attended by Queen Mary, the choir sang the hymn – which comprised William Blake's 1804 poem 'Jerusalem: And did those feet in ancient time', set to music by Sir Hubert Parry in 1916. Barr writes that the following year it was sung at a suffrage demonstration, and that it 'would become emblematic of women's perseverance in their fight for the vote'. Standing at the Royal Albert Hall, she said: 'I could imagine the words echoing throughout the curved building, filtering beyond its walls and into the streets of London.'[6]

I will not cease from mental fight,
nor shall my sword sleep in my hand,
till we have built Jerusalem
In England's green & pleasant land.

In my earliest months of motherhood, where I thought I had lost myself, I found solidarity and freedom in song alongside a group of mothers in south-east London. The first time I walked into the community centre where the Hummy Mummies – a community choral group – met, it felt like heaven. There were babies crawling around on the floor, rolling around on playmats, being breastfed by their mums. There were babies crying. There were babies having their nappies changed. Then there were the mothers. They were free. As I walked into the chaos, I exhaled; because here I did not have to shush my baby, or feel shame at not having it all together. Most wonderfully of all, here I got to sing with others. Pop and rock classics that made us feel good: from Cyndi Lauper's 'True Colours' to Bon Jovi's 'Livin' on a Prayer'. Years after that first maternity leave, I reach out to Hummy Mummies' founder Richard Swan and thank him. I tell him it was life-saving for me, and ask what led him to set it up. 'I know from experience how much singing can bring people together and foster community,' he tells me. 'Mothers – particularly new mums – can often feel isolated and lonely, and I thought that a baby-friendly choir would really help with that.'

In her book *Why We Sing*, Julia Hollander details Swedish singer and neuroscientist Björn Vickhoff's experiment exploring the effects of social singing on the rhythms of the singers' hearts. Vickhoff found that 'even allowing for the variability in each individual's cardiac oscillations, they were sharing common patterns . . . In other words, singing together makes our hearts beat as one.'[7] Hollander describes such communal singing as being like a murmuration – a collective of birds that flock together, swooping, swirling and shapeshifting as one:

> It felt as though we were in our own version of a murmuration.
> With our hearts as the hub, from the soles of our feet to the
> crowns of our heads, our blood is all pumping in the same rhythm.
> Even if we didn't know it, our bodies must have felt that common
> beat through our skin: in our veins and our arteries. In the pulsing
> of our singing hearts there must be some ancient survival instinct,
> not so different from the birds'.

Perhaps what I was experiencing in that moment of collective motherhood with the Hummy Mummies was that singing together with
other mums felt like a murmuration, too. A maternal murmuration.
When women sing together, it can make a difference.

Writing about women's role in radical theology in the seventeenth-century English Revolution, Sarah Apetrei notes that women
engaged in prophetic singing: 'Spiritual singing was considered a
manifestation of the new birth, like the Magnificat: the proclamation
of the living Christ incarnate in the saints, and heaven's condescen-
sion to earth. With Mary, female prophets played a particular role as
singing heralds of the kingdom of Christ, breaking forth within all
humanity.'[8] A singing prophetess was 'the herald of revolutionary
change, not only in the world around her, but in herself: the site of
the living temple, where the songs of Sion could be sung anew'.[9]
Speaking of Mary's song, womanist Hebrew scholar Dr Wil Gafney
notes:

> She professes faith in a God whose mercy transcends time and is
> not limited to her and those who see the world exactly as she sees
> it. She proclaims a God who is partial to the plight of the poor and
> is a terror to the tyrant. The Magnificat recalls an ancestral prom-
> ise and she bears witness, in her very body, to a God of
> promise.[10]

Mary's song joins with the prophetic singing of women in Scripture
who had gone before. Theologians have noted the similarities
between Mary's Magnificat and Hannah's song in 1 Samuel. Some

have suggested that Hannah's song is a harbinger of Mary's, with both using their gratitude at their divinely ordained motherhood to sing praise to God and declare a coming kingdom that bears little resemblance to the unjust one in which they live. The Magnificat is also a song addressed to another woman – Elizabeth – who, like Hannah and Mary, has become pregnant. For Hannah and Elizabeth, their pregnancies follow years of infertility. The Magnificat is a declaration for all humanity, but it is also the song of mothers, the song of women. As a group of feminist theologians declared in 1994: 'This song, the Magnificat, announces a complete change in the present, patriarchal order. This means moral, social, political, economic and cultural reversals. The woman who sings this song is a liberated woman, standing in the line of the strong women of Israel . . . There is great encouragement for women in the support and solidarity that women give to one another.'[11]

Mothers rise up

One of the four Marian dogmas of the Catholic Church is the belief in the Assumption of Mary. Defined by Pope Pius XII in 1950, it comprises the idea that 'the Immaculate Mother of God, the ever-Virgin Mary, having completed the course of her earthly life, was assumed body and soul into heavenly glory'.[12] The word 'assumption' here derives from the Latin word *assūmptiō*, which translates as 'taking up' – in Mary's case, into heaven. The dogma does not define whether Mary died first and was then taken up, or whether she did not face bodily death but went straight to heaven. The earliest beliefs about Mary's assumption arose around the fifth century, and much of the dogma has been shaped by apocryphal and early writings. The main scriptural reference is taken from Revelation 12:1–2: 'A great sign appeared in heaven: a woman clothed with the sun, with the moon under her feet and a crown of twelve stars on her head. She was pregnant.' This speaks to me of a magnificent mother who rises up and is propelled into a future hope – the hope that all of us will be called into, according to the Christian faith. It speaks of a future in which the world will be as it should have been all along. The

Catholic belief is that, having left her children – the Church – Mary, from this heavenly viewpoint, is interceding on our behalf, seeing the hurt and the pain and the fear and the brokenness. As mothers, we too look to the future for our children. When I became a mother, I was consumed with a visceral urge to fight for a better one for my children. If I'm being honest, the future doesn't look too great right now; and I find myself racked with guilt and fear and helplessness. I have a recurring image of my two little boys wandering alone on a barren planet that has been destroyed by climate change. I imagine them trudging through the greyness just as the boy and his father walk through the end of the world in Cormac McCarthy's *The Road*: 'Where men can't live gods fare no better.' It is bleak and hopeless. It is the desolate scene that flashes up in my mind when I find myself crippled to the point of despair when I think about what we have done to the planet, and why we can't just stop.

Having children spurred me into action about the future. I found there was no longer any room for my complacency. I want to do everything in my power to make sure the bleak vision does not come to pass. I need the world to be better because it is the world that my babies will inhabit once I am gone.

It was this thought that drove me to join the Mothers Rise Up march in 2019. I had made a sign: 'Now this is what I call a mothers' meeting.' And I, my husband and our son walked through the streets of London surrounded by thousands of other mothers, and fathers, marching for the sake of their children's futures. I did not know it at the time, but also on the march was writer Joanna Wolfarth, who wrote in her book *Milk* about the power of breastfeeding during that protest, and 'feeling transformed by my maternal status, which lent me a greater urgency in addressing catastrophic climate change'.[13] She writes about the 'nurse-in' held by Extinction Rebellion climate protesters in London, in which mothers blockaded the road as they breastfed their babies and demanded action to protect the environment for the sake of their children. Wolfarth also recalls the now iconic image of doula Kyla Carlos breastfeeding her newborn child while holding up a power fist at a Black Lives Matter protest in Virginia. In 2024, six mothers from the group Mother's Manifesto held a five-day hunger strike outside the UK Houses of Parliament to stand in solidarity with British families who could not afford to feed their children, calling on the government to enforce universal free school meals for children. They had held a similar protest the previous year.[14]

Time and time again, it has been mothers who – foretelling of future danger – have demanded better of the powers that be, for the sake of their children, and for all our children. At times, women have not just protested from the sidelines, they have got their hands dirty and brought about the change themselves. I remember coming across a striking photo of Sierra Leonean women wearing hard hats. It accompanied an article about a new maternity centre that was being built in the country, which has the highest maternal mortality rate in the world; 60 per cent of the labourers on the hospital construction site were women. 'It is for us, the women who will give birth here. That's why we are putting in effort to build the hospital,' said twenty-one-year-old Hawa Baryoh.[15] Sometimes Mary's motherhood has particularly lent itself to the environmental movement. Andrew Greeley writes of the way in which the world is likened to Mary's garden in some church traditions, explaining:

> If the earth is Mary's garden, you don't rip it up or rip it off. Respect for the physical environment is not just a new notion dug up to give relevance to an outmoded symbol that one is trying to rehabilitate for the modern world. Respect for the environment, on the contrary, is at the very core of the Mary myth – though the phrase 'respect for environment' is new. If 'all things rising' [from the Manley Hopkins poem *The May Magnificat*] reflect through Mary the life-giving love of God, then all the rising things on earth are mystery. To pollute, abuse, corrupt, destroy these things is a sacrilege.[16]

When Mary declares in the Magnificat that 'all generations will call me blessed' (Luke 1:48), she is looking far ahead into the future. Not just to the next generation, but to generations to come. Motherhood propels us into that future, looking not just to the needs of today, but to those of the days and years and centuries to come. It is why it is often women who have foretold of future dangers, including in technological advancement. Take Mary Shelley's warnings in her Gothic tale *Frankenstein*, or those of the women working in tech in Silicon Valley about the dangers of artificial intelligence. Good motherhood looks not just to its own interests, but to those of the whole of humanity, now and in the future.

At the turn of the twenty-first century, author Toni Morrison gave a speech in which she talked about her fear for humanity's future. The human imagination was no longer able to think beyond what comes immediately next, she said. Writing about Morrison's fears, Jennifer Banks said: 'People could speak of *their* children, but not of all children, born into a future no single person would live to see. Humans could think forward only a few generations at best; after that, the horizon had become impenetrable to the human imagination.' But, Banks adds, Morrison thought that we could change this future perspective to a longer view:

> That future entailed generations, connected one after the other like Hebrew Bible lineages, with births acting as fertile renewals. History, she prophesied, 'is about to take its first unfettered breath'. The future would be hospitable to the human race, but it would demand of us that we think not just of our own children and of their children, following forward through our own family lines, but of all the children alive today and all the children that might be born.[17]

We cannot care about the future of all children without thinking about the future of the planet as a whole – by which I mean in particular the physical earth, the environment, or creation. The Greek word from which the word 'ecology' is derived is *oikos*, which can mean household, environment or habitat. Ecological concerns therefore move us from thinking about the needs of just our own household to those of the world around us. Ecology is literally a global family business.

As well as literal motherhood, Mary's divine motherhood has often also represented the renewal or rebirth of creation. It is why she has been an emblem for ecological movements around the world, and how she has found her place there in the twenty-first century. At a time of existential crisis, and in a period in which the influence of the Church in the West is much less than it has ever been, Mary finds herself in these surprising places, with feminists from across all religions and none discovering what she might say for our times.

While – as we saw earlier in this book – the comparisons between Eve and Mary have often relied on negative perceptions and caricatures of women, the idea of Mary as the 'new Eve' can help us as we think about motherhood in relation to the world around us. Just as Eve was crowned 'the mother of all the living' (Genesis 3:20), so too does Mary symbolise the interconnectedness and mutuality of all living things.

Rather than being a passive bystander in the new creation, Mary's part is an active one. 'In the figure of Mary, creation, church, and pregnancy all entwine as images of one another,' writes Natalie Carnes. Mary's 'yes' to God in the Annunciation has been used to send a message to women that they should consent, that they should do as they are told. But some read it differently. Some are able to intentionally see past the construction of Mary that calls for the perfection of all mothers, and instead carve out meaning for themselves about what she and her story represent. For some, therefore, Mary's 'yes' is an active one, not a passive 'OK'. It is a mother rising up to the challenge of getting stuck in to the new thing God is doing. In her book *Motherhood: A Confession*, addressed to God in the style of St Augustine's own *Confessions*, Carnes writes:

> Mary's body is presented as a new creation. Mary's words 'let it be done to me' (*fiat mihi* in the long-time language of the Church) echo Your words at creation 'let there be light' (*fiat lux*) . . . The incarnation is a new creation, and theologians and artists have over the centuries dramatized its echoes of and parallels to the first creation. The first creation gave us Adam; the second, the new Adam, Christ. From the body of a woman, the Spirit makes a new creation . . . With all creation, the Mother-Church groans in her birth pains, waiting for the arrival of Christ that will end her labor.[18]

She adds: 'With the *fiat lux*, light is created that makes physical sight possible. In the *fiat mihi*, a babe enters Mary's womb, invisibly. The world looks absolutely the same, and yet the world has entirely changed. Can I imagine anything more transcendent? Humanity has been re-created, reborn by Mary's words.'[19]

For much of the past two millennia, Mary of Nazareth has resembled her son. Or at least the mythical version of her son: meek and mild, fair-haired and blue-eyed. Because patriarchy has long been dominant in western society, she has also taken on the compliant stance of the women in whichever age she has found herself: quiet and submissive. This Mary is the self-sacrificial, doting, ever-gentle, loving, perfect mother. But there is another Mary.

Mary of Nazareth was no wallflower. Peel back the layers of patriarchal construction and we find in the pages of history an extraordinary woman, who gave birth to a son, yes, but also to a movement that changed the world. Among the earliest Christian writings and drawings, we see a Mary who was very much a leader in her movement, empowered and freed from the misogynistic chains around her. She was not just liberated herself, she freed others too. Early Christian writings described her as a 'defender of women'. The salutation 'Hail, Mary, through whom and by whom all the women in the world have acquired freedom of speech with her Lord!' is attributed to Demetrius, the third-century archbishop of Antioch. As Ally Kateusz states, the fourth-century poet Ephrem the Syrian wrote: 'In Mary there has come hope for the female sex: from the insults they have heard and the shame they have felt she has given them freedom.'[20]

What might this freedom mean for the daily lives of mothers today?

No mum left behind

One of my favourite things to do during both my maternity leaves was one of the most favoured activities of middle-class London mums: going to baby cinema. It was the highlight of my week. I would scan cinema listings across London and choose whichever film showing would best suit my baby's current schedule and not clash with doctors' appointments or other baby classes or social gatherings. There are two golden windows in which baby cinema works: first, with a newborn, who sleeps pretty much all the time, so that you can just hold them and feed them and watch the film. And then again when your baby's naps become predictable and you can park them in a buggy carrycot and live the dream of having your baby sleep throughout the movie. Once your baby is old enough to crawl, then, sadly, your baby-cinema days are up. I loved a particular cinema in North London. I would trek across on the Tube, navigating the labyrinth of buggy-accessible routes on the London Underground. I would always exhale when I walked through the doors and was greeted by an attendant who took my order for a hot drink and cake outside the door to the seats. Once I was settled, one of the staff would deliver a steaming hot coffee, along with a freshly baked cake, to my seat. Instead of the usual uncomfortable bucket seats, this cinema had comfy sofas that mothers could relax into. It was bliss, and I am convinced this cinema experience must have been created by a mother, who knew exactly what new mothers need.

What made these baby-cinema experiences such a vital part of my week was the sense of escape they created. The opportunity to watch a film not only reminded me of the life I had before, but momentarily took me away from the day-to-day roller coaster of new motherhood. I fondly remember these cinema trips, but there were also times when it was hard – when the baby did not follow his schedule; when a poonami happened right in the middle of the most important part of the film and I had to shuffle out to find the baby-changing toilets.

The beauty of baby cinema was in the simple fact of just being alongside other women who were going through the same things; who were in this very particular window in their lives too. Covered by the darkness of the auditorium, we fed and burped and bounced and shushed our children. In the flicker of the screen lighting, we caught glimpses of our sisters. There was peace despite mewling newborns and tiny ones crying; in this particular liminal space their noises felt more manageable, less shaming, because these mothers all knew what it was like.

I will never forget one mother, though, who was getting

increasingly agitated by her baby. Perhaps it was one of those days we have all experienced – when the baby isn't sleeping, when nothing satisfies them. Perhaps she was a first-time mum on her first cinema trip with her baby. Perhaps she had done all this before and was frustrated at the fact that she still couldn't master the art of perfect motherhood. She may have been experiencing what we were all experiencing – the things that come with the territory of being out and about with a baby – but for some reason she just couldn't handle it that day. Maybe it was owing to sleep deprivation or postnatal depression or simply that feeling of having had enough. Whatever it was, in that moment, not long after the film had started, this mum picked up her baby, along with all her things, and started to shuffle her way down the aisle. I could tell she was crying. We could all sense her frustration. But this is what this space was for, for us to be together in challenge, to let each other be, without judgement or pressure to conform. A place to let the tears fall. As this exhausted mum made her way up the stairs, one woman shot up and ran after her, shouting, 'No! You stay!' A few others of us joined in with encouragement for this mum not to leave. 'This is what it's for!' one woman shouted. 'No judgement here!' cried another. Soon, most of us were imploring the woman to stay. In the end, she carried on walking, and left.

I think about this woman sometimes. I hope that she heard acceptance in the cries of her mother-sisters. I hope that our collective willing of her to stay went some way towards shattering the myth of perfect motherhood that may have seeped into her subconscious and made her feel hot with shame when she thought in that cinema that morning that she was the only one failing.

I was also proud of the rest of us who were there that morning. I get goosebumps when I think of the mothers rising up from their seats to rail against this idea that we can't let the challenges and so-called imperfections of what it is to be a mother out in public. When mothers rise up, demanding a better way, we can not only free ourselves, we can change the world.

The myth of Mary's motherhood is that she is 'alone of all her sex'. Her set-apartness, her perfection, has separated her from all other women, while simultaneously telling us all that we are like her, or at least *should* be perfect like her. The beauty of Mary is that she never really is alone. She is at the side of her Christ-child, the Saviour of all humankind. She is part of the Holy Family. But she is also one in a long line of women stretching back to the beginning and forward to today. When we recognise that we too are not islands of mother-hood, that we need each other to flourish, Mary's song becomes a chorus, not a threat. It is when mothers – those who have children, and all those who care for others – rise up, together, that we can change the world.

When I met Margaret Hebblethwaite – author of *Motherhood and God* – for the first time in the foyer of the British Library, we hugged. This was our Visitation. As we sat over coffee I wondered what other people there might guess our connection was – this unlikely pairing: me, a tall, Black, 40-year-old woman; she a tiny, red-haired, white grandmother, with a voice so soft you might mistake her for some-one who was not a force to be reckoned with. But here we were both simply mothers, who spoke in one continuous murmuration of Mary and her divine motherhood, and our motherhood, and God's. Towards the end of her book, Margaret writes:

> In the end what I have wanted to write about is God, and I have wanted to write about motherhood as a way into writing about God . . . I shall be satisfied if I have helped anyone to find a God who is even a fraction more real, more loving, more warm. There is no point at all in calling God our mother, unless it can lead to that. But then it is also true that in the end what I have wanted to write about is motherhood, and I have wanted to write about God as a way – the only way – to find the full, true meaning of motherhood. I have written, not for Christians first, nor for mothers first, but for both groups, in the belief that a deeper understanding of God is at the same time a deeper understanding of humanity, and a deeper understanding of humanity is at the same time a deeper understanding of God.[21]

This has been my aim too in writing about this profound experience of motherhood and God; and, like Margaret in her subsequent words in the book, I too will end where I began: in the twilight hours in which the world seems dark and I feel inadequate and my babies will not sleep; when I feel the rage about my failures and my lack of control over the state of my own home and the world outside our four walls, and the shame of not living up to an impossible standard. Then may I think of Mary, who birthed Life itself in her womb, and who points me to a freedom that is found only in God's mother-love.

Afterword

The Miracle That Saves the World

> One need not be a saint, or even a mother, to become
> a bearer of God. One needs only to obey. The divine
> resides in all of us, but it is our choice to magnify it or
> diminish it, to ignore it or to surrender to its lead.[1]

— *A Year of Biblical Womanhood*, Rachel Held Evans

Here is my dilemma. The world is groaning. Climate catastrophe hovers just around the corner. I fear for my children's futures, and some mothers – already on the front line of it in places around the world – fear for their children's present. We are told that there are too many people, that there is too much consumption, too much destruction of the earth. I am doing what I can: flying less, recycling, driving a hybrid electric car, and teaching my children about how we need to look after the planet. I applaud those people who are choosing to not have children, or to limit their family size for the sake of the planet. The terror of climate change aside, the planet is burning with fear of the other, growing political unrest: broken, powerful men with the authority to take lives in their thousands being handed the keys to do just that. Our children are watching.

But I also see the ways in which having children of my own has opened my eyes to the world around me, and given me a new insight into the nature and being and love of God, and of humanity. Motherhood is, of course, not the only lens through which one's views can change or expand; but for me it has been my most profound altering.

Perhaps the truth about Mary is that not only does she birth God in her body, but she brings new life in the metaphorical sense too. Many people have believed this. Hannah Arendt, though she did not have children of her own, understood what it meant to give birth in our bodies and in our world, and how important that was. Living in the aftermath of the brutality and horror of the Nazi regime and the Second World War, she said that renewal, birth, new life could lead to a more positive future: 'The miracle that saves the world, the realm of human affairs, from its normal, "natural" ruin is ultimately the fact of natality.'[2]

There is something of the divine that resides in the reality of motherhood. This God-infused motherhood calls us not to a perfection with which we beat ourselves over the head only to find ourselves falling short. Divine motherhood does not draw a narrowly defined line around what it is to be a woman. This motherhood welcomes all of us into a loving, grace-filled embrace. Divine motherhood does not rest in easy answers or binary choices. Instead, it rises to the challenge of what it is to be human, to live out daily the messy, unpredictable, beautiful, transcendent tasks of interdependence and vulnerability. To care for another person you see not as separate from you, but as part of you, and you of them. It is in this togetherness that God dwells – in the dance of relationship, in the reaching out of incarnation, in the hope of renewal. Motherhood – which carries the hope of new life and a more fruitful future – is the miracle that saves the world – over and over, time and time again.

Just as there is more to Mary's motherhood than we have been led to believe, so there is more to our motherhood than we dare to believe.

Notes

1 Kate Baer, *What Kind of Woman: Poems,* (Harper Perennial, 2020), p. 70.
2 Cole Arthur Riley, *Black Liturgies: Prayers, Poems, and Meditations for Staying Human,* (Hodder & Stoughton, 2024), p. 267.

Introduction

1 Molly Millwood, *To Have and to Hold: Motherhood, Marriage and the Modern Dilemma* (HarperCollins, 2019), p. 56.
2 Rachel Cusk, *A Life's Work* (Picador, 2003), p. 136.
3 Definition from Oxford Languages Dictionary.
4 Pew Research Center, 'Parenting in America Today: A Survey Report', 2023.
5 Lucy Jones, *Matrescence: On the Metamorphosis of Childbirth, Pregnancy and Motherhood* (Penguin Random House, 2023), p. 5.
6 Millwood, *To Have and to Hold,* p. 52.
7 Mary C. Gray, 'Reclaiming Mary: A Task for Feminist Theology', *The Way* (1989) 29: 334–40 (theway.org.uk).
8 Tom Holland, 'We Swim in Christian Waters', interview, 27 September 2019, churchtimes.co.uk.
9 Catherine McCormack, *Women in the Picture: Women, Art and the Power of Looking* (Icon, 2022), p. 81.
10 Jones, *Matrescence,* p. 182.
11 Nicola Slee, *The Book of Mary* (SPCK, 2007), p. 1.
12 Ibid.
13 Ibid., p. 7.
14 Jones, *Matrescence,* p. 135.
15 Adrienne Rich, *Of Woman Born: Motherhood as Experience and Institution,* (W. W. Norton & Company: 2nd edn. 1986), p. 39.

16 Mary Gordon, 'Coming to Terms with Mary', *Commonweal Magazine*, 1982.

17 Amy Peeler, *Women and the Gender of God* (William B. Eerdmans, 2022), p. 6.

18 Kimberly VanEsveld Adams, *Our Lady of Victorian Feminism: The Madonna in the Work of Anna Jameson, Margaret Fuller, and George Eliot* (Ohio University Press, 2001), p. 226.

19 Theodore Roszak, *Where the Wasteland Ends: Politics and Transcendence in Post-Industrial Society* (Doubleday & Co., 1972), cited in Andrew M. Greeley, *The Mary Myth: On the Femininity of God* (Seabury Press, 1977), p. 11.

20 Karen Armstrong, *A Short History of Myth* (Canongate Canons, 2018), p. 10.

21 Andrew Greeley, *The Mary Myth* (Seabury Press, 1977).

22 Jennifer Banks, *Natality: Towards a Philosophy of Birth* (W. W. Norton & Company, 2023), p. 179.

23 Elina Vuola, *The Virgin Mary Across Cultures: Devotion among Costa Rican Catholic and Finnish Orthodox Women* (Routledge: Taylor & Francis Group, 2019), p. 2.

24 Vuola, *Virgin Mary Across Cultures*, p. xii.

25 VanEsveld Adams, *Our Lady of Victorian Feminism*, p. 11.

Chapter 1: The Making of Mary

1 Dante Alighieri, Paradiso 33, 1318–1321.

2 Rachel Held Evans, *A Year of Biblical Womanhood* (Thomas Nelson, 2012), p. 70.

3 Lucy Winkett, 'Cultivating Wisdom – Women and Authority in a Post Feminist Society', https://www.greenbelt.org.uk/talks/cultivating-wisdom-women-and-authority-in-a-post-feminist-society/ (Greenbelt Festival, 2006).

4 Marina Warner, *Alone of All Her Sex: The Myth and the Cult of the Virgin Mary* (Oxford University Press, 1976), pp. xxxiv–xxxv.

5 Clarissa Atkinson, *The Oldest Vocation: Christian Motherhood in the Medieval West* (Cornell University Press, 2019), p. 118.

6 Beverly Roberts Gaventa, *Mary: Glimpses of the Mother of Jesus* (Fortress Press, 1999), p. 2.

7 Ally Kateusz, *Mary and Early Christian Women: Hidden Leadership*, (Palgrave Macmillan, 2019), p. 5.

8 The Council of Ephesus, AD 431, https://www.papalencyclicals.net/councils/ecum03.htm (Papal Encyclicals Online).

9 Tina Beattie, *God's Mother, Eve's Advocate* (Continuum, 2002), p. 89.

10 Atkinson, *The Oldest Vocation*, p. 118.

11 Vuola, *Virgin Mary Across Cultures*, p. 26.

12 Beattie, *God's Mother, Eve's Advocate*, p. 89.

13 Atkinson, *The Oldest Vocation,* p. 117.

14 Marina Warner, *Alone Of All Her Sex*, p. xxxvi.

15 Kateusz, *Mary and Early Christian Women*, p. 2.

16 Atkinson, *The Oldest Vocation* p. 118.

17 Kenneth Clark, *Civilisation*, Episode 7: Grandeur & Obedience, https://www.bbc.co.uk/iplayer/episode/b0074r50/civilisation-7-grandeur-and-obedience (BBC iPlayer, 1969).

18 Ibid.

19 Marilyn J. Westerkamp, *Women and Religion in Early America, 1600–1850: The Puritan and Evangelical Traditions* (Routledge, 1999), p. 5.

20 Beth Allison Barr, *The Making of Biblical Womanhood: How the Subjugation of Women Became Gospel Truth* (Brazos Press, 2021), p. 103.

21 Martin Luther, *The Estate of Marriage*, p. 40, cited in Atkinson, *The Oldest Vocation*, p. 210.

22 Atkinson, *The Oldest Vocation*, p. 161.

23 Ibid., p.162.

24 Marina Warner, *Alone of All Her Sex*, p. 192.

25 Singapore Conference, 'Summary Statement on Feminist Mariology', in Ursula King (ed), *Feminist Theology from the Third World: A Reader* (SPCK/Orbis Press, 1994), pp. 272–3.

26 Cited by Cardinal John Henry Newman, *Mary – The Second Eve* (E. Breen, comp.) (Tan Books, 1982), p. 3.

27 Vatican Council II, *Lumen gentium* [On the Church], in W. M. Abbott & J. Gallagher (eds), *The Documents of Vatican II* (Guild Press, 1966), pp. 14–101.

28 Gloria Thurmond, 'Ecology and Mary: An Ecological Theology of Mary as the New Eve in Response to the Church's Challenge for a Faith-Based Education in Ecological Responsibility', *Journal of Catholic Education* (2013), 11(1), p. 33.

29 Vuola, *Virgin Mary Across Cultures*, p. 29.

30 Adrienne Rich, *Of Woman Born: Motherhood as Experience and Institution* (W. W. Norton & Company, 2nd edn, 1986), p. 34.

31 Kateusz, *Mary and Early Christian Women*, p. 2.

32 Rich, *Of Woman Born*, p. 34.

33 Kristin Kobes Du Mez, 'The Most Important Christian Feminist You've (Probably) Never Heard of', *Feminism & Religion*, 15 June 2015 [accessed online].

34 VanEsveld Adams, *Our Lady of Victorian Feminism*, p. 7.

35 Elizabeth A. Johnson, 'In Search of the Real Mary', *Catholic Update* 1–4 (2001), p. 1.

36 Pope Paul VI, *Marialis Cultus: For the Right Ordering and Development of Devotion to the Blessed Virgin Mary,* February 1974 https://www.vatican.va/content/paul-vi/en/apost_exhortations/documents/hf_p-vi_exh_19740202_marialis-cultus.html

37 Nadia Maria Filippini (trans. Celia Boscolo), *Pregnancy, Delivery, Childbirth: A Gender and Cultural History from Antiquity to the Test Tube in Europe* (Routledge: Taylor & Francis Group, 2021), p. 2.

Chapter 2: Mother Superior

1 Sarah Hubert and Isabelle Aujoulat, 'Parental Burnout: When Exhausted Mothers Open Up', *Frontiers in Psychology* (2018), 9: 1021.

2 Margaret Hebblethwaite, *Motherhood and God* (Chapman, 1984), p. 37.

3 Tanya Klich, 'The New Mom Economy: Meet the Startups Disrupting the $46 Billion Millennial Parenting Market', *Forbes*, May 2019.

4 Hilda C. Graef, *Mary: A History of Doctrine and Devotion* (Sheed and Ward, 1963), p. 74.

5 Edith Stein, *Woman* (ICS Publications, 2017), p. 189.

6 Elise Loehnen, *On Our Best Behaviour: The Price Women Pay to Be Good* (Bloomsbury Publishing, 2023), p. 37.

7 Catherine McCormack, *Women in the Picture: Women, Art and the Power of Looking* (Icon Books, 2021), p. 81.

8 Andrea O'Reilly, *Feminist Mothering* (State University of New York Press, 2008), p. 11.

9 Vuola, *Virgin Mary Across Cultures*, p. 56.

10 Therese Oneill, '"Don't Think of Ugly People": How Parenting Advice Has Changed', *The Atlantic*, 19 April 2013.

11 Joanna Wolfarth, *Milk: An Intimate History of Breastfeeding* (Weidenfeld & Nicolson, 2023), p. 44.

12 Cusk, *A Life's Work*, p. 119.

13 Sirin Kale, '"I felt rage. I had traded my sanity for milk": what happened when I breastfed despite the pain', *The Guardian*, January 2024.

NOTES

14 Wolfarth, *Milk*, p. 111.

15 Clarissa Atkinson, *The Oldest Vocation*, p. 202.

16 Ibid., p. 111.

17 Annabelle Hirsch, *A History of Women in 101 Objects* (Canongate, 2023), p. 128.

18 Ibid., p. 129.

19 Shannon K. Evans, *Rewilding Motherhood: Your Path to an Empowered Feminine Spirituality* (Brazos Press, 2021), p. 9.

20 'Breastfeeding/Nursing Aversion and Agitation (BAA), https://kelly-mom.com/bf/concerns/mother/breastfeeding-nursing-aversion-agitation-baa/ (KellyMom.com)

21 Sarah Blackwood, '"Little Women" and the Marmee Problem', *The New Yorker*, 24 December 2019, https://www.newyorker.com/culture/cultural-comment/little-women-and-the-marmee-problem

22 Anne Lamott, *Operating Instructions: A Journal of My Son's First Year* (New York Pantheon, 1993), p. 37.

23 Rich, *Of Woman Born*, p. 166.

24 Blackwood, '"Little Women" and the Marmee Problem'.

25 Rich, *Of Woman Born*, p. 46.

26 Rebecca Etherington, 'Mothering and its Absence in a Group of Nineteenth-century Novels', *Arts and Culture* (brighton.ac.uk), http://arts.brighton.ac.uk/projects/brightonline/issue-number-four/mothering-and-its-absence-in-a-group-of-nineteenth-century-novels

27 Adrienne Auslander Munich, 'Queen Victoria, Empire, and Excess', *Tulsa Studies in Women's Literature*, 6(2), *Woman and Nation* (Autumn 1987), pp. 265–81, https://www.jstor.org/stable/464272

28 Virgina Woolf, *Killing the Angel in the House: Seven Essays* (Penguin Books, 1993), p. 3.

29 Sandra Gilbert and Susan Gubar, *The Madwoman in the Attic: The Woman Writer and the Nineteenth-Century Literary Imagination* (2nd edn) (Yale University Press, 1979), p. 20.

30 VanEsveld Adams, *Our Lady of Victorian Feminism*, p. 5.

31 VanEsveld Adams, *Our Lady of Victorian Feminism*, p. 226.

32 Peeler, *Women and the Gender of God*, introduction.

33 Tertullianus, *De Cultu Feminaru* (On the Apparel of Women), Modello (documentacatholicaomnia.eu).

34 Barr, *Making of Biblical Womanhood*, p. 32.

35 Ibid., p. 16.

36 John Piper, 'Honoring the Biblical Call of Motherhood', *Desiring God*, May 2005).

37 Ibid.

38 Marina Warner, *Alone of All Her Sex: The Myth and the Cult of the Virgin Mary* (Oxford University Press), p. 71.

39 Ibid., p. 72.

40 '500 Years of Virgin Mary Sightings in One Map', *National Geographic*, https://www.nationalgeographic.com/science/article/151113-virgin-mary-sightings-map

41 Marguerite Duras, 'Motherhood Makes You Obscene', *The Paris Review*, 1 October 2019, https://www.theparisreview.org/blog/2019/10/01/motherhood-makes-you-obscene/

42 Margo Lowy, 'A Silenced Part of Mothering', British Psychological Society, 15 April 2021.

43 Rozsika Parker, 'Maternal Ambivalence', *Winnicott Studies* (1994), no. 9:3-17, cited in Orna Donath, *Regretting Motherhood: A Sociopolitical Analysis*, 2014.

44 Cited by Margo Lowy, 'A Silenced Part of Mothering'.

45 Hebblethwaite, *Motherhood and God*, p. 55.

46 Ibid., p. 30.

Chapter 3: Mother God and Divine Revelation

1 *The Prayers and Meditations of Saint Anselm with the Proslogion*, trans. with introduction by Sister Benedicta Ward (Penguin, 1973), pp. 141–56.

2 Justin Brierley and Tom Holland, 'Are We Witnessing a Rebirth of Belief in God?' London Institute for Contemporary Christianity, 18 March 2024, https://www.youtube.com/watch?v=VG6xIvxrd2o

3 Sheila Nonato, 'Peterson Finds Her New Home in Mary', *Catholic Register*, 3 April 2024, https://www.catholicregister.org/item/36618-peterson-finds-her-new-home-in-mary

4 'A Mary For All: New evidence on links between Judaism, Christianity and Islam, *The Economist*, December 2003, https://www.economist.com/christmas-specials/2003/12/18/a-mary-for-all

5 Richard Rohr, *The Universal Christ: How a Forgotten Reality Can Change Everything We See, Hope for and Believe* (SPCK, 2019), pp. 124–5.

6 Ibid., p. 124.

7 Edmund Colledge & James Walsh (eds), *Showings: Julian of Norwich*, (Paulist Press, 1978, p. 299.

8 Christena Cleveland, *God is a Black Woman*, (HarperOne, 2022), p. 22.

9 Marianne Katoppo, 'Challenging Traditional Theological Thinking', in King (ed), *Feminist Theology*, p. 245.

10 See Sara Ruddick, *Maternal Thinking: Toward a Politics of Peace* (Beacon Press, 1995).

11 Feminist activist bell hooks intentionally wrote her name in lowercase letters. Some say it was because she did not want her name to overshadow her message, while others say that it was a deliberate protest against societal power and oppression.

12 bell hooks, *Feminist Theory: From Margin to Center*, 2nd edn (Pluto Press, 2000), p. 139.

13 John Piper, 'The Frank and Manly Mr Ryle – The Value of a Masculine Ministry', *Desiring God*, 2012, https://www.desiringgod.org/messages/the-frank-and-manly-mr-ryle-the-value-of-a-masculine-ministry

14 Katoppo, 'Challenging Traditional Theological Thinking', p. 246.

15 Peeler, *Women and the Gender of God*, pp. 102–03.

16 Ibid., p. 101.

17 For a detailed exploration of the arguments regarding male pronouns for God, see Richard S. Brigges in *The Melios*, 29(2), https://www.thegospelcoalition.org/themelios/article/gender-and-god-talk-can-we-call-god-mother/

18 *Tosefta* refers to a compilation of oral rabbinic law, from the late second century

19 Julian of Norwich, 'The Fourteenth Revelation', *The Revelations of Divine Love of Julian of Norwich*, trans. James Walsh (Harper and Brothers, 1961), ch. 59 (long text), p. 162.

20 Sarah McNamer, 'The Exploratory Image: God as Mother in Julian of Norwich's *Revelations of Divine Love*', *Mystics Quarterly* (1989), 15(1), 21–28, http://www.jstor.org/stable/20716905

21 Greeley, *The Mary Myth*, p. 17.

22 Wolfarth, *Milk*, p. 40.

23 Wolfarth, *Milk*, p. 40 - or Ibid.

24 Kathryn Jezer-Morton, 'Mother's Day Is About the Posse', *The Cut/Brooding*, 10 May 2024, https://www.thecut.com/newsletter/2024/05/brooding-may-10-2024.html.

25 Jennifer Banks, *Natality: Toward a Philosophy of Birth* (W. W. Norton & Company, 2023).

26 Theodore Roszak, *Where the Wasteland Ends: Politics and Transcendence in Post-Industrial Society* (Doubleday, 1972), cited in Greeley, *The Mary Myth*, p. 11.

27 Melanie McDonagh, 'A Mess: British Museum's Feminine Power – the Divine to the Demonic Reviewed', *The Spectator*, June 2022, https://www.spectator.co.uk/article/a-mess-british-museum-s-feminine-power-the-divine-to-the-demonic-reviewed/

28 Elizabeth Johnson, 'A Theological Case for God-She', *Commonweal*, 29 January 1993, https://www.commonwealmagazine.org/theological-case-god-she

29 Wil Gafney, 'Biblical Language for a God Who Transcends Gender', TheoEd Talks, February 2020, https://youtu.be/zLfpaRhsSUI?si=e84pAIhBMSyrqalY

30 Julian of Norwich, *Revelations*, Ch. 61, p. 603.

31 Presbyterian Mission, 'Firing Up Our Sanctified Imagination', 3 May 2022, https://www.presbyterianmission.org/story/firing-up-our-sanctified-imagination/

32 Joby Martin, Eleven22, 17 April 2023, https://youtu.be/ZkJlSxMnH5k

33 Warner, *Alone of All Her Sex*, p. 197.

34 Wolfarth, *Milk*, p. 111.

35 Cited in Wolfarth, *Milk*, p. 111.

36 Edmund Colledge, *Julian of Norwich: Showings* (Paulist Press, 1977).

37 Hebblethwaite, *Motherhood and God*, p. 39.

38 Wil Gafney, 'This Is My Body: The Womb of God', *Womanists Wading in the Word*, 19 August 2018, https://www.wilgafney.com/2018/08/19/this-is-my-body-the-womb-of-god/

39 Dana Raphael, *The Tender Gift: Breastfeeding*, (Schocken Books, 1955), p. 19.

40 Jennifer Fulwiler, 'Atheist Convert, Why I'm Catholic', November 2011, https://whyimcatholic.com/index.php/conversion-stories/atheist-converts/item/103-atheist-convert-jennifer-fulwiler

41 Trudelle Thomas, 'Becoming a Mother: Matrescence as Spiritual Formation', in *The official journal of the Religious Education Association*, Vol 96, 2001 – Issue 1, p. 93 Becoming a Mother Matrescence as Spiritual Formation (4).pdf

42 Banks, *Natality*, p. 91.

Chapter 4: This Is My Body

1 Lamott, *Operating Instructions*, p. 36.

2 Toni Morrison, *Beloved* (Plume, 1988), p. 88-9.

3 Toni Weschler, *Taking Charge of Your Fertility: The Definitive Guide to Natural Birth Control, Pregnancy Achievement and Reproductive Health* (Vermilion, 2016).

4 University of Strathclyde, published in the journal *Obstetric Medicine*,

October 2021, https://www.strath.ac.uk/whystrathclyde/news/2021/
pregnancysicknessdriveswomentoterminationandsuicidalthoughts/

5 Rich, *Of Woman Born*, p. 39.

6 Laura Fabrycky, 'Motherhood and the Intellectual Life', *Comment*, 2024, https://comment.org/motherhood-and-the-intellectual-life/

7 St Bonaventure (attrib.), *Meditations on the Life of Christ* (Paris, Bibliothèque Nationale MS. Ital. 115), trans. Isa Ragusa, eds. Isa Ragusa and Rosalie B. Green (Princeton, 1961), pp. 32–3.

8 Atkinson, *The Oldest Vocation*, p. 148.

9 Nadia Maria Filippini (trans. Celia Boscolo), *Pregnancy, Delivery, Childbirth: A Gender and Cultural History from Antiquity to the Test Tube in Europe* (Routledge: Taylor & Francis Group, 2021), p. 34.

10 Atkinson, *The Oldest Vocation*, p. 148.

11 Esther Cohen, 'The Animated Pain of the Body', *American Historical Review* (2000), 105(1), pp. 36–68 (p. 46).

12 Ibid., p. 61.

13 'Queen Victoria Uses Chloroform in Childbirth, 1853', *Financial Times*, https://www.ft.com/content/1e2ce5d6-aad3-11dd-897c-000077b07658

14 The landmark Ockenden Review gave detailed information about the state of maternity services in the UK, and was published in 2022, https://www.gov.uk/government/publications/final-report-of-the-ockenden-review/ockenden-review-summary-of-findings-conclusions-and-essential-actions

15 Pope Pius XII, 'Text of Address by Pope Pius XII on the Science and Morality of Painless Childbirth', *The Linacre Quarterly* (May 1956), 23(2), https://epublications.marquette.edu/cgi/viewcontent.cgi?article=3786&context=lnq

16 Grantly Dick Read, *Natural Childbirth* (William Heinemann [Medical Books], 1933), p. 23.

17 Elinor Cleghorn interviewed in episode 14 of Child – a podcast by BBC Sounds, https://www.bbc.co.uk/programmes/pohcsngs

18 Emmanuel Royidis, *Pope Joan: A Romantic Biography*, trans. Lawrence Durrell (Andre Deutsch, 1960), p. 1.

19 In *Purity and Danger: An Analysis of Concepts of Pollution and Taboo* (Praeger, 1966), p. 2, Mary Douglas argues that 'dirt is essentially disorder'.

20 Clément, Catherine, *Opera, Or, The Undoing of Women* (University of Minnesota Press, 1988), p. 105.

21 Fernand Leroy, *Histoire de naître: de l'enfantement primitif à l'accouchement médicalisé* (De Boeck Supérieur, 2001), pp. 100–01.

22 For more on this subject, see Paula Gooder, *Body: Biblical Spirituality for the Whole Person* (SPCK, 2016), p. 26.

23 Ibid., p. 127.

24 Atkinson, *The Oldest Vocation*, ch. 2, p. 3.

25 In December 2023, the app Peanut devised a new glossary of terms to replace outdated and sexist language within obstetrics and gynaecology. The Renaming Revolution included suggestions for changing 'infertile' to 'reproductive struggles', 'incompetent cervix' to 'early cervical dilation', and more. https://www.peanut-app.io/blog/renaming-revolution-glossary

26 Karen O'Donnell and Claire Williams (eds), *Theologies from the Inside Out: Critical Conceptions of Pregnancy and Childbirth* (SCM, 2023), offer the term *un/pregnant*, 'which we felt helpful in articulating something of the ambiguity both of the body that is capable of becoming pregnant, but is not pregnant, or was pregnant but isn't now. Or the body that longs to be pregnant but is not. Or the body that has given birth but is still birthing. This term *un/pregnant* helps us to articulate the messiness and fluidity of the kinds of bodies we are talking about in their volume'.

27 Ibid., p. 8.

28 Tertullian, 'On the Flesh of Christ', in *The Writings of Tertullian*, vol. 1, ANCL 11 (1869), as quoted in Beattie, *God's Mother, Eve's Advocate*, p. 96.

29 Olivier Laurent, 'A Portrait Expert Analyzes Beyoncé's Pregnancy Photos', *Time*, February 2017, https://time.com/4657982/beyonce-pregnant-2017-photo-analysis/

30 'House of the Dragon' Creators Showed Birth Scene to Women to See If It Was Too Violent, https://www.businessinsider.com/house-of-the-dragon-birth-scene-too-violent-shown-to-women-2022-8

31 Plutarch, 'On Affection for Offspring' 3.496c (translation from Plutarch, *Moralia*, vol. 6, trans. W. C. Helmbold, LCL 337) (Harvard University Press, 1961), p. 349). Cited by Amy Peeler, https://blogos.wp.st-andrews.ac.uk/2018/02/05/the-humility-of-god-by-amy-peeler/#_ftn9

32 Iris Marion Young, *On Female Body Experience: 'Throwing Like a Girl' and Other Essays* (Oxford University Press, 2005), p. 57.

33 Jane Austen, *Northanger Abbey* (Little, Brown & Company, 1903), p. 5.

34 Clarissa Atkinson, 'Motherhood Reformed: The Parson's Wife and Her Children', in Atkinson, *The Oldest Vocation*.

35 https://libquotes.com/joseph-hall/quote/lbe3a4v

36 World Health Organization, 'Maternal Mortality', 26 April 2024, https://www.who.int/news-room/fact-sheets/detail/maternal-mortality

37 Office for National Statistics, 'Families and households in the UK: 2022', https://www.ons.gov.uk/peoplepopulationandcommunity/births deathsandmarriages/families/bulletins/familiesandhouseholds/2022

38 Veera Korhonen, 'U.S. average number of own children per family with own children 1960–2023', 5 July 2024, https://www.statista.com/statistics/718084/average-number-of-own-children-per-family/#:~:text=The%20typical%20American%20picture%20of%20a%20family%20with,under%2018%20per%20family%20in%20the%20United%20States

39 Why We Don't See More Pregnant Women in Art History | Artsy

40 Alice Watson, 'The (Re)Ritualisation of the Transition to Motherhood within the Church of England, 2019' – dissertation shared with thanks.

41 Jones, *Matrescence*, p. 153.

42 Joanna Wolfarth, *Milk: An Intimate History of Breastfeeding* (Weidenfeld & Nicholson, 2023) - all the quotes in this paragraph are from p. 18.

43 Jones, *Matrescence*, p. 153.

44 Danielle LaSusa, 'Death Was a Theory, Until I Became a Mother', *New York Times*, January 2021, https://www.nytimes.com/2021/01/14/parenting/baby/existential-crisis-motherhood.html

45 Wendy Hollway, *Knowing Mothers: Researching Maternal Identity Change* (Palgrave Macmillan, 2015), p. 81.

46 Natalie Carnes, *Motherhood: A Confession* (Stanford University Press, 2020), p. 14.

47 Jones, *Matrescence*, p. 5.

48 Irene Oh, 'The Performativity of Motherhood: Embodying Theology and Political Agency', *Journal of the Society of Christian Ethics* (Fall/Winter 2009), 29(2), pp. 3–17.

49 Anna McInerney, Mary Creaner, and Elizabeth Nixon, 'The Motherhood Experiences of Non-Birth Mothers in Same-Sex Parent Families', *Psychology of Women Quarterly* (2021), 45(3), pp. 279–93.

Chapter 5: Hashtag Blessed

1 https://www.tiktok.com/@heidimontag/video/7166869750008663339?_r=1&_t=8XR3gsIwgbo&is_from_webapp=v1

2 Liza Tsaliki, 'The Exoticisation of Motherhood: The Body Politics of

Pregnant Femininity Through the Lens of Celebrity Motherhood', *Feminist Encounters: A Journal of Critical Studies in Culture and Politics* (2019), 3(1–2), p. 6, https://doi.org/10.20897/femenc/5913

3 Nylah Burton, 'Black "Tradwives" Say Marriage is the Key to Escaping Burnout', *Refinery29*, December 2022, https://www.refinery29.com/en-us/2022/12/11161942/tiktok-black-tradwives-burnout-marriage-capitalism

4 hooks, *Feminist Theory*, p. 133.

5 Catherine McCormack, *Women in the Picture: Women, Art and The Power of Looking* (Icon Books), p. 82.

6 Karen Danna Lynch, 'Advertising Motherhood: Image, Ideology, and Consumption', *Berkeley Journal of Sociology* (2005), 49, pp. 32–57, http://www.jstor.org/stable/41035601

7 'Rewriting Motherhood: How TV Represents Moms and What We Want To See Next', Geena Davis Institute, 20 March 2024, https://geenadavisinstitute.org/research/rewriting-motherhood-how-tv-represents-moms-and-what-we-want-to-see-next/

8 Orsini, abbé (Mathieu) – translated by Frederick Charles Husenbeth, 'The history of the Blessed Virgin Mary', (London: R. Washbourne), p. 102.

9 Bonnie Fox and Elena Neiterman. 'Embodied Motherhood: Women's Feelings about Their Postpartum Bodies,' *Gender and Society* (2015), 29(5), pp. 670–93, http://www.jstor.org/stable/43670009

10 Eva Wiseman, 'Will Maternity Leave Make Me Invisible?' *Guardian*, 22 March 2020, https://www.theguardian.com/lifeandstyle/2020/mar/22/will-my-second-maternity-leave-make-me-invisible-eva-wiseman

11 Rose Capdevila, Charlotte Dann, Lisa Lazard, Sandra Roper and Abigail Locke, '#mothersday: Constructions of motherhood and femininity in social media posts', *Feminism & Psychology* (2022), 32(3), https://doi.org/10.1177/09593535221107832

12 Sarah Hooper, 'Mum Died Days After Having Twins From Suffering Postpartum Depression', *Metro*, 20 December 2023, https://metro.co.uk/2023/12/20/mum-died-days-twins-suffering-postpartum-depression-20001219/

13 Pope John Paul II, Apostolic Letter *Rosarium Virginis Mariae*, 2002, https://www.vatican.va/content/john-paul-ii/en/apost_letters/2002/documents/hf_jp-ii_apl_20021016_rosarium-virginis-mariae.html

14 Celeste Ng, *Little Fires Everywhere*, (Little Brown, 2017), p.287

15 Ursula King (ed.), *Feminist Theology from the Third World: A Reader* (SPCK/Orbis Books, 1994), p. 273.

16 Ruth Graham, 'It's Hilarious That the Pope Called Mary the "First Influencer," but It's Also Totally Something He Would Do', *Slate*, 28 January 2019, https://slate.com/human-interest/2019/01/pope-mary-first-influencer-social-media.html

Chapter 6: This Woman's Work

1 Caitlin Moran, *More Than a Woman* (Penguin Random House, 2020), p. 100.

2 mother_pukka, 'Quick reminder in case you are losing your mind/ hair / sanity somewhere in simply trying to exist as a family. Listen to @ bonnieparsons . . .', https://www.instagram.com/p/C2r4Ufzogd7/?igsh=MTUocGJxNW1sOGpmaQ%3D%3D

3 Oliver Salt, 'Chiefs owner's wife Tavia Hunt breaks her silence on Harrison Butker controversy . . . and appears to BACK under-fire star after "sexist" speech', *Daily Mail Online*, 17 May 2024 https://www.dailymail.co.uk/sport/nfl/article-13431389/harrison-butker-chiefs-tavia-hunt-kansas-city.html

4 Clementina Black (ed.), 'Married Women's Work: Being the Report of an Enquiry Undertaken by the Women's Industrial Council (Incorporated)' (G. Bell and Sons, 1915).

5 Ibid., p. 10.

6 Melissa Hogenboom, 'The Hidden Load: How "Thinking of Everything" Holds Mums Back', *BBC Worklife*, 18 May 2021, https://www.bbc.com/worklife/article/20210518-the-hidden-load-how-thinking-of-everything-holds-mums-back

7 Andrea O'Reilly, 'Matricentric Feminism: A Feminism for Mothers', *Journal of the Motherhood Initiative* (2019), 10(1–2), pp. 13–15.

8 S. Thébaud, S. Kornrich and L. Ruppanner, 'Good Housekeeping, Great Expectations: Gender and Housework Norms', *Sociological Methods & Research* (2021), 50(3), pp. 1186–1214, https://doi.org/10.1177/0049124119852395

9 Soraya Seedat and Marta Rondon, 'Women's Wellbeing and the Burden of Unpaid Work, *British Medical Journal (BMJ)* (2021), 374, doi: https://doi.org/10.1136/bmj.n1972

10 Triantafyllia Kadoglou and Katerina Sarri, 'Women, Motherhood and Work', *Simone de Beauvoir Studies* (2013–14), 29, p. 39.

11 Thomas, 'Becoming a Mother'.

12 Mark Landler, 'Quoth the Raven: I Bake Cookies, Too', *New York Times*, 23 April 2006, https://www.nytimes.com/2006/04/23/weekin-review/quoth-the-raven-i-bake-cookies-too.html

13 Madeleine Davies, 'Maternity provision for Church of England clergy is chaotic, report suggests', *Church Times*, 8 May 2024, https://www.churchtimes.co.uk/articles/2024/10-may/news/uk/maternity-provision-for-church-of-england-clergy-is-chaotic-report-suggests

14 Atkinson, *The Oldest Vocation*, p. 171.

15 Isak Collijn (ed.), *Acta et Processus Canonizacionis Beate Birgitte*, SUSF, ser. 2, Lat. skrifter 1 (Almqvist & Wiksells, 1 924–3 1 1, p. 305), cited in Atkinson, *The Oldest Vocation*, p. 171.

16 Atkinson, *The Oldest Vocation*, p. 172.

17 Ibid., p. 175.

18 Ibid., p. 179.

19 'The Quiverfull: The Evangelical Christians Opposed to Contraception', *BBC News*, 17 May 2013, https://www.bbc.co.uk/news/magazine-22526252

20 Barna, 'The Powerful Influence of Moms in Christians' Households', 7 May 2019, https://www.barna.com/research/moms-christians-households/

21 Singapore Conference, 'Summary Statement', pp. 272–3.

22 Although Luke's account suggests that Mary originally came from Nazareth, Matthew writes that the family went to live in Nazareth instead of returning to Bethlehem to escape King Archelaus, who might have killed Jesus (Matthew 2:21–3).

23 Cited in Margaret Hebblethwaite, 'The Mary Enigma', *The Tablet*, December 2020, pp. 12–13.

24 Hebblethwaite, 'The Mary Enigma', pp. 12–13.

25 Laura Saetveit Miles, 'The Origins and Development of the Virgin Mary's Book at the Annunciation', *Speculum* (2014), 89(3), pp. 632–69, http://www.jstor.org/stable/43577031

26 Slee, *Book of Mary*, p. 64.

27 Nadya Williams, 'The Pink Scandal of the Evangelical Mind', *Christianity Today*, 29 November 2023, https://www.christianitytoday.com/2023/11/pink-scandal-of-evangelical-mind-women-intellectual-life/

28 Giacomo Vagni, 'Bringing It All Back Home. Social Class and Educational Stratification of Childcare in Britain, 1961–2015', *Journal of Time Use Research*, 2023, 18(1), pp. 37–57.

29 Sharon Hays, *The Cultural Contradictions of Motherhood* (Yale University Press, 1996), p. 8.

30 Nikhil Swaminathan, 'Fact or Fiction?: Babies Exposed to Classical

Music End Up Smarter', *Scientific American*, 13 September 2007, https://www.scientificamerican.com/article/fact-or-fiction-babies-ex/

31 M. Konsam, S. R. B. D'Souza, S. K. Praharaj et al., 'Effectiveness of Music on Perinatal Anxiety Among Pregnant Women and Newborn Behaviors: A Systematic Review and Narrative Synthesis', *Indian Journal of Psychological Medicine* (2023), 45(1), pp. 565–72, doi:10.1177/02537176231167077

32 Jane Lankes, 'Negotiating "Impossible" Ideals: Latent Classes of Intensive Mothering in the United States, *Gender & Society* (2022), 36(5), pp. 677–703, https://doi.org/10.1177/08912432221114873

33 Hubert and Aujoulat, 'Parental Burnout'.

34 Alison Gopnik, *The Gardener and the Carpenter: What the New Science of Child Development Tells Us about the Relationship Between Parents and Children* (Vintage/Penguin Random House, 2016), p. 18.

35 Jonathan Haidt, *The Anxious Generation: How the Great Rewiring of Childhood is Causing an Epidemic of Mental Illness* (Allen Lane/Penguin Random House, 2024), p. 268.

36 Banks, *Natality*, p. 185.

37 Kateusz, *Mary and Early Christian Women*, p. 2.

38 Hubert and Aujoulat, 'Parental Burnout'.

39 Ibid.

40 Hebblethwaite, *Motherhood and God*, p. 49.

41 Heather Thompson Day, 'Guest Column: How Can the Church Be the Community Mothers Need?', 5 May 2021, https://www.barna.com/guest-column-mothers/

Chapter 7: The Black Madonna

1 Audre Lorde, *Poetry Is Not a Luxury* from *Sister Outsider: Essays and Speeches,* (Crossing Press: Berkeley), p. 38.

2 Some translations say I am dark 'but' lovely, while others translate this passage as dark 'and' lovely.

3 Quoted in Melanie Rose Landman, *An Investigation in to the Phenomenon of the Black Madonna,* University of Roehampton (doctoral thesis), 2012, p. 23.

4 Marija Gimbutas, *The Language of the Goddess: Unearthing the Hidden Symbols of Western Civilization* (Thames and Hudson, 2001), p. 144.

5 Landman, *An Investigation*, p. 10.

6 Christena Cleveland, 'My Soul-Soaring Pilgrimage to Visit the Black Madonnas of France', *Oprah Daily*, 22 March 2022, https://www.

oprahdaily.com/entertainment/a39503554/black-madonnas-france-journey/#_edn1

7 Cleveland, *God Is a Black Woman*, p. 220.

8 Malcolm X, 5 May 1962, Los Angeles speech: 'Who Taught You to Hate Yourself?' https://www.mic.com/articles/141642/here-s-the-malcolm-x-speech-about-black-women-beyonce-sampled-in-lemonade

9 Stephanie E. Jones-Rogers, *They Were Her Property: White Women as Slave Owners in the American South* (Yale University Press, 2019).

10 Eric Kyere, 'Enslaved People's Health was Ignored from the Country's Beginning, Laying the Groundwork for Today's Health Disparities, *The Conversation*, 30 July 2020, https://theconversation.com/enslaved-peoples-health-was-ignored-from-the-countrys-beginning-laying-the-groundwork-for-todays-health-disparities-143339

11 Parul Sehgal, 'White Women Were Avid Slaveowners, a New Book Shows', *New York Times*, 26 February 2019, https://www.nytimes.com/2019/02/26/books/review-they-were-her-property-white-women-slave-owners-stephanie-jones-rogers.html

12 James Cone, *The Cross and the Lynching Tree* (Orbis Books, 2013), p. 150.

13 Gloria Thurmond, 'Ecology and Mary: An Ecological Theology of Mary as the New Eve in Response to the Church's Challenge for a Faith-Based Education in Ecological Responsibility, Journal of Catholic Education' (2013), 11(1), pp. 27–51 (p. 37).

14 Jeanette Rodriguez, *Our Lady of Guadalupe: Faith and Empowerment Among Mexican-American Women* (University of Texas Press, 1994), p. xxii.

15 Cleveland, *God Is a Black Woman*, p. 223.

16 Leonard W. Moss and Stephen C. Cappannari, 'The Black Madonna: An Example of Culture Borrowing', *The Scientific Monthly* (June 1953), 76(6), p. 323.

17 Delores S. Williams, 'Womanist Theology: Black Women's Voices', in King (ed.), *Feminist Theology*, p. 82.

18 Rachel Mann, 'My Struggle with Mary', *The Christian Century*, 8 December 2023, https://www.christiancentury.org/voices/my-struggle-mary

19 Safe Families (safefamilies.uk) is a charity that works with over thirty-five local authorities around the UK, offering hope, belonging and support to children, families and care leavers, primarily, but not exclusively, with and through local churches. Its 'Family Friend' volunteering

programme matches individuals with time with parents and children who need support, helping them to feel less isolated.

20 *The Drew Barrymore Show*, 29 April 2024, https://www.youtube.com/watch?v=d_XCKpxsp5k

21 'Misogynoir' is an early-twenty-first-century term coined by US scholar Moya Bailey. It is a blend of 'misogyny' and the French word for 'black', *noir*.

22 Melissa V. Harris-Perry, *Sister Citizen: Shame, Stereotypes, and Black Women in America* (Yale University Press, 2011), p. 72.

23 Carolyn M. West, 'Mammy, Jezebel, Sapphire, and Their Homegirls: Developing an "Oppositional Gaze" Toward the Images of Black Women', in J. Chrisler, C. Golden and P. Rozee (eds), *Lectures on the Psychology of Women*, 4th edn (McGraw Hill, 2012), p. 289.

24 Ibid.

25 Ellen E. Jones, 'From Mammy to Ma: Hollywood's Favourite Racist Stereotype', *BBC News online*, 31 May 2019, https://www.bbc.com/culture/article/20190530-rom-mammy-to-ma-hollywoods-favourite-racist-stereotype

26 Guy Hepner, 'Andy Warhol: *Mammy* from *Myths*, 1981', https://guyhepner.com/artists/31-andy-warhol/works/1193-andy-warhol-mammy-f.s.-ii-262-from-myths-1981/

27 Banks, *Natality*, p. 179.

28 Vuola, *Virgin Mary Across Cultures*, p. 1.

29 Linda Matchan, 'The Statue of a Doctor Who Experimented on Enslaved Women Still Stands in Alabama. But Now There's Also a Monument to His Victims', *Washington Post*, 2 October 2021, https://www.washingtonpost.com/entertainment/mothers-gynecology-alabama-memorial-statue/2021/10/01/cca0a788-21fd-11ec-8200-5e3fd4c49f5e_story.html

30 Annalies Winny and Rachel Bervell, 'How Can We Solve the Black Maternal Health Crisis?' Johns Hopkins, Bloomberg School of Public Health, 12 May 2013, https://publichealth.jhu.edu/2023/solving-the-black-maternal-health-crisis

31 Tobi Thomas, 'Stark Disparities': Why Black Mothers Are More at Risk of Perinatal Mental Illness in England', *Guardian*, 6 May 2024, https://www.theguardian.com/world/article/2024/may/06/stark-disparities-black-mothers-more-risk-perinatal-mental-illness-england

32 All-Party Parliamentary Group on Birth Trauma, 'Listen to Mums: Ending the Postcode Lottery on Perinatal Care', May 2024, https://www.theo-clarke.org.uk/sites/www.theo-clarke.org.uk/files/2024-05/

Birth%20Trauma%20Inquiry%20Report%20for%20Publication_
May13_2024.pdf

33 Banks, *Natality*, p. 127.

34 This short documentary shows the reunion of the Black Madonna with the Christ-child she had been separated for from for centuries: https://www.youtube.com/watch?v=k_vaqVNioSk&t=15s

35 Carnes, *Motherhood*, p. 57.

Chapter 8: A pierced soul

1 Joan Taylor and Helen Bond, *Women Remembered: Jesus' Female Disciples* (Hodder Faith, 2022), p. 133.

2 Brené Brown, Twitter post, 3 May 2017.

3 Claudia Dey, 'Mothers as Makers of Death', *Paris Review*, 14 August 2018, https://www.theparisreview.org/blog/2018/08/14/mothers-as-makers-of-death/

4 Jones, *Matrescence*, p. 112.

5 Kathryn Mannix, Twitter/X on 25 January 2024: 'Tweeps, can you help? Are there words worldwide for a parent whose child has died? A sibling whose sib has died? If so, do you know anything about the derivation of the words that name such a difficult bereavement? The absence of words in English renders it literally unspeakable.'

6 Qianlan Yin, Zhilei Shang, et al., 'An Investigation of Physical and Mental Health Consequences among Chinese Parents Who Lost Their Only Child', *BMC Psychiatry* (2018), 18(45), doi: 10.1186/s12888-018-1621-2

7 'The Sorrowful Mother', Страдальна Мати (Ukrainian Lenten Hymn), https://www.youtube.com/watch?v=ruPqbsRacoo

8 Karla Holloway, 'Giving a Name to the Pain of Losing a Child', 26 June 2006, https://www.npr.org/2006/06/26/5511147/giving-a-name-to-the-pain-of-losing-a-child

9 Karla Holloway, 'A Name for a Parent Whose Child Has Died', *Duke Today*, 26 May 2009, https://today.duke.edu/2009/05/holloway_oped.html

10 'Panel: On Death and Dying', Greenbelt Festival, 2023, https://www.greenbelt.org.uk/product/on-death-and-dying/

11 Karen O'Donnell, *The Dark Womb: Re-Conceiving Theology Through Reproductive Loss* (SCM Press, 2022), p. 138.

12 Ibid., p. 139.

13 Warner, *Alone of All Her Sex*, p. 225.

14 Atkinson, *The Oldest Vocation*, p. 162.

15 George Shuffelton (ed.), Item 30, 'The Lament of Mary', from *Codex Ashmole 631: A Compilation of Popular Middle English Verse* (Medieval Institute Publications, 2008), https://d.lib.rochester.edu/teams/publication/shuffelton-codex-ashmole-61

16 Clarissa Atkinson, '"Mother of Love, Mother of Tears": Holiness and Families in the Later Middle Ages', in Atkinson, *The Oldest Vocation*, p. 162.

17 'It meant a great deal to her': the Catholic faith of the woman voted "greatest Black Briton"', *Catholic News Agency*, 8 July 2020, https://www.catholicnewsagency.com/news/45090/it-meant-a-great-deal-to-her-the-catholic-faith-of-the-woman-voted-greatest-black-briton

18 Gregory Eiselein, *Literature and Humanitarian Reform in the Civil War Era* (Indiana University Press, 1996), p. 93.

19 Lonnae O'Neal, 'George Floyd's Mother Was Not There, But He Used Her as a Sacred Invocation', *National Geographic*, 30 May 2020, https://www.nationalgeographic.com/history/article/george-floyds-mother-not-there-he-used-her-as-sacred-invocation

20 Diana Spalding, CNM, Author at Motherly (https://www.mother.ly/author/diana-spalding-cnm/)

21 Jules Evans, 'Peter L. Berger on "signals of transcendence"', *Philosophy for Life*, 20 January 2015, https://www.philosophyforlife.org/blog/peter-l-berger-on-signals-of-transcendence

22 Mark L. Yenson, 'Battered Hearts and the Trinity of Compassion: Women, the Cross and *Kenōsis*', *The Way*, 5–11 January 2006, pp. 51–66, https://www.theway.org.uk/back/451yenson.pdf

23 Tish Harrison Warren, 'What Mary Can Teach Us About the Joy and Pain of Life', *New York Times*, 12 December 2021, https://www.nytimes.com/2021/12/12/opinion/what-mary-can-teach-us-about-the-joy-and-pain-of-life.html

24 Sarah Apetrei, *The Reformation of the Heart: Gender and Radical Theology in the English Revolution* (Oxford University Press, 2023), p. 74.

25 Richard Coppin, *The Exaltation of All Things in Christ* (London, 1649), p. 38-9, cited in Sarah Apetrei, The Reformation of the Heart, p. 57.

26 Malka Z. Simkovich, 'Who is the Mother of Israel?' *The Christian Century*, 10 August 2022, https://www.christiancentury.org/article/features/who-mother-israel

27 Apetrei, *Reformation of the Heart*, p. 60.

28 John W. Fountain, 'Mamie Mobley, 81, Dies; Son, Emmett Till, Slain in 1955', *New York Times*, 7 January 2003, https://www.nytimes.com/2003/01/07/us/mamie-mobley-81-dies-son-emmett-till-slain-in-1955.html

29 Maureen Corrigan, ' "Let The People See": It Took Courage To Keep Emmett Till's Memory Alive', *NPR*, 30 October 2018, https://www.npr.org/2018/10/30/660980178/-let-the-people-see-shows-how-emmett-till-s-murder-was-nearly-forgotten

30 Cited in Warner, *Alone of All Her Sex*, p. 222.

31 Greeley, *The Mary Myth*, p. 200.

32 As recounted by her colleague, Tjada D'Oyen McKenna, on X, 7 May 2024, https://x.com/Tjada/status/1787878521022607836

33 Angela Denker, 'For Mother's Day, I don't want brunch. We need a cease-fire', *Minnesota Star Tribune*, 8 May 2024. For Mother's Day, I don't want brunch. We need a cease-fire. (startribune.com)

34 Banks, *Natality*, p. 203.

35 Toni Morrison, 'The Future of Time: Literature and Diminished Expectations', The 25th Jefferson Lecture in the Humanities, 1996, https://neh.dspacedirect.org/server/api/core/bitstreams/1ef1ae0e-dcd8-4298-9eaa-40d8f78d6ab9/content

Chapter 9: Mothers Rise Up

1 Judith Wilson, 'A Conversation with Toni Morrison,' in *Conversations with Toni Morrison*, ed. Danielle Taylor-Guthrie (Jackson: University Press of Mississippi, 1994), p. 136.

2 Margaret Hebblethwaite, in conversation with the author, April 2024.

3 Ursula King (ed.), *The Bible as a Source of Empowerment for Women*, in King (ed.), *Feminist Theology*, p. 208.

4 Vuola, *Virgin Mary Across Cultures*, p. 80.

5 Winkett, 'Cultivating Wisdom'.

6 Barr, *Making of Biblical Womanhood*, pp. 215–16.

7 Julia Hollander, *Why We Sing* (Atlantic Books, 2023), p. 142.

8 Apetrei, *Reformation of the Heart*, p. 137.

9 Ibid.

10 Wil Gafney, 'Live Your Theology Out Loud in Public', *Womanists Wading in the Word*, 16 December 2017, https://www.wilgafney.com/2017/12/16/live-your-theology-out-loud-in-public/

11 Singapore Conference, 'Summary Statement', pp. 272–3.

12 Pope Pius XII, *Munificentissimus Deus*, 1 November 1950.

13 Wolfarth, *Milk*, p. 156.

14 'Mothers Staging Hunger Strike at Parliament for Parents Who Cannot Feed Children', *ITV News*, 10 March 2024, https://www.itv.com/news/2024-03-09/mothers-staging-hunger-strike-at-parliament-for-parents-who-cannot-feed-children

15 Katy Fallon, 'It is for us, who will give birth here': The Women Breaking Barriers to Build Sierra Leone's New Maternity Unit', *Guardian*, 4 September 2023, https://www.theguardian.com/global-development/2023/sep/04/it-is-for-us-who-will-give-birth-here-women-breaking-barriers-to-build-sierra-leone-new-maternity-unit

16 Greeley, *The Mary Myth*, p. 122.

17 Banks, *Natality*, p. 197.

18 Carnes, *Motherhood*, pp. 180–1.

19 Ibid., p. 180.

20 Ephrem, 'Hymn on Mary', no. 2, 10 (Brock, *Bride of Light*, 36), cited in Kateusz, *Mary and Early Christian Women*, p. 8.

21 Hebblethwaite, *Motherhood and God*, p. 141.

Afterword

1 Evans, *A Year of Biblical Womanhood*, p. 72.

2 Hannah Arendt, *The Human Condition*, 1st edn (University of Chicago Press, 1958), p. 77 and p. 247.